D1419158

942.
259

Falkirk Council Library Services

This book is due for return on or before the last date indicated on the label. Renewals may be obtained on application.

Bats
in the
Larder

Memories of a
1970s Childhood
by the Sea

Jeremy Wells

This book was largely created by the indefatigable nagging of two extraordinary women. It was my mum who got behind the idea of writing it; it was my girlfriend who kicked my behind until I did write it. So, Peggy Wells and Ginny James, what follows is your fault. It's also dedicated to you both with much love and respect.

The right of Jeremy Wells to be identified as the Author
of this work has been asserted in accordance with the
Copyrights, Designs and Patents Act 1988.

British Library Cataloguing in Publication Data.
A catalogue record for this book is available from the British Library.

ISBN 978 0 7524 5705 5

Typesetting and origination by The History Press
Printed in Great Britain
Manufacturing managed by Jellyfish Print Solutions Ltd

Contents

Author's Note

lthough the towns of Hastings and St Leonard's-on-Sea comprise a number of separate locales, I have, in general, used the terms 'Hastings' and 'the town' to mean the overall borough of Hastings and St Leonard's.

In addition, I should warn readers of a gentler disposition that they will find some mild profanity and general vulgarity in the pages that follow. What has been included is not wilfully gratuitous and is there either because it constitutes a direct quote or because I have attempted to represent not just the context of a particular thought or image but its emphasis, too.

Preface

This is a book of memories. Had I become a superstar in any chosen field, were I rich and famous today, they would be called memoirs. But I didn't . . . and I'm not . . . so they aren't. Thus, what follow are simply humble memories but, and this is the important bit, they are *my* memories.

There may be some irony in the fact that their genesis came of an exodus: when my mother was diagnosed with terminal cancer in early 2002 there seemed little point in talking about the future so, on my daily visits to her at St Michael's Hospice and, latterly, in St Augustine's Nursing Home, we reminisced about the early days of our 'new life' in St Leonard's; all those incidents and accidents we'd experienced, the people we'd met and the neighbours alongside whom we had lived.

We laughed – how we laughed! – and, given the circumstances, that laughter was worth more than gold. It was mum who suggested I write down all the anecdotes and, as each recollection by the one of us triggered another from the other, we realised that life had, all things considered, been pretty good to us after we made the move to the fading seaside resort which we came to love for its quirky individuality and the personality it had revealed to us as we lived our ordinary lives by the sea.

Mum had found the friends that were as necessary to her as the air she breathed, particularly after dad died in 1975, and my sister and I grew up safely and in an ordinary way. Convention and routine reassured us while fleeting moments of excitement, drama, humour and tragedy flecked the predictability of life with that very unpredictability which gives us all pause both to think and to examine ourselves and our living environments.

I'm not quite sure at what point in life the word nostalgia becomes significant to us as individuals and I've also wondered how to define the difference between nostalgia and memory. The answer to the first question is that there is no precise answer. For some people, I think, nostalgia is borne of seeing their own children passing through those phases of life that gave them, in years past, the moments of mental and emotional extreme that constitute growing up and leaving behind the comforts, safeties and protections on which we all rely unconditionally as children; for others it is, perhaps, the dawning knowledge that there is less time on the planet ahead than they've hitherto enjoyed at that particular point in time. And there are those who find themselves unexpectedly relocated to a new dimension, to a new perspective of things past by something as innocuous as a sight, a sound or a scent. As to a definition: well, the word nostalgia has come to us from ancient Greek via modern Latin and originated as *nostos* which means 'going home'. For me, then, while memory is of the mind, nostalgia is of the mind and of the heart – a Gordian knot of selective recollections of the past intertwined with powerful emotions of the present – sadness, happiness, comfort, shame, triumph, warmth, anger . . . you name it. In any event, memories are personal possessions and, for me, now a middle-aged man who has known both the aces and the deuces that the Great Dealer in the Sky can place before one, they are grown to surprisingly precious things.

Now, I'm quite sure that astute readers of this book (should I be lucky enough to have any readers at all) will pause at certain passages and say things such as: 'Wait a minute, that building was on the other side of the road . . .' or: 'Actually, I'm sure that happened in 1973 not 1974 . . .' And they'll probably be right. If they are, more power to their mental elbows – but I don't really want to know; for what I have tried to encapsulate in these pages is as much the spirit of our story as its dry chronology.

Bats in the Larder is neither sociology nor local history but the simple tale of a family who relocated to a town which seemed, in many ways, just a couple of decades behind the booming London suburb from which that family arrived. If it is peppered with a few unreconstructed opinions on life as it is today, I apologise in advance; but I am what I am.

So, having said that, if anything that follows brings you, the reader, the warmth of nostalgia or the comfort of comradeship: if any of the anecdotes brings a smile to your lips or, better still, a laugh to your throat, then I venture to suggest that you will not have wasted your time in the reading and I will not have wasted my time in the writing.

Jeremy Wells, St Leonard's-on-Sea,
New Year's Day, 2010

Prologue:
Departures and Arrivals

The journey of a thousand miles begins with a single step, say the philosophical Chinese. My journey was 64 miles and it began with a sausage roll on New Year's Eve, 1970.

For me, just turned eleven years old, that was a highly promising start; but for my parents, embarking on the last day of a dramatic relocation from the London suburbs to a retirement bungalow by the sea, that sausage roll was the physical manifestation of a disaster – and an ominous one at that.

After all, this was their first house move in twenty-five years and, as far as they were concerned, it was going to be their last. My father's teaching post had become redundant when the preparatory school at which he taught English and History had closed at the end of the summer term of 1970. He had, for some years, fought the long defeat against arthritis and had, earlier that year, decided that enough was enough. He was 62 years old and he was retiring.

The proceeds of the sale of our three-bedroomed semi-detached in Denziloe Avenue, Hillingdon, had bought a bungalow in St Leonard's outright and, with care and some possible part-time work on the part of my mother supplementing the domestic economy, looked set to allow the family to live in basic comfort henceforth. Of their three children, my brother had long since flown the nest; I, as a pupil at the same school at which my father had taught, the highly regarded Rutland House, on Hillingdon Hill, was bound to find a new school for obvious reasons and my sister, it was hoped, would slot into whichever seaside primary school was closest to us – her confidence bolstered by the presence of 'big bruv' who was still the best part of a year away from needing a secondary school place.

The Hillingdon home had been stripped bare and the contents sent forth in an impressive Pickford's lorry. The residue of those contents, the Wells family itself, should have been similarly sent forth by courtesy of a British Rail service from Charing Cross to Hastings on a bitingly cold last-day-of-the-year. Unfortunately, the train had the appalling effrontery to depart exactly on time and the luggage-laden Family Wells bumped to a halt at the platform entrance to see its smug rear-end disappearing from the station, diesel engines booming as it rumbled over the Hungerford Bridge, across the black glitter of the Thames and into the darkness of the South-East London suburbs. So much for dad's theory that 'trains never arrived on time because they never left on time.' Thus, we found ourselves an hour behind schedule before even leaving the capital and were forced to wait in the overheated, over-priced Formica forest of the Charing Cross buffet for the next – indeed the last – service to Hastings.

But a sausage roll . . . well, that was a treat, indeed! I began to have reinvigorated hopes for the whole adventure as I munched away oblivious to the fact that it was in my possession only to shut me up so my parents could bicker and blame each other for the travel cock-up without whingeing children interrupting their flow.

And it was an adventure. Eleven-year-olds are not afflicted with the curse of nostalgia. Yes, I was leaving familiar faces and familiar places but the promise of what was to come was infinitely more enticing that what I was leaving behind. After all, how many of us have had wonderful holidays and wished with all our hearts that we could actually move to live in that holiday heaven? We were doing just that; about to turn our annual two weeks by the sea into fifty-two weeks by the sea. In my mind, life was about to become one long holiday – the more so as dad was retiring and what was retirement other than one unending holiday?

While I enjoyed my sausage roll, dreamed of a seaside Arcadia and revelled in the excitement of a main line station's hustle and bustle, mum was queueing for a pay-phone to let our host for that night, an old friend in St Leonard's called Joyce McIntyre, know that we had missed our train. By coincidence and very conveniently, Joyce lived just a couple of hundred yards from the bungalow that awaited us and it could even be seen from her windows.

We finally boarded, lodged the suitcases and found seats, even mum and dad finally infected by the excitement of the children chorusing: 'Goodbye, dirty old London . . . Bye-bye River Thames . . . Good riddance noise and smoke and dog poo . . .' and so forth. The train weaved, creaked, squeaked and clanked through the nineteenth-century junctions, squeezing its way through the grime and soot-encrusted warehouses of Borough Market and New Cross to Lewisham and beyond where the light-stippled high-rise blocks gave way to the ordered ranks of sodium-orange street lamps and the hump-backed terraces of suburbia. All the while, the distinctive thump-thump of the train's diesel engine seemed to beat a tattoo of advance as we headed to our new life. Indeed, the train itself seemed part of that new life, as it was one of the unique Hastings Diesels built specifically for that journey, partly because the line after the Tonbridge junction was not at that time electrified and partly because BR's existing rolling stock was too wide to use the tunnels between Tunbridge Wells and Hastings. I felt like we'd even been given our own special train for the journey.

Unfortunately, British Rail had one last trick to play on us and it came from the very nature of our dedicated train

– a six-carriage multiple unit which, when coupled to one of its brothers, formed a twelve-car train which was just one carriage too long to fit neatly between the tunnel mouths at either end of St Leonard's Warrior Square station. This resulted in the last carriage remaining in Bo-Peep Tunnel while the eleven others were cheerfully discharging their weary passengers onto the platform of journey's end.

Guess who'd found seats in that twelfth carriage?

It was gone ten o'clock and we knew our journey was nearly done but when the train squealed to a halt we assumed it was waiting for a signal that would allow it into the station. Then the engine started to thump again and my parents wearily began to gather coats and cases into the gangway. Our carriage emerged into the all-but-deserted station, disconcertingly gathering speed rather than slowing down. As we sped along the platform we spotted the muffled figure of Aunty Joyce searching each window for a sign of her guests, clearly resigned to the fact that we'd missed yet another train. She spotted us at last and made frantic gestures which, although they seemed meaningless to me, were correctly identified by my parents as: 'Get off at Hastings and come back one stop.' Fortunately, an understanding guard at Hastings spotted the bewildered 'Grockles' with their suitcases and bickering children and held up his London-bound train long enough for us to cross the platform and join it. We were lucky, for it was the last of the night. By this time we were all dog-tired, hungry and, in my father's case, deeply depressed at his lack of transport management skills. Matters weren't helped by the guard on our saviour-train finding the whole business highly amusing and repeatedly telling us that: 'All you trippers get caught out like that.' Checking our tickets, he leaned forward conspiratorially and, as though revealing one of the secrets of the universe, said: 'Train's too long for the platform, see. Oughtn't to have sat right up the arse-end, see! Happy Noo Year, to you . . .'

Aunty Joyce was waiting for us at Warrior Square and, fortunately, she dispensed all the sympathy that we required, although for me, that sympathy was promptly curtailed when it became clear that we could not all fit into her car – an aged Mini Estate that looked like it had probably come off the production line at about the same time as the Kaiser abdicated – the more so as she'd brought one of her strapping teenage sons, Paul, with her to help with the luggage. To my pouting outrage, it was decided that I should walk to Joyce's flat with Paul – and carry my own bag – from the deserted station. The tail-lights of the car disappeared down Western Road and fourteen-year-old Paul manfully picked up my case. 'Come on, it's not far,' he said.

It wasn't; but it was all uphill as Joyce's flat was in Helena Court, that highly imposing (or monstrous – depending on your architectural preferences) redbrick edifice that dominates the skyline at the top of Pevensey Road. I forgot my ire at being excluded from the car by the nature of that walk up the long, curving hill from London Road. The temperature must have been well below freezing and the sky was studded with stars, the brilliance of which astonished me. I'd never seen them in such profusion or pin-point clarity and that fact, coupled with the deep silence that seemed to have settled over a darkened St Leonard's, was faintly unnerving. This wasn't like being in London. Hillingdon was never really dark and it was certainly never silent. Here, it seemed, dark was dark; the stars were stars and silence was just that – silent; awesomely silent.

Within fifteen minutes, Paul and I arrived at his home, my overnight accommodation. There was no lift in Helena Court and I had to trudge up seemingly endless flights of dimly lit and creaking stairs to Joyce's top-floor flat. The darkness suddenly ended at a golden threshold and, as I stumbled into light and warmth, I saw mum and dad turn towards me with smiling faces and I promptly burst into tears. It was all a bit too much. Those stars, that searingly cold air, that deep silence over the town; all new, all strange because now this was our town. For the first time, a sharp sense of no-going-back had come over me. This was it; I was part scared, part excited but, above all, completely exhausted. That exhaustion, and the excitement of the day, finally had its way with me. I was falling asleep on my feet and my sister had long since drifted into slumber.

I was dimly aware of being taken to Paul's attic bedroom amid numerous hushed 'Happy New Years' and the muted chink of glasses. There, a camp-bed had been made up for me in one corner under the eaves. I recollect a hot water bottle passed to me wrapped in my pyjamas and I remember looking out of the window to see the sweep of a lighthouse beam far over the sea. I also recall being strangely comforted by its rhythmic repetition. Then mum was shooing me into my little bed with its crisp, clean sheets. The light in the room was turned off and silence settled; but that lighthouse continued to pierce the darkness and paint the faintest glow on the walls of the room. I asked Paul where it was and listened drowsily as he told me that it wasn't a lighthouse but the old *Royal Sovereign* lightship moored some 15 miles out on the treacherous Royal Sovereign shoals. It was there as a serious warning to all mariners, of course, but it was a strangely welcoming first anchor for me. A new town, a new life; but somehow, somewhere, someone was wakeful and watchful, bringing safety and security to the empty hours of the night. I fell asleep to dream vividly that I was alone on a dark and rolling sea with only a pin-point of golden light to draw and welcome me into a port that I had never visited before. Mum told me later that she had popped her head round the door fearing that I would be troubled in my sleep by the strangeness of it all. Apparently, she found me lost to the world with a happy, peaceful smile on my face.

The next morning I stood shivering and bare-footed at the tiny eaves window of Joyce's landing seeking my first glimpse of our new home. It was Friday, a monochrome New Year's Day – everything seemingly black and white because of the light fall of snow in the small hours that lay undisturbed on footway, roof and road. It seemed as though a deep, fur-lined silence had wrapped the world. As it was a Bank Holiday we could not expect the removal men with all our worldly goods until the next day. However, we were all eager to take possession – symbolically, at least – and I was bursting to explore the house so I pulled on my clothes and clattered down the narrow stairs just as mum appeared.

'Come on,' she called, packing two thermos flasks into a shopping basket. 'Grab one of these bags down here and look sharp! We can have breakfast in our new home!'

We set out through the freezing air, our breath steaming in clouds about us as we talked rapidly and loudly about what we would find within the house and how we intended to make our marks upon it; but any illusions I'd had that moving home was simply transferring one's creature comforts from one set of bricks and mortar to another were about to be rudely challenged.

1
The House That Had Been Hit On The Head

Now, it's a strange fact to relate but, on that cold first morning of 1971, as we stood in front of our new home, it was the very first time that three of the four family members had so much as set eyes on the place.

For the choice of 17 Boscobel Road North had been mum's alone. Having voted to quit the capital for good, my parents quickly agreed they wanted to be by the sea. That decided, the list of possibilities was swiftly whittled down to two – Sussex or the West Country and, in the case of the latter, it was, specifically, Devon or Cornwall. The Sussex option stemmed from mum's friendship with Joyce McIntyre, a friendship which had brought her to St Leonard's on numerous occasions over the years. Devon and Cornwall made the cut because mum had a sentimental attachment to the peninsula. She'd had an aunt who bequeathed her tiny, two-bedroomed chalet – it wasn't substantial enough to be classed a cottage – to mum. To her enduring regret, mum had been forced to sell the chalet for needed cash following the birth of my sister. There had been a number of happy holidays in that chalet, perched on a cliffside at Downderry, when my brother was a child and I was a baby and mum had always loved the idea of relocating there permanently. But the choice of Sussex was made with me and my sister in the forefront of my parents' minds. Dad warned mum: 'If they end up at college or in London and we're more than

90 minutes away on a train they won't come home and we'll never see them.'

Wouldn't we? Wouldn't they? Who can say? However, the argument was clearly a sufficiently cogent one for mum and she bought into it. Even so, Devon and Cornwall weren't ruled out entirely and mum and dad spent our two-week summer holiday of 1970 in split house-hunting. He went to Devon and based himself in Newton Abbot while she brought my sister and me to St Leonard's. We had a wonderful time entertained by Aunty Joyce while mum ran her proverbial arse ragged viewing the short-listed properties which had been sent up to London by estate agents positively salivating at the prospect of a cash sale. Consequently, it was mum who inspected the bungalow and it was on her recommendation that the couple made their decision, put in their offer and signed the contract. It was an extraordinary act of faith on the part of my father – in all respects the archetypal husband and head of the house – and the more so as he had quite made up his mind that this new location would be the one from which his two younger children were launched into the wider world.

'Well . . .?' said mum encouragingly as we stood on the grass verge in front of the house.

'It looks like it's been hit on the head, doesn't it, dad?' said my sister. Funnily enough, that's just what it did look like. A square 1930s bungalow with an apex roof, a centred bay window under eaves – clearly one of the bigger living rooms – and a steep, stepped path down to the front door – which was actually set in one side of the house.

Dad chuckled; mum smiled in relief and we raced down the path to be first inside, clamouring at the door while the house keys, still attached to the paper luggage label, were produced. The door was duly opened – a door to a new home and a new life.

Familiar only with the two-up, two-down semis and terraces of the London sprawl, my sister and I were puzzled and intrigued by the curious geography and the illogical configuration of just about every aspect of this new-fangled 'bungalow' thing. One element in which we took an inordinate pride was the fact that no. 17 had two entrance gates, one on either side of the front garden. The one on the left, as you faced the house, sported the house number and led to the front door which was actually set in the side of the house. The other gate led to the door into the house which was diametrically opposite the front door. This was, then, we logically deduced, the back door (although the actual back of the house didn't have any doors at all). Thus, the gate that led to the back door had to be the back gate although it was clearly at the front. It made sense in a curious way and was something dad dubbed 'Hastings Logic' – a way of thinking and perceiving things that we found rather different from that to which we were accustomed. Hastings Logic was fun, though, because even the most everyday conventions and utilities tended to provide their own unique twists. We loved having a back gate at the front of the house – and if proof were needed that it was indeed the back gate, it was provided by a small embossed metal sign saying 'Tradesmen' – and everyone knew that tradesmen had to use your back door. We'd seen it on *Upstairs, Downstairs* a thousand times. It was The Law.

Mum was partly delighted and partly embarrassed to find herself chatelaine of a house with a bespoke tradesmen's entrance and we were soon to discover that there were quite a few tradesmen to use it, too. Back then, one could have just about anything brought to your door – as long as it was the back door, of course! Coal was delivered, the rubbish taken away; there was a milkman, naturally; a fishmonger and a delivering baker. There was even a grubby individual with hands permanently decorated with sticking plaster who offered to sharpen our knives, shears and lawnmowers. Dad reckoned he couldn't be doing very well out of the business because of the amount of time he must have been spending in hospital having blood transfusions. By arrangement, meat, fruit and vegetables could be summoned to your house and there were those hardy perennials: the football pools collector; the Avon Lady; the insurance man – the legendary Man from the Pru' – and, of course, the postman. Our postman was quickly dubbed the 'Whistling Postie' (for reasons I'm sure I don't need to explain). We'd hear him when he was still a considerable way off, his friendly, avuncular form whistling sinister ditties like the theme tune from *The Good, The Bad and The Ugly* or the latest James Bond film. Like the buses, as we were to discover, the postal service in the town seemed to operate at its own untrammelled pace, Royal Mail's finest more than happy to accommodate those of his customers disposed to chat with the melodic mail-maestro as he made his relaxed way along the road.

He'd dump his bag on our garden wall and come sauntering down the path, smiling in all weathers, and calling out: 'Mornin' Mrs Wells. Just a bank statement and a letter from your son in London. He's sent you some photies!'

We half expected him to tell us what the photographs showed and how much money we had in the current account. Dad rather disapproved of this informality, as he saw it, and thought that anyone compelled to go to work in a peaked cap should conduct himself in the manner of a Coldstream Guardsman on Household duty. Mum, on the other hand, thoroughly enjoyed it. On top of the intrinsic flirting (and I've never met a woman immune to that pastime – within reason, naturally), I think it created in her mind that sense of close community that she associated with her dream existence of the 'small holding-small village' in which people lived close-knit and everyone knew each other – and each other's business.

There were more opportunities to play at small-holdings in no. 17 – or rather, outside no. 17 – in the form of the back garden. Mum fell in love with it on that first exploratory day, principally because it had grass – a proper lawn – as well as apple trees, a rose bed and flower borders. On top of that, the garden backed on to the Marina Estates Allotments which created the impression that the garden, beyond its ancient boundary fence, stretched into the distance offering a pleasing prospect of hazel, hawthorn and hedgerow. That view was further enhanced by the fact that the land sloped away so that no ultimate border was visible, the lie of the land offering a countrified aspect sitting below the distant beaches at Bulverhythe and Glyne Gap with Eastbourne and the Beachy Head promontory on the horizon.

But my admiration for the view would have to wait: I had spotted something much more interesting and much closer to home – quite literally. We had sheds! Not a shed but sheds plural. There were two of them and the male members of the family were thrilled.

Now, here we encounter one of those curious but universal bifurcations of the sexes: for the average woman, a shed is a purely functional edifice used for storing lawnmowers and sundry garden tools. Sheds are to be avoided if possible because they are dirty, dusty and almost certainly have splinters. Worse, they have spiders and moths – if not rats and mice. They are also viewed with deep suspicion because they provide a ready-made bolt-hole and an escape route through which husbands can swiftly go AWOL when unexpected visitors turn up or wives start chatting casually about redecorating. For men, a shed is something else . . . much more. Maybe it's the old caveman thing – the territorial domain; it's the frontiersman's cabin; the commando's operational base; the outlaw's hideout. The shed is a masculine preserve where tobacco can be smoked, world conquest can be planned and a free-born Englishman can belch, fart and scratch his knackers without fear of reprimand or sanction.

So while mum was examining the flower beds and mentally planting-out, envisioning the quiet riots of colour that would burst forth in this sunny, sheltered corner, dad and I were exploring the larger of the two sheds at the bottom of the garden. It had a sturdy workbench running along the windowed side and was clearly water-tight and in a good state of repair. Dad stood looking around him and nodding in approval, muttering: 'Armchair over there . . . radio to hang on the wall there . . . few shelves . . . can use the workbench as a desk . . .' He came out looking pleased with himself.

'What's it like in there?' asked mum.

'Loads of spiders,' said dad.

'And very big moths,' I chipped in and, in a moment of male-bonded inspiration, added, 'Lots of mouse poo, too.'

Dad looked down at me gravely: 'Those mice might be rats, son. Probably best if we take care of that shed. The one up the top there will do for the bikes and the tools.'

'Hmmm,' said mum. She scanned our faces dubiously while we returned her interrogation with innocent sincerity.

Our excitement at our new back garden was not so surprising when you bear in mind that the one we'd had in Hillingdon was basic in the extreme. There, a narrow path from the back door was bordered on one side by a row of rickety outhouses which functioned as coal-holes and, on the other, by a small piece of muddy grass about the size of a Subbuteo football pitch. There was an area of crazy paving beyond that which dad had laid himself; it wasn't so much crazy as utterly demented. The garden ended in a dilapidated garage which was still filled with the rotting timber off-cuts which were there when my parents took possession of the house. It was a north-facing garden, too, and so not conducive to verdant growth. Mum tried runner beans the year they moved in but the shoots stuck their heads out of the stony London soil, took one look at their dank, chilly surroundings, took one sniff of the sooty reek and promptly keeled over and died on the spot. Its one redeeming feature was an old and abundant plum tree. Apart from us children playing out there, that garden was seldom visited except for the occasional bonfire and the memorable occasion on which dad lent his assistance to the midwife for the birth of my sister.

She was born during the first week of April 1963. It was the worst winter since the famous freeze of 1948 and, in many towns up and down the country – including Hastings and St Leonard's – 1962/3 remains the coldest winter since records began. In Hillingdon, snow and ice blocked most of the suburban streets and when the baby decided to come it was clear that no ambulance would be able to make it to our house. Fortunately, the local midwife was made of sterner stuff and trudged her way through the snow to deliver my sister in the traditional way – freezing back bedroom, lots of towels and bewildered father running up and down stairs with gallons of hot water. When Miranda had been successfully brought into the world, the midwife came down stairs and informed dad in that brisk, business-like way of the medical professional. She then handed him a parcel wrapped in a copy of *Titbits*. Dad looked blank and the midwife told him: 'It's the baby's luggage, Mr Wells.'

Dad continued to look blank. The midwife sighed and whispered to him: 'It's the placenta, Mr Wells, the afterbirth. Now then, hygiene is paramount with a new baby just arrived. Please take the parcel and burn it immediately . . . and not in here!' she added quickly, seeing dad's gaze drift to the fireplace.

Mum told me years later that the midwife then rejoined her and my baby sister in the bedroom and went straightaway to the window overlooking the back garden. She promptly dissolved into laughter. In driving wind and swirling snow dad was out on the crazy paving, the newspaper-wrapped afterbirth on the ground in front of him. He was lighting match after hopeless match, trying, at arm's length, to set fire to the parcel as if it was some biological firework likely to explode in his face.

So much for the gardens of our new seaside domain. Just as initially perplexing as the exterior of this curiously smitten home was the inside. The solid wooden front door opened onto a small vestibule where coats could be hung. Another door, almost equally substantial but this time set with panels of frosted glass from top to bottom, opened onto the hallway proper. This double-doored entrance was dubbed 'The Airlock' on that first day and we called it that for the next twenty years. The house comprised nine rooms in all, each of them featuring dark wooden beams, approximately four inches square, running across the ceilings. Dad's investigations proved that they were not load-bearing so were there only for decoration; but they were a striking feature and mum loved them because they were another nod to the idea of the country cottage. Because all the rooms opened off a double L-shaped hallway, there were, by definition, no windows between the hall and the external walls. Consequently, with the front door shut and all the doors to the internal rooms closed the hallway was in complete darkness. From day one, that front door was hooked open when the first member of the household was up and abroad and not closed until the last person retired for the night. For years, our home was secured by nothing more substantial than the sprung ball-and-socket catch on 'The Airlock'. Anyone could have walked into our home: no one ever did and it never occurred to us that anyone ever would.

At least that glass-panelled door provided some natural light – and the place needed it. What was it with our grandparents and great-grandparents and their ideas on interior decor? No. 17, like so many other houses occupied by that generation, was overwhelmingly brown. The doors were painted dark brown, the floors were covered with brown linoleum and all the internal walls treated to an earth-coloured distemper. Even the light switches and power points were in mahogany Bakelite. (Incidentally, Bakelite – a forerunner of modern plastic – has the technical name of

Polyoxybenzylmethylenglycolanhydride. It's not the sort of thing one needs to know in an everyday context, I appreciate, but if you're playing Scrabble it will absolutely slaughter the opposition!). I often wonder how the estate agents of a century ago attempted to sell such gloominess:

> We feel that we shall in no way distract the discerning viewer's earnest appreciation of the fabric of this fine residential edifice by drawing his respected attention to the splendid interior décor. Walls are washed in a delicate shade of Burnt Sienna while doors are cloaked in the ever-distinguished Vandyke Brown. Subtle contrast is offered by the Burnt Umber of the wainscoting and picture rails, the whole completed by the visually restful ochre shade offered by that miracle floor material of the future, Linoleum.

But brown is brown. 'It'll be like living in a hollowed out turd,' dad muttered to himself. Then, addressing the family, he opined that this was precisely the sort of environment he was anticipating when he was six feet under and that he had no intention of living in a world of loam before that time came. A gallon of white emulsion was the first thing to go down on the 'things to buy' list.

Even with the aid of the limited natural light, it was still some days before we had mastered the internal geography of the place. I'd never dreamed that a simple square could prove so complex. That front room with the bay window was earmarked as 'the dining room', in effect the family's living room. A space for dad's throne-like armchair was reserved, its location decided by the preferred siting of that single most critical item of furniture, the TV. That was to prove an entertainment in its own right – but more on that later. Mum and dad ummed-and-ahhed in the gloomy dust and echoes of the bare-boarded room, allocating floor space to the other components of our second-best, three-piece suite, the dining room table – an ugly and knee-knocking example of Second World War utility furniture (highly collectable now – detested as a relic of times better forgotten, then) and the equally ugly and junk-cluttered sideboard that contained the best china and a superb canteen of wedding-gift cutlery. Mum point-blank refused to use either, too terrified that some component part would somehow be damaged, scalded, chipped, stained, broken, marred or lost. A royal visit might conceivably have swayed her, but I wouldn't have bet my half-crown pocket money on it.

If there were items in the dining room that weren't to be touched, there was a whole room that was out of bounds to the whole family other than on very special occasions. In our new home it would be, confusingly, the 'Front Room'; I say 'confusingly' because it was actually at the back of the house. It was called the Front Room because it was, as far as possible, a facsimile of the front room at Hillingdon (there, it was at the front of the house). I mention this front room specifically because it was a curiosity of my parents' class and time. Front rooms were the best rooms in a house; they had the best carpets, the best furniture, the cabinets containing such valuable antique silverware and china as were possessed and the best curtains and pictures. They stayed 'best', too, because no-one ever got to see them, touch them, walk on them or generally come into close proximity to them.

The front room, lounge, best room – different families had different terms for it – stayed as a weird and utterly useless inner sanctum; a reception room that received nothing and no one for 99 per cent of the time and was used only when guests – and guests of some substance – were to be entertained. I say 'weird' because one might have thought that such a room, pristine, immaculate and showing off the best the Wells family had gathered over the years, might just reflect something of the family's history and tradition; at the very least clues as to my parents' collective past. But it didn't.

For some 360 days of the year it remained a sterile chamber like a business boardroom, always ready for use, but rarely pressed into service.

Mum and dad both came from houses which had, in their turn, featured front rooms. As a child, my dad set foot over the threshold of his family's seasonal sepulchre only on Christmas Day. Mum's parents were more relaxed. She and her siblings were allowed into their front room on Sundays but only to peruse the educational books collected therein – principally the Bible and her father's prized possession, a copy of Foxe's *Book of Martyrs* presented to him as a school prize when he was thirteen. Mum recalled how she and her brother would leaf through that mighty tome – for 200 years the officially sanctioned record of the Catholic persecution of the pioneers of Protestantism – their sides aching with silent mirth. They tried not to catch one another's eyes while trying to fix their faces into studies of grave compassion as they examined the artists' impressions of gruesome executions at Smithfield and Jews being burned in chains at Northampton. 'We only laughed because we were expected to be so serious,' mum recalled to me once. 'What use is a book like that to nine-year-olds – all church language and tiny print? We didn't realise the artist had drawn those poor old Jews writhing in torment. We thought they were dancing. If they weren't dancing, why were all the people in the background clapping and cheering?' Unfailingly, one or the other of them would lose control of their features and they would be expelled from the room with stinging slaps to arms and legs.

By my time, the front room had become less of a chilly chamber of high manners and low usage but it was still a room reserved for special occasions and one which we were not even allowed to enter without permission. It was a shame, too, for that front room at the back of the house, south-facing, had the best view of all and, after redecoration, with walls emulsioned a pale creamy orange, the skirting boards and picture rails a brilliant gloss white and with a green three-piece suite, the room seemed to be filled with a permanent glowing sunset. Even the print of Millais' *Boyhood of Raleigh*, with its maritime theme and sited discreetly to one side of the chimney-breast, seemed to fit perfectly with the view from the windows – low-tide sands at Bulverhythe, Glyne Gap and the whale-backed promontory that was Eastbourne, Beachy Head and the southernmost reaches of the Downs.

Things were to change, though, and sooner than we might have expected. But as we installed ourselves in no. 17, allocating a room to be the front room was high on the agenda. To this day, I know families who have maintained that same tradition; now, of course, the untouchable icons of style and success are HD TVs with surround-sound audio, £5,000 Chesterfields and hand-styled Art Deco table-lamps which cost more than the 1930s originals from which their designs have been shamelessly stolen.

But if the front room was for other people, the dining room had always been for us – it was our living room although for the most part we lived in the kitchen – certainly, for those twelve weeks of winter before the spring arrived. The dining room had a coal fire but that would not be lit until early evening so, for the children, the day began and ended in that kitchen. It was the room that saw the greatest transformation in the shortest space of time. On that first day of exploration, it was also the room that stopped us dead in our tracks because we'd seen nothing like it. It was a kitchen dominated by a huge porcelain sink with a single cold water tap, a wooden draining board and an enamel gas cooker that looked suspiciously like the same model used by King Alfred to burn those cakes. There was also a stone-flagged floor, dipped and cracked in more than one place; but of fridges, freezers and washing machines there was no sign; they were mod cons of which our 'new' kitchen had never dreamed. Storage space comprised a Welsh dresser painted pale green and lined with very yellow pages from a 1943 edition of the *Daily Telegraph* and a marble-shelved larder built into the north wall containing a perforated-zinc meatsafe – and five slumbering pipistrelle bats.

They had ensconced themselves neatly into a small hole in the plaster high up on the right-hand side and had clearly accessed their 'des res'. via a small painted-out window which had cracked and allowed part of itself to splinter away. The access and egress hole was miniscule, but so were the lodgers. The pipistrelle is a tiny animal in terms of its body which is rarely larger than the top joint of a man's thumb. With their wings open, of course, they're a little more substantial but when roosting upside-down in some snug niche those wings fold neatly round the animal's furry body to create a very efficient, draft-proof leather jacket. At mum's soft call we all gathered quietly at the door of the larder and peered into the gloomy recess.

'I barely noticed them,' said mum in an excited whisper. 'I thought it was a hole in the wall blocked by old dusty cobwebs. Then the big one on the end yawned and half opened its wings.' She was a natural mother and loved anything she perceived as weak, helpless or generally disadvantaged by the wider world.

'They can't stay there, can they,' I said, more statement than question. 'Dad won't like it.'

'Hmm,' said mum. 'Where is he?'

'He's getting those dead birds out of the fireplace.'

'Hmm,' she said again.

There was a silence.

'Dad won't like bats, mum,' I said in my most grown-up and warning voice.

'Why not?' said mum, still peering up at our chiropteran squatters.

I dredged up all my knowledge of bats. 'They drink blood, they spread rabies and . . . and . . .' I struggled to summon another example of the battish bad habits that would undermine our possession of the house. 'And . . . and . . . they get tangled in your hair!'

Mum turned a thoughtful face to me and said: 'Well, I don't think that will worry your dad. He hasn't got any hair.'

My finger shot out accusingly. 'But you have,' I said darkly. 'I'll take my chances,' said mum.

So we quietly closed the door on the bats and let them be. Without having his attention drawn to them it was highly unlikely that dad would discover them. After all, the kitchen was the preserve of women, children and those domesticated animals that a family allowed into its house – no man had any business there. I'm not sure what he would have done had he been apprised of their presence. He would no doubt have regarded them as, at best, unhygienic and, at worst, vermin. But he wasn't generally as stern in deed as he was in word. We, on the other hand, were thrilled; appalled at the dishonesty and, at the same time, delighted at this bizarre situation. Before coming to this funny place, we'd never even seen a bat in the flesh. Now we had five of them living in our larder of all places! What next? Owls in the attic? A family of foxes in the laundry basket? A unicorn in the bottom shed? We were determined that the bats would not be betrayed to their destruction – or even their eviction. Today, the welfare and requirements of those tiny interlopers would come before those of the occupying humans. The 1981 Wildlife and Countryside Act wrapped the bat – there are more than a dozen different types native to the UK – in swathes of legislative protection and one interferes with them at one's peril. Whole building projects have ground to a costly halt because a roost of bats has been found in an old building or a hollow tree on site. Back then, though, unwanted guests could be dealt with summarily and mum clearly had no intention of training a spotlight on one of those encounters with nature which encouraged her to see the move to St Leonard's as the closest she was going to get to that bucolic idyll.

As I've already indicated, she had always loved the idea of being a farmer's wife, living both on and with the land and I think it was more than just Marie Antoinette playing at shepherdesses, too. She did have a natural feeling for the earth whether it was the modest flowers in the sole sunny spot in the front garden at Hillingdon or her expanding ambitions with the allotment she later secured at the very foot of the back garden at no. 17. Born twenty years later she might well have been a hippy chick; thirty years later, a Greenpeace or Friends of the Earth activist. She would never have been radical or extreme but she would have stayed true to the ideals of the movement. I think it was because she had such a simple view of everything on the planet living together harmoniously that she was able to ensure that she never constrained her liberality of feeling with a straightjacket of theory or polemic – unlike her husband. Dad had all the political theory in his soul but he had the mind and hand of the arch-pragmatist. The two make uneasy bedfellows and he could never suspend the practicalities of life sufficiently to embrace mum's vision. I think it rather irritated him. He would not have seen why five bats in our larder was such a triumph for mum and such a thrill for us kids; but, generally, he indulged us all as far as he was able. Indeed, he didn't raise a word of complaint when, during that first spring, mum acquired a pair of disreputable-looking and rather thuggish chickens – Warren Studlers – and installed them in the bottom shed – his shed.

So, in theory at least, although the future of our very own bats might have been balanced on a knife-edge, they were never in any real danger. We kept quiet about them for several weeks but someone, ultimately, had to let the bat out of the bag. Ironically, by then spring had sprung, the bats were venturing forth into the milder evenings and we'd all but forgotten about them anyway. Dad screwed up his face and swivelled his eyes briefly from the 2.30 at Haydock Park.

'Bats? Where did they come from? I suppose they're looking for nests now the weather is warmer,' he ventured vaguely.

I opened my mouth but mum was too quick. 'Yes, I think that's it. We'll just wait until they go out in the evening and block the hole.'

'Good idea, love. You can manage that, can't you? Better do it sooner rather than later. Can't be hygienic.'

'Oh, I don't know, Jim. There's no mess and they've always gone by the time I start dinner.'

'They've obviously seen you cooking.'

Mum withdrew with the victory she had, refusing to rise to the bait. And, of course, the bats left of their own volition anyway. They had used the larder as expedient winter quarters and now, awake and alert in the softer, scented air that reached their tiny twitching noses, they started to make exploratory excursions into the lengthening dusk. One day they just didn't come back. Interestingly, they didn't deplete individually. On Monday they were in residence all five; on Tuesday they were gone. We children soon forgot about them – there was too much else of a surprising and an enchanting nature to explore and investigate. But I caught mum looking into that little hollow in the larder wall on more than one occasion with a look in her eyes that I couldn't have hoped to identify then and which I can only guess at today. She was a great admirer of the poet A.E. Housman. Read his collection *A Shropshire Lad* and you might just catch a glimpse of what I saw in her then.

The adventure of those tiny bats was the first of our encounters with the abundant wildlife we were to discover in and around our new home – but we'll look at that in more detail a little later on.

The departure of the bats, then, was some months in the future on that grey, snow-dusted day during which we clumped and echoed through the freezing rooms of our earth-distempered, linoleum-floored palace. But we kept returning to that out-of-time kitchen and it was there, again, that we spotted one curious fixture-and-fitting that greatly intrigued us. It was a smallish wooden box fitted above the inside of the kitchen door. The front of it seemed to be black glass with three clear windows, each about one inch square, ranged side by side and marked 'dining room', 'front bedroom' and 'back bedroom' respectively. Here, then, was a clue to the previous occupants and a suggestive one for, as mum pointed out, the box was the visual identifier to a bell system that must have been set up in the house at sometime in the past. The box on the wall was clearly the last vestige of it to be seen. Mum explained to us that wealthy people who had servants summoned them by pulling a bell-cord or pressing a bell-push. The minion in the kitchen would hear the bell and look at the box on the wall. A red flag would drop into the clear glass window indicating in which of the three rooms the bell was being rung.

Mum told us that the original occupants of the house had been three women; two elderly spinsters – sisters it was popularly believed – who lived with their 'companion' although she had gathered, from the pursed lips and discreet nods of the estate agent, that the term companion was really a euphemism for servant.

'These so-called "companions" were what were known as distressed gentlewomen,' said dad. 'They were usually daughters who had stayed at home to look after elderly parents and, when the parents popped off, the gentlewomen were left seriously distressed.'

'Why were they distressed, dad? Because their parents had died?'

'Well, partly that and partly because, by then, they'd turned into scrawny, ugly old hags who no man was going to look at. No money, no property, no husband.'

'I'm not so sure missing out on the last of those would be so distressing,' mum sighed under her breath.

Dad ignored her. 'You see,' he said. 'Everything was inherited by the sons back then.'

This struck me as eminently sensible and no more than the practical administration of natural justice. My sister, however, was outraged. She demanded forcefully: 'So what were the gentlewomen supposed to do?'

'They had to make a living by skivvying on a daily basis – usually for ungrateful families who didn't pay them and never lifted a finger to help them,' dad replied.

Mum looked up from examining one of the kitchen drawers and said thoughtfully. 'So, not really any different from getting married and having children of their own, then . . .'

It was a unique, exhilarating day filled with discoveries. As well as exploring all the nooks and crannies of our new home, there had been the excitement of planning where everything would be placed – albeit tempered by frustration at not actually having any things to place. Slowly, the winter's dusk began to gather in the corners of the rooms and flow across the bare floorboards. We took a last turn around the property and watched the sun set from the back garden, the sky turning to jam roly-poly and custard. Tired but elated, we trudged back to Aunty Joyce's flat to find she had cooked us all a fish and chip supper. I even got a can of Pepsi which I couldn't drink because cans didn't have ring-pulls then and Joyce couldn't find her can-piercer. I didn't mind; it was all too exciting. Dad tucked in and said between mouthfuls, 'Just the right day for this meal.'

'Why, dad?'

'Because Fridays are fish days.'

'Why, dad?'

'It's traditional.'

'Why, dad?'

At this point a lot of tired, hungry parents attempting to eat a meal would have dismissed this sort of inquiry with brutal brevity but dad was extraordinarily patient with youthful interrogation. I think it's what made him such a good teacher. In any event, he was happy to explain.

The custom of eating fish on Fridays (he said) came as a consequence of people abstaining from meat on Fridays – a devotional tradition that went back to the earliest days of the Christian Church and maintained by the Roman Catholics. Despite this association, it survived the Reformation and was further cemented into the structure of English domestic life by an Act of 1548 which legally enforced Fridays as fish days. England got distinctly fish-focused and, later on, Wednesdays and Saturdays were included. In fact, more than half the year ended up as official fish days. And all this, said dad, some years before the first potatoes had even reached English shores. I was aghast: all that fish and not a chip to be seen in the realm. As for pickled eggs . . . It didn't bear thinking about!

But these fish days had little to do with religion, dad revealed, and were a canny ploy on the part of the first Queen Elizabeth's ministers. They gave a real boost to the country's coastal towns like Hastings (where, even 400 years previously, unemployment had been a persistent problem) and the nation's limited livestock had a chance to increase which helped reduce the need to import meat from the Continent. No real imposition was laid upon the 'Great Unwashed' (as dad compassionately dubbed the Tudor working class) because the peasants couldn't afford meat anyway. Dad said he really enjoyed this story because it was one of the few occasions he knew of in history in which the wealthier classes – or 'nobs', as he termed them – were the ones called upon to make the sacrifice.

'You should know these things, son,' he told me as he lit an Embassy cigarette. 'You live in an ancient town where men have been fishing the Channel for hundreds – maybe thousands – of years and pretty much in the same way. England's heritage is a maritime heritage!'

His prandial lecture rather went over my head at the time – but not completely. There was an association between this quiet fishing town and the momentous events of English history that went deeper than 1066 and, in time, I was to build the substantive links that enabled me to connect one to the other. Enforced fish days are, of course, a residual curiosity of the distant past but it's interesting to note how a law of the land, although defunct as such, remains with us today as an idiosyncratic custom which many people still observe without the faintest notion as to why. It's still going, too. There are a large number of school cafeterias and works canteens up and down the country which are still providing a fishy option of the fifth day of the week. As to something as mundane as fish playing a part in defining who and what we are as a nation . . . well, there was an intriguing path to be discovered there, too, but more of that later.

I retired for the night in an exhausted but highly complacent frame of mind. I drifted into slumber, licking the salt and vinegar from my lips and counting the hours until the morrow and the arrival of all our household goods – including my games, books and precious Airfix models which I was desperate to suspend from those curious wooden beams across the ceiling of my new bedroom.

Saturday morning saw me, once again, at that attic window surveying an almost identical scene to the one I had encountered on the previous morning. Not quite, though, for today the undisturbed white coverlet of the road surface featured two black lines which led along Pevensey Road below my vantage point and turned right into Boscobel Road North. They ended at the rear of that same massive Pickford's removal van to which we had waved goodbye in Denziloe Avenue. Even as I watched, the still, silent morning was animated by a little puff of smoke that emanated from the window of the lorry driver's door. Almost immediately, the clamour of my parents' dismay echoed up the stairs.

They, too, had realised that the removal van had arrived at no. 17 while the new occupants had not. It was a day of semi-organised chaos. No, who am I trying to kid? It was a shambles. Things did not get off to a propitious start. As the removal men were swinging open the doors of their lorry, dad disappeared into the gloomy depths of the hall. Mum came through the front door with a dangerously sagging cardboard box and asked, 'Where's dad?'

'Gone to park his breakfast,' I told her.

'Really, Jem, I do wish you wouldn't use that sort of express—'. Her eyes widened. 'Oh my God!' she shrieked. 'The water's not turned on yet . . .' She ran off down the hall shouting: 'Jim! Jim! Wait . . . Don't go into the loo!' She was too late. Dad was ex-RAF; shall we say that his bomb doors had already opened and he had deposited one of his infamous '500 pounders'. The dry, clanking sound of a toilet chain being fruitlessly pulled echoed from the depths of the house. A couple of minutes later they both returned and dad said rather sheepishly: 'I . . . err . . . wouldn't go in there for a while. Not until I've found the stopcock and got the water turned on.'

Of course, immediately we were told the toilet was out of bounds, both my sister and I were consumed with the need 'to go'.

'You'll just have to wait,' said mum irritably as one of the removal men attempted to manoeuvre an iron bedstead into the room designated as the dining room and took a chunk out of the architrave while doing so.

'But I need a number two!' wailed my sister.

'You didn't need anything two minutes ago,' argued mum unwisely.

'No, I started needing it one minute ago,' my sister retorted, clenching her buttocks theatrically while standing on tip-toe.

'Well, you'll just have to wait. Now make yourself useful!'

From somewhere outside came a large bang followed by the tell-tale tinkle of broken glass.

'Oh Lord,' sighed mum. 'Where's dad now?'

'He's gone up to the loft to find the tap thingy that turns on the water,' I said and ducked quickly out of the house.

Five minutes later my sister, who had fled from the house howling, returned with a rather smug smile on her face.

'What are you looking so pleased about?' I demanded suspiciously. 'I thought you were bursting for the loo.'

'I've been,' she said simply.

'You can't have done,' I retorted hotly. 'We're not allowed to use the loo until dad's found the stopwatch and we can flush it.'

'I didn't need to wait,' she said with a superior air. 'I used the other toilet – the one outside the back door.'

Mum was furious. 'Brilliant! What if any of the removal men want to go? What then?'

'Well, stop giving them so much tea,' said dad's voice from the black square of the loft entrance. 'I'll find the stopcock in a minute. It can't be far away,' he added with a hint of desperation in his voice. Unfortunately, the toilet flushes were supplied by a gravity tank in the attic. With the kitchen taps working perfectly, it hadn't occurred to anyone that the toilets wouldn't be working just as efficiently. Fortunately, dad found what he was looking for and mum could breathe easily again. In fact, everyone could breathe more easily – quite literally – as anyone who had ever attempted to follow my father into a lavatory in the mornings would readily confirm.

All this time, a steady stream of furniture, disassembled beds, tables and other items were making their way into the house to be stacked in the centre of every room. It all looked highly incongruous. Fixtures and fittings which had been installed in the house at Hillingdon since before I was born, immoveable and as solid as granite cliffs, seemed curiously diminished and even frail. These were things whose territorial rights were senior to mine; items on which I had banged my head, chipped my teeth and stubbed my toes on freezing winter mornings. It gave me another of those small but sharp shocks of transition such as I had experienced on that first night in St Leonard's at Aunty Joyce's flat. And it said: 'No Going Back!'

Carrying a box into the house, I collided with my sister. She gave me a venomous glare and ran off before I could tell her that her cardigan had caught on the rough edge of my burden. I dropped the box and ran after her. She thought I was chasing her and squealed in alarm. She headed for the kitchen and the garden. By the time I caught her, she was wearing half-a-cardigan and that end of the house looked like a badly done cat's cradle. Mum didn't have time for her normal inquisition as one of the removal men, looking just a tad embarrassed, was inquiring, 'Could we . . . err . . . borrow a dustpan and brush, Mrs Wells?' Looking behind him, he added, 'Actually, better make that a broom.'

Mum seemed to be in a state of permanent motion and would suddenly appear holding the most odd and abstract items in her hand. On one occasion, she rushed into the kitchen holding a golliwog soft toy and demanded, 'Has anyone seen the box with the breakfast cereal?' Without waiting for a reply she rushed out again.

'Looks like Golly missed out on his breakfast,' one of the removal men suggested to me with genuine concern in his slow, deep voice.

At 12.30 the removal men broke for lunch and some sort of calm seemed to descend on the place. Once more, mum appeared, pushed her hair back from her face and demanded irritably, 'Where's your father?'

'Not sure,' I said cautiously, trying to catch my sister's eye. I was too late.

'He's in his shed, mum,' said Miranda.

'*His* shed, is it?' muttered mum and disappeared out of the back door calling: 'Jim! Jim!' in that voice we all knew as 'The Paint Stripper'. Funnily enough, we saw a lot more of mum zipping about that day than we did of dad. I decided he had obviously been supervising the removal men out front and that the strong smell of cigarette smoke in the bottom shed was probably my imagination. At about four in the afternoon the chief removal man poked his head round the kitchen door, proffered the three empty tea mugs that had been replenished heaven knows how many times that day and announced to our surprise that 'everything was in' and that the crew 'would be off now, then, missus.'

So, after dumping the items of furniture in rough – very rough – approximations of their desired positions and stacking the tea chests wherever floor space presented itself, the chief remover presented mum with a form on which she could claim for the breakages.

'What breakages?' asked mum in alarm.

'Mr Wells knows all about that,' said the top man reassuringly. At that, dad muttered something in his ear, pressed something into his hand and ushered the team out of the house with his thanks. They drove away into obscurity – but not oblivion; for mum informed us later that the instructions given to the removal men that 'everything was to go' from the old house had been carried out with unbending zeal as was witnessed by the presence of a half-eaten sausage which, found under the dining room table, had been carefully wrapped in aluminium foil and put into one of the tea chests marked 'Dining Room – Miscellaneous'. Mum told that story for years; it was the personal anecdote which, for her, encapsulated everything that was noble about the British working man and which, at the same time, illustrated precisely why the country was going down the drain. Today, I can see her point – or points.

We were finally alone in our new home and the grown-ups immediately attempted to comfort each other with the mutual assurance that establishing the house as they wanted it would be neither a long nor an arduous job. They had decided that there wasn't a great deal of furniture anyway and that we would manage it all ourselves quickly enough.

'After all,' they had agreed. 'It's really just the beds and wardrobes, the dining room table and chairs and the three-piece suites . . .' Yes, it was; plus all the lamps, fire irons, pots and pans, bed linen, curtains, washing machine, rugs, kitchen chairs, TV, kitchen utensils, tumble drier, canteens of cutlery, kids' toys, garden tools, laundry baskets, emergency paraffin heaters, clothing, garden tools, pot-plants and a monster 1950s radiogram. On top of that, there was a round dozen tea chests containing books, records and assorted domestic bric-a-brac. Unfortunately, they had fallen into that trap which awaits so many of us when we move house. The furniture and the household items which they believed themselves to possess were just a fraction of what was really there. I mean, no one really takes into account things like ironing boards, bathroom towels, garden tools and all the accumulated crap of decades which, although stored out of sight at the previous address, nevertheless has to be transported to the new home and provided with somewhere to live there. Thus it was with the Wells' miscellany; it had all been duly transported to the new home and now it sat variously on bare boards in echoing rooms and looked highly uncooperative and really rather formidable.

But it was at this point that another of those quirky, odd incidents – and quirky, odd people – that were to become so synonymous with Hastings Logic and with our new life – arrived on our doorstep – again quite literally. To this day, I'm still not sure how or why Sidney arrived to help us on that day. I think he was known to Joyce McIntyre who, ever the subtlest of friends and most practical of helpers, had sent him to us to lend his portly but energetic frame to the furniture-humping fray. And he was a God-send; for Sidney's physical strength was as mighty as his mental strength was meagre.

Sidney. Those six letters can give no indication of that extraordinary man's zest for life and verbal brio. Never before or since have I met anyone who could keep up such a scintillating monologue of complete and utter bollocks. Sidney's running commentary on Life, the Universe and Sidney made one soaring leap after another, taking us all to new planes of ever more rarefied inanity.

But boy, did he work!

Within a couple of hours, with Sidney as the power-house, mum as director and the rest of us functioning as rather weedy cogs in the gearbox of Sidney's mighty motor, we had the house pretty much as it was intended to be and, in Sidney, we had made a loyal friend for life. And he was always welcome because he never failed to make us laugh – whether he meant to or not. He even got the nod of approval from dad, not the most sociable of humans and always rather jealous of any dealings mum had with other men. On one occasion, after a particularly insightful Sidney discourse on the best way to deal with the IRA, I found dad in the back garden, doubled-up, gasping for breath and with tears streaming down his face. I thought he was having a heart attack. He looked at me, red-faced and speechless, shook his head hopelessly and dissolved into a fresh series of convulsions. That was the effect Sidney had on people. No one could dislike him because he was one of those wonderful people who was interested in everything and everyone, whose imagination was permanently on the wing and whose only fetter to mundanity was his total inability to master his native tongue. He got pretty much everything wrong. People roared; Sidney roared with them. He never took offence. Everything going on was just too interesting to waste time navel-gazing over the impressions he was casting.

'Hello, Sidney,' mum said one day. 'Had your dinner?'

'I have that, missus,' a beaming Sidney affirmed.

'What did you have?'

'The wife done us a chicken arserole. It was right peachy.' Everything was 'peachy' in Sidney's life.

'Arse— Do you mean a casserole, Sidney?' asked mum, the corners of her mouth twitching.

'That's right, missus. What did I say, then? Steak and kidney pie?' Sidney beamed at us generously as we dissolved into laughter.

I went back to my homework but Sidney had noticed my books spread out over the floor. 'What's that, then, young 'un? You doin' your overtime? Ah, looks like clever stuff. Science, is it? Is it chemical or just the physicals? They never learned us that at my school but I seen this telly programme about Albert Eisenower. Clever bloke. Had a theory about rear entry. Eisenwossname's theory of specific rear entry, he called it. Clever bloke. Tell you another clever bloke. Leonardo da Vincent. He was an Eye-talian bloke, too. He done paintings like the Moaning Lisa and invented all sorts of stuff like sumbarines and parakeets. Peachy.'

He became a fixture for a number of years although we never met Mrs Sidney. Once, when I was coming up for my O-Levels, he asked me, 'What you goin' to do then when you leave that school? Doctor, is it? Pilot?'

I couldn't resist the temptation, 'Actually, Sidney, I want to be Regius Professor of Molecular Systematics at one of the better Oxford colleges.'

Sidney didn't bat an eyelid, 'Good on you, young 'un. Peachy! That'll bring in a few quid for your old mum. I hear there's a lot of money in them molecules.'

We tried to make a collection of the malapropisms that Sidney bestowed upon us but we soon lost count. Ridiculous was rickidoodalus; a certificate was a serstifikit and, of course, there were endless sumbarines, skellingtons and chimbleys for chimneys. Sidney's word for a squirrel simply defies reproducing but I think my favourite was, and remains, a comment he made about our cat, Timothy. Observing the animal asleep on a chair, Sidney started to tickle his ears. Timothy stretched his legs, as cats do, and started to purr in quiet contentment.

'Aaahhh' said Sidney in delight. 'Happy cat, that one. Listen to him scribbling up his nose.' A cat's purr is casual but intimate, soft but intense and mechanically complex. Sidney caught the phenomenon perfectly in four words with a simple quality of poetry. I've yet to hear a better description of the sound made by a happy feline.

The man was as guileless as a six-year-old and just as enthusiastic for what he saw about him each day. He never did anything as such and our association with him tended to report a net loss on the basis of the vast quantities of tea, biscuits and cake he consumed but he was always willing to help in any way he could and, on top of that, he was what mum and dad's generation referred to as 'a tonic' – and you couldn't put a price on that.

We were to encounter a number of these weird and wonderful people as time progressed and I'll introduce you to some of them a little later on. There seemed to be something curiously liberating about St Leonard's. The eccentricities, the pace of life, that Hastings Logic . . . they all contributed to making life so much more interesting than it had hitherto been. It was as if, previously, everything had been seen, heard and experienced through some strange muslin filter. Now, the filter was off and all the sights and sounds of life and humanity, as they should be, hit us full in the face. It did me good, personally, and of that I'm quite certain. I had always been nervous, prone to taking on irrational fears at the drop of a hat. As a young child, my most dramatic phobia had been the fear of my mother's prized black tulip that she had nurtured into bloom at the front of the house. I had to be led past it, down the garden path, legs wobbling and with tear-stung eyes averted. Then there was having my hair cut, going to the shoe shop, airborne helicopters, dragonflies, old women in wheelchairs and even a weird-shaped crack in the ceiling of my bedroom – all left me in a state of deep and senseless fear. Physical deformity was also something

I shied away from and although I had started to leave these fears behind on reaching double figures and although the move to St Leonard's undoubtedly emboldened me, boosted my confidence and fired my sense of adventure, this last fear remained and, what's more, it very nearly cost me my life.

Our first Hastings friend, good old Joyce McIntyre, had two sons. Paul I have already mentioned. He was at boarding school and was at his mother's home only during the school holidays. The other boy was Duncan. He must have been eighteen or nineteen when we arrived in the town and he, like his younger brother, was only at home occasionally because he had joined the Royal Navy and visited only when on shore leave.

Although Paul was nearer my age and shared my passion for Airfix construction kits, Duncan was the one I really admired and whose company I sought. He smoked, he swore in front of his mother and he was, to boot, a skilful mimic who did convincing impersonations of the politicians of the day such as Harold Wilson, Ted Heath and Dennis Healey. His world-weary cynicism was probably a horribly adolescent contrivance but to me, an eleven-year-old, it was about the coolest thing I'd ever seen. The 'Paul and Duncan' double-act was both hilarious and edgy and, after we'd settled in at the bungalow, I did my best to hang about with them whenever I could.

But there was a problem and it came in the form of the man who effectively acted as the concierge at Helena Court and who checked in and checked out the householders and their visitors alike. He was a permanent presence in his little cubby-hole office under the stairs and I dreaded having to pass him. Poor man! He had been badly burned while on active service with the RAF during the Second World War. He flew Hurricanes during the Battle of Britain and his plane was shot down. Although he got away with his life and his sight, the cockpit inferno had taken a heavy toll on the skin of his head and his neck. He had, apparently, been one of the famous 'Guinea Pigs' sent to the Queen Victoria Hospital in East Grinstead, where such fantastic pioneering work was done in reconstructive plastic surgery. They'd given him back a face of sorts, I suppose, but it wasn't much of one with its ruined ears, red-rimmed eyes and stretched, shiny skin that seemed to pull his mouth into an expression of continual leering pain.

Dad had been part of Bomber Command during the war and with the hero-worship I reserved for his fellow RAF Titans and my boy's fascination for all things military, I should, by rights, have elevated this battle-scarred survivor straight into my personal pantheon of heroes. I'm ashamed to say that I shunned him like the plague and lived in terror of encountering his twisted smile as he softly patrolled the gloomy entranceways of the building. So great did my unreasoning terror of this unfortunate man become that I couldn't bring myself to go through the front door and, just a couple of months after the house move, my visits to the McIntyre home simply stopped; but I still craved the company of Paul and Duncan. There would have been no point in trying to articulate my reticence to mum or dad. They would either have told me to 'stop being silly' or they would have offered to escort me – both options really rather missing the point of my anxiety.

Then I hit upon a plan. I would surprise the brothers by arriving not at their door but at their window! I'd use the fire escape to climb up to the top storey of their block of flats and knock on their lounge window. That would take them by surprise and my stock as a weird and exciting guy would rise dramatically. Best of all, I wouldn't have to use the front door and run the risk of encountering *him*.

It was a cold, winter's night and even as I approached the towering building a sea mist was rolling in. The darkness at the front of the house was bad enough but as I tremulously made my way to the back it completely submerged me. Beginning seriously to doubt the brilliance of my idea, I finally found the wrought-iron fire escape and started to climb. The mist made the metal wet and slippery and my head began to buzz with the increasing height that I could feel rather than see. I seemed to climb for ever until I realised I could go no further and was perched on a narrow walkway with just a low railing separating me from a plunge into foggy oblivion. All my thoughts of bursting through the net curtains to rain down 'BIG SURPRISE!' on the astonished faces within evaporated as I stood trembling on that fire escape hardly daring to move.

Finally, I managed to tap on the curtained windows and call out a 'Hello there' in a sort of croaking squeak. Nothing happened and suddenly I was convinced that I was going to be stuck on the fire escape all night, unable to make myself heard by those inside and too terrified to attempt the descent. In panic, I started to hammer on the window, shrieking, 'Let-me-in-let-me-in-let-me-in-let me in!'

Suddenly, there was a flare of light as a curtain was pulled aside and I caught a glimpse of a highly alarmed Duncan. Then something hit me full in the face. I took a step back, bent almost to ninety degrees over the railing and found myself looking into utter blackness. I grabbed wildly at anything, felt my feet slipping and screamed in blind panic. Then something had me by the scruff of the neck and I seemed to be floating in light and warmth. When I focused my eyes, I saw faces observing me with obvious concern while Joyce's voice was speaking urgently into the telephone. Mum came to collect me and heard the story in silence and some embarrassment.

Duncan no longer looked quite the world-weary cynic; more a frightened teenage boy who had realised that, by opening the window so violently, he had very nearly catapulted me 150 feet to my death. He was wretchedly apologetic although there was no one to blame but myself.

The boys, not unreasonably, believed they were being burgled and had decided to come out fighting. The burning question, of course, was: 'What the bloody hell did I think I was doing?' I couldn't say. How could I explain that the whole silly escapade had stemmed from my fear of encountering a man with a burned face? Mum took me home soon afterwards. As we started down the stairs, Joyce said to her, 'Paul will come down to the door with you. It's dark down there and it's the caretaker's night off.'

2
Settling In

Moving house in the dead of winter would not be most people's preferred season for doing so. January is a rotten month; its one redeeming feature being that it's marginally better than February. By the time one is bogged down in the freezing mud of the first calendar month, Christmas is just a memory. Decorations come down on Twelfth Night leaving the house looking bare and drab; the 'New Year' is now just 'the year' and all those well-intentioned resolutions have crashed ignominiously – as have the family finances. It's when those credit card statements start to arrive in January that we realise just how overly festive we were.

In those first days of 1971, though, my thoughts were focused very much on a positive future. I had a new school to start, a new environment to explore and new friends to make. My concept of family finances was no broader than the half-crown pocket money (two shillings and sixpence in old money; twelve-and-a-half pence in the decimal abomination that was shortly to arrive) that was doled out to me every Friday evening with the same unchallengeable regularity with which the sun rose each morning. For my parents, though, the prime concern was getting the kids bedded in at a new school so, whatever their plans and dreams for their new home, continuity was the order of the day and we found that post-Christmas holiday life was pretty much as it had been before the move. And if one thing hadn't changed, it was the misery of hauling myself out of bed to face another week in the less than sunlit glades of Academe. And it was cold.

I know I'll be accused of going into 'Old Fart Mode' here, but I really don't think that the current crop of youngsters appreciates just what life was like before the advent of common central heating and how tough it was in winters when parents watched every penny spent on power like hawks and kids could get a cold roasting for so much as leaving the toilet light on. Indeed, for the children of today the concept of a house without central heating is unthinkable. It's on a par with a house with no roof. It does not compute. On those early days at no. 17, school mornings followed the same routine: a knock on the door from mum in the raw darkness, the struggle to don the school uniform before emerging from under the eiderdown – no duvets back then. Mind you, there was precious little warmth in our school uniforms. As I recall, they were made almost completely of nylon – nylon socks, undies, trousers, shirts and jumpers. In fact, it seemed that everything was made of nylon on those freezing mornings – including the carpets, curtains and bed sheets. It was the wonder material of the twentieth century and was the basis of a lot more than just women's stockings which, thanks to the mini-skirt, had all but disappeared by the time I was old enough to take an interest in such things. The Democratic Republic of Nylon was a horrible, slippery, rustling world which a generation of children was forced to inhabit because the material was hugely popular with mums. It was tough, it washed easily and it didn't need ironing. However, it did have its entertainment value. I remember the indoor pyrotechnics we set off when changing for bed. My sister and I would race around the room, rough and tumbling; mum would then turn off the light and we'd scramble to rip the jumpers off each others backs, the nylon material crackling while pretty blue sparks of static electricity flew in all directions from our flailing limbs. I suppose that workhorse, all-purpose 'miracle fibre' was another future vision that got overtaken by the future. Can one get nostalgic for a nylon bedroom carpet that was permanently crunchy with the pieces of plastic sprue from my Airfix kits that became immutably entangled in its fibres? I fear I am going that way.

Then it was the transition from crunchy carpets to freezing linoleum on the stumbling run down the hallway and into the kitchen where mum would have the oven of the gas cooker full on and with the door wide open. We would perch on chilly plastic chairs alternately putting our feet on the edge of the oven doorway (until the heat became unbearable) and then putting them back onto the icy stone tiles of the kitchen floor (until the cold became unbearable). We would mechanically munch through our eggs on toast while Tony Blackburn presented the Radio 1 Breakfast Show with his legendary and inexhaustible exuberance.

It must seem strange to today's kids that people were prepared to tolerate that level of discomfort in their own homes and I suppose, in a way, we were the last generation to have it inflicted upon us. For me, it was quite natural to press the button on an aerosol can and see what looked like a jet of cat's pee emerge from the nozzle – the temperature in the bedroom too low to allow the contents of the can to vaporise on contact with the freezing air. I was used to prising my face-flannel from the side of the bathroom wash basin where it had frozen into a solid ball during the night. Mum was always the first member of the household to get up in the mornings and her first vitally invigorating cup of tea depended on her having remembered to put the bottle of milk back into the fridge on the previous evening. Inside, the contents would stay in liquid form; if left on the worktop the milk would be a miniature white iceberg by the time it was required for breakfast. I can remember one morning when dad came into the kitchen to be greeted by mum's shriek of horror.

'Jim! What on earth's happened?'

'What are you talking about? Nothing's happened,' replied dad looking round anxiously.

'Your face . . . all that blood!'

Dad hurried back to the bathroom, returning ten minutes later with his face positively tessellated with tiny squares of toilet paper. He'd shaved in cold water, the immersion heater not having been turned on the previous evening, and, in the numbing cold, had been quite oblivious to the fact that he had shaved off a large part of his face along with the overnight bristles.

If getting up in the mornings was a misery, going to bed at night wasn't much better. My sister and I both had fan heaters in our bedrooms and we were allowed to have them on for ten minutes (strictly ten minutes) before we turned in – just long enough to take the chill off the room and to warm up our pyjamas. We also had our 'hottle-bottles' – our hot water bottles – to take to bed with us. Even today, the smell of an old-style rubber hot water bottle is one so evocative that it projects me straight back to my childhood. On winter nights, the sound of the kettle on the hob as it started to sing was the death knell of the day for when the hottle-bottles were filled, we were going to bed. In those days, bedrooms were for sleeping in and we spent the rest of the time either in the dining room or the kitchen – the only rooms of the house in which winter could be kept at bay with any success. Consequently, those bedrooms had minimal – if any – heating and the hot water bottle was an essential. As kids, we developed the habit of shoving them down to the bottom of the bed and toasting our chilled feet on them before pushing those same feet out from under the bedclothes and into the icy air when our toes felt like they were on fire. The inevitable result of this activity, coupled with the kitchen toe-toasting in the mornings, was chilblains: angry, red inflammations which, by turns, throbbed, ached and itched and were caused directly by the extremities being exposed to too much heat and too much cold. One doesn't hear much about chilblains these days, especially among children, but they were a veritable plague to the post-war generations who had to endure freezing cold houses in the days before central heating was a given rather than a luxury.

My parents had led tough lives. Neither had been forced to endure the truly grinding poverty that was endemic in the capital through the depression of the 1930s, but they'd witnessed it at first hand and had grown up in families which had fought tooth and nail to maintain their precarious finances. Depression, war, rationing and reconstruction had all left their mark. Consequently, expansive and expensive purchases went against the grain but I think even mum and dad conceded that something in the way of a heating system was required in the bungalow. The result was an act of rather craven bravado that saw a pair of storage heaters bought and installed in the new home. One was put in my parents' bedroom and the other in the labyrinthine hall. They proved about as useful as the proverbial chocolate teapot. In fact, a teapot may well have put more heat into the house for those storage heaters were rubbish with a capital 'C', a capital 'R', a capital 'A' and a capital 'P'.

Their attraction to my dad was the fact that they ran off the cheap-rate Economy 7 electricity tariff – something which appears to be making a come-back in these cash-strapped days. Economy 7 became very popular in the 1960s and '70s and was originally introduced to encourage consumers to use excess electricity produced by coal-fired and nuclear power stations which had to be kept going through the night, even though demand for power was relatively low during those hours. Enter the storage heater . . . a stamped metal box containing about three tons of breeze blocks threaded through by an electrical element. The element used the cheaper electricity, available through the night, to heat up the blocks which then, in theory, radiated out the stored heat during the period that the leccy went back to full price. I say 'in theory' because the wretched things never did anything of the sort. They were ugly, obtrusive, out of keeping with the dark-wood décor mum strived to achieve in the hallway, at least, and left everywhere they were supposed to heat stone cold.

I remember the misery of a 'flu attack that first winter which saw me desperately huddling up to the storage heater in the hall in a vain attempt to keep warm. I was running the sort of temperature that would have allowed you to fry an egg on my backside but those damned piles of bricks stayed steadfastly tepid as the frost bit into the fabric of the house and I wished I was dead. In the end, even mum and dad had to concede that the storage heaters were a waste of time, space and money; but it was with great excitement and no little incredulity that we learned, as the next winter loomed large on the horizon, that dad had sanctioned the installation of gas-fired central heating. It took a little while for the significance of this news to sink in. Hot water on demand and an end to those miserable winter mornings! I had visions of flinging back the bedclothes to saunter casually from my 75-degree bedroom, along a 75-degree hallway and into a 75-degree kitchen. Indeed, the kitchen would no longer be needed in the mornings. Like those happy families we constantly saw tucking into their Sugar Puffs on the TV advertisements, we would all be able to sit round the dining room table, actually able to see the day broadening instead of having the light of our lives filtered through a thin frosting of ice on the inside of the glass. And central heating was a revelation. It's difficult to convey to those who take such a facility for granted just how significant a change it prompted in the Wells' day-to-day life and routine. For the first time ever, mum could be heard singing along to the radio at 6.15 on an Arctic January morning and I could get dressed after getting out of bed instead of before. From that point our time in the house was reckoned as either BC – Before Central (Heating) – and AC

(After Chilblains)! And the fun didn't stop there because, as the installation neared completion, we looked forward with malicious pleasure to taking revenge on the storage heaters that had promised so much and delivered so little. But they were as resistant to destruction as they were to giving out heat. We hammered them, prised them and broke them open only to discover we then had to dispose of all the bricks inside. They were lying round the back garden for ages. As for the elements, they uncurled into a continuous length of wire long enough to run to the moon and back. It steadfastly refused to stay put in the dustbin, defied any attempts to push it under the workbench in the shed without springing out to trip people up and broke out of every bin-liner and carrier bag into which it was forced. The metal casings were equally intractable. The dustbin men refused to touch them and they ended up being pushed behind the shed at the top of the garden where they probably remain to this day, doggedly refusing to rust away and probably still waiting for the chance to slip out again and gash somebody's shin.

Dad reckoned we could have shortened the war by years if we had dropped Economy 7 storage heaters on the Germans while they were dropping bombs on us. Half the population of Berlin would have frozen to death, he reckoned, while the other half would have gone insane trying to dismantle the damned things and hide them behind various garden sheds in Poland and Russia. Mum said his idea would have probably been against the Geneva Convention as it would have constituted a terror weapon of mass destruction as well as psychological warfare waged on civilians with children and chilblains.

All was well in the home, though; we had central heating. But, the wildly extravagant capital expenditure that saw those blessed radiators decorating the walls of every room stopped there. My parents' parents had been Victorians and the Victorian fruit doesn't fall far from the Victorian tree. Apart from mum's John England mail order catalogue there was no credit in our household. Credit and debt were the same thing and to be in debt was the ultimate mark of failure and humiliation. The 'catalogue', as it was referred to, was only tolerated because it was interest-free and earned mum commission when family, friends or neighbours bought something through it. Thus it could be argued that running that catalogue was almost like running a business and that was earning a living. That's how dad saw it, anyway. Mum, though pretty much of a kidney with dad and their generation's general attitude, was also a pragmatist. She had to be; she was a housewife and mother. Dad may have been the one who changed the light bulb, but he had absolutely no concept of what a light bulb cost. That catalogue with its 38-week terms was a life-saver.

Green Shield Stamps played their part, too. We had many trips to Castle Street to the building now occupied by Argos to redeem the books that we had licked ourselves dry to fill. For those too young to remember them, Green Shield Stamps were a very big deal. Thousands of outlets across the country issued them – from supermarkets to petrol stations. One was given a set number of stamps for every pound one spent in-store. The stamps were gummed on one side and had to be licked and pasted into the books issued to contain them. When we had filled a book we started a new one and eagerly searched the Green Shield catalogue to see what we could get for the number of books we'd managed to fill. There was a touch of opulence about that catalogue because mum and dad used the stamps for items which, if not exactly luxuries, were lifestyle embellishments rather than household necessities. Our first set of bathroom scales was a good example. Garden tools, a hairdryer for mum and – another first for the Wells family – an electric kettle also came into the house as a result of much licking and pasting. Ironically, Green Shield Stamps remain in my mind not so much for what they provided as for the company's famously maladroit advert of the 1970s. In 'happy family' vein, it showed a mum and dad leading their little darling by the hands atop the slogan 'Suddenly it's yours with Green Shield Stamps'. I tormented my sister for ages with the suggestion that she had been acquired in exchange for 25 filled books. She was a bargain, I told her. After all, mum and dad could have carried on saving for the 1,350 books needed for a Ford Cortina!

Being a customer of the Midland Bank, my father was an early recipient of the new Access credit card – the first real rival to the Barclaycard. It arrived unbidden in the post one day. Dad examined it with suspicion and grunted, 'Access? The only access this will give us is an open door to the workhouse.' Dad threw it onto the fire with some satisfaction, a temptation banished to the nether regions where it belonged. Mum, I think, would have banished it to the top drawer of the sideboard on the basis that principles were admirable things but they didn't pay for the mending of burst pipes three weeks after Christmas or the holes in the children's shoes a week before the start of the school term. Mum and dad were, in essence, the last of the cash generations. In their inherited financial philosophy, if you couldn't pay cash for something it was because you didn't have the money to buy it. If you didn't have the money to buy it, you couldn't have it. Full stop. Even cheques were reserved for serious transactions like the payment of the utility bills or special purchases. They represented transactions on a higher financial plane. When, later on in that first year, I was offered a place at Hastings Grammar School, the school uniform had to be bought and it wasn't cheap. In fact, there were two sources for that uniform – Wards, the old-style outfitters in Queens Road, or the Co-op. Wards sold the grammar school blazer finished with shiny brass buttons; the Co-op's version had black, plastic ones. Dad never actually said: 'No son of mine is going to a grammar school with plastic buttons on his blazer,' but he certainly thought it, for I was dispatched with mum to Wards for my blazer, my cap and my regulation mackintosh fittings and the lot was paid for with an immaculately completed cheque filled in with dad's best Papermate ball-pen (which was, itself, reserved for writing things of significance!). He would never have written a cheque for anything from the Co-op. After all, the Co-op was a thinly disguised fund-raising organisation for the Labour Party. It wouldn't have got dad's money on principle; it certainly wouldn't have been allowed to create an incriminating 'paper-trail' through which his bank could observe his patronage of an organisation he regarded as borderline seditious and barely a step away from Bolshevism.

Even at the age of eleven I remember having an awkward feeling that such rigidity of views didn't sit comfortably with my perception of my father's expansive intellect. It smacked of closed doors and shuttered windows when one of the things I most admired about him as a child was his breadth of perception and his understanding of why the world worked liked it did. I probably wouldn't have been able to explain the concept of snobbery then and would have hotly denied any accusations of it directed at me or my family. All the same, I still remember the sense of suppressed glee I felt on my first day at the grammar when I sat down in morning assembly and found myself next to a boy whose blazer was fastened with those tell-tale plastic buttons.

It was, of course, many years before I realised just what a struggle my parents had endured with dad's failing health and his increasing depression at his perceived failure to provide for his family. That, in turn, was intensified by my mother's enforced employment. To make matters worse the nation had already set a course towards political crisis: inflation, price-rises and the Three-Day Week. For me, though, blissfully ignorant of the knife-edge on which millions like us were balancing their finances, there was a feeling of quiet sufficiency in the house – as sufficiency was understood by children who had never previously known central heating and who drank Coca Cola only when the adults drank champagne.

My family never owned a car. Dad could drive but never managed the wherewithal to acquire a vehicle. Later on, his arthritis got to the point at which driving was no longer an option, anyway. Mum had never learned and didn't want to. Until we made one particular friend who did have a car, for the most part we walked down to St Leonard's and caught a bus when we needed to go into Hastings. Taxis were only for emergencies. To my mind, they had an ominous quality because they seemed synonymous with an unwelcome urgency. If my parents were prepared to pay for a car to drive them non-stop from A to B, then whatever was at B was pretty damned important. Mind you, we found the buses more expensive than we were used to because they were all 'one-man operated' with drivers who took your fare before you could sit down. Now, on London Transport's celebrated Routemaster double-deckers, the driver was secluded in his cab and the tickets were dispensed by a conductor with a leather satchel for his money and a hand-operated ticket machine hanging round his neck. It's not that we deliberately avoided paying our fares by hiding under the seats or ducking down in the hope that the conductor wouldn't spot us; but sometimes, if you were only going a short distance and the bus was full, you would actually reach your destination before the conductor reached you. It was one of those things that was just accepted as, at times, unavoidable. Because the LT driver didn't have to mess about with tickets and change, the buses moved away from bus stops very quickly. In Hastings, though, it was a different story.

Maidstone and District Motor Services Ltd operated the local buses and, as I recall, they were all single-deckers except, for some reason, the no. 76 which was the circular route going round the town. The bus we used most often, though, was the no. 74. That came up from West St Leonard's station and stopped at the top of Boscobel Road North just round the bend from that curious edifice stuck in the middle of the road, outside Highlands Mansions, known as 'The Chimney'. It was called 'The Chimney' because that's what it was – and is. The round, brick beehive with the sawn-off top set in the middle of Pevensey Road is the stack at the top of the ventilation shaft for the Bo-Peep railway tunnel, some 100-plus feet below the surface of the road. In the days of steam locomotives it was a very necessary thing: even when diesel engines came along it was still useful to help clear exhaust fumes from the tunnel which is a fairly long one at 1,318 yards. Oh dear, once a trainspotter, always a trainspotter!

The no. 74 bus was populated largely by old people – as, it seemed to us, was pretty much everything. The bus would pull up at the stop and we would wait an age for the elderly alighters to gather their bags and belongings and fall down the rather sharp flight of three steps to the pavement. Dutifully, we would allow the elderly bus-boarders to go ahead of us. All of them had spent as long as 20 minutes at the bus stop gassing away but only when they had actually climbed the steps to confront the driver did they begin the prolonged rummage through their bags to find their purses. Having found those purses, they would then begin the ticket-buying process.

'One ticket to the London Road post office please, driver.'

'Don't stop at the post office,' the driver would say. 'You'll have to get off at Christ Church and walk down the hill or jump off at Norman Road and walk back a bit.'

'I can't walk. That's why I need your bus.'

'No love, what I mean is . . .'

And so it would go on, the driver cheerfully welcoming his regulars on board, particularly on pension day when the old dears headed for the post office en masse. On one occasion, we'd all finally sat down ready for the off when the driver craned his head round to the passengers and said: 'Where's Lilly, then?'

'Oh dear!' said one of the recent additions. 'I saw her with her dog this morning and she said she was coming down today.'

'Here she comes!' croaked someone else.

We all peered as best we could through the rear window to see an old lady with a string bag in one hand, a walking stick in the other and three or four library books jammed under her arm. She came on at a swift hobble. Every few steps she would pause, wave her stick in the air and mouth something as urgent as it was inaudible. At that point at least one of the library books would escape its armpit imprisonment and fall to the pavement. She would stoop to gather it up whereupon she would let go of the string bag and two oranges plus a ball of wool would make their own bid for freedom. She finally made it to the doors. By this time the driver had come out of his cab and was on the pavement to assist the panting passenger up the stairs.

'Just sit down Lilly, love. We'll sort out the ticket at the other end.'

Gasping for breath, poor Lilly still paused in the gangway to bid everyone . . . pant . . . Good Morning and . . . gasp . . . apologise for holding . . . wheeze . . . everyone up.

How that no. 74 bus maintained its timetable I'll never know but I remember it as being pretty much where it was supposed to be when it was supposed to be there.

'They build in "O.F.F. Time" when they're calculating the timetable,' said dad casually on one occasion when mum was moaning about the length of time it seemed to take to get anywhere by bus.

'Off?' I asked. 'What's off-time?'

'Not off-time,' he corrected me. 'O.F.F. Time.'

'What does O.F.F. stand for?' I asked, puzzled.

'It stands for Old Farts' Fumbling time,' said dad straight-faced.

'Oh Jim,' said mum looking away quickly. 'Don't tell him things like that. He'll believe you.'

I did believe him and, what's more, I still do – although I'm sure Maidstone and District's timetable calculating pointy-heads had a much more scientific name for it – and certainly a politer one.

The buses were frustrating and entertaining by turns but, as I have already hinted, at eleven years old I was in love with the railways. I had been brought up just a stone's throw from the old Great Western Railway which ran from the mighty Paddington station through the West London sprawl of Acton and Southall and onto Reading, Swindon, Bristol, South Wales and the far-flung outposts of Devon and Cornwall. There that great railway, that measure of Victorian engineering brilliance and British civilisation, penetrated a strange and mysterious land where the towns and villages had curiously un-English sounding names; Luxulyan, Penryn, Crows-an-Wra, Probus, Tywardreath. They were strange names for strange places, as I imagined them, clinging to the very edge of the country and bracing themselves against the measureless might of the Atlantic Ocean. In Hillingdon, dad would take me to nearby Hayes station where I would stand, endlessly thrilled, as the mighty diesel locomotives flashed into view. The lines would start to hiss menacingly as the express trains approached before crashing through the station at nearly 100mph with a sound like the end of the world.

But again, the quirky little town that we had made our home had already made its own impact on the nation's railways despite being, in effect, little more than a green extension of the busy reticulation that was the commuter network. For Hastings had its own specially built trains – the Hastings Diesels – and they were to be found nowhere in the country other than on the line that ran from Charing Cross and London Bridge, via Sevenoaks and Tunbridge Wells, to St Leonard's and Hastings. They were another example of

Hastings Logic – and they were famous. Indeed, there were many occasions on which I met fellow anoraks who had travelled the length of the country to ride and photograph the unique Hastings Diesels. Some of them even brought tape recorders to catch the distinctive engine beat which had earned the trains their nickname of 'The Thumpers'. The trains themselves, it must be admitted, were hardly style icons of the railway world and were purely functional creations which had appeared for two reasons. The more prosaic of them was that the line between Tonbridge Junction and West St Leonard's had never been electrified. Consequently, when steam evaporated into the pages of history, diesel power was required. The second reason was more interesting and based on some distinctly dark and dodgy dealings – quite literally. Apparently, the companies building the Mountfield and Wadhurst tunnels on the Charing Cross to Hastings line, south of Tunbridge Wells, decided they could sharpen up their profit margins by building those tunnels with a brick-skin lining depth of two bricks when at least four were actually required. The murky skinflinting was exposed to the glare of revelation when a section of the Mountfield Tunnel lining collapsed in 1855, just three years after it was opened. The tunnels had to be relined with a new brick-skin. Unfortunately, the tunnel bores were such that, when properly finished, they became too narrow for existing trains to pass one another safely inside them.

What to do? The solution arrived at was to build slim-line trains that could pass one another safely deep under the earth and, in the late 1950s, a new fleet of diesel multiple units, built narrower than their existing counterparts, were introduced. These were the Hastings Diesels, and they came as six-car units – six carriages with an engine apiece in the first and the sixth carriages. And it was these very trains, as twelve-car combinations, that were just that teensy-weensy bit too long to fit the platform of Warrior Square station and which caused the Wells family, a number of our visitors and, I've no doubt, many other first-time visitors to the town, to realise that they had arrived at Warrior Square only as the train accelerated out of the station on its way to Hastings.

I shall always have a sentimental soft-spot for those trains. They disappeared in the mid-1980s when the Tunbridge Wells line was finally electrified and the problem tunnels were converted to single track but the 'doomp-doomp-doomp' of the Thumpers lives on in my memory as one of those background sounds of my childhood, just like 'Moaning Minnie', the dreary, inexhaustible fog-horn on board the old *Royal Sovereign* lightship. I remember dad telling me, in a rare confessional moment, that when he lay awake at night, the pain in his joints preventing his sleeping, and those dark and silent hours of the middle-night bearing down on him, he would listen to the first of those trains as it emerged from Bo-Peep Tunnel, knowing that it was 5.30 a.m., that night was on the wane and that the dawn, in the winter months at least, was just below the eastern horizon. Then, and only then, would he sink into the light slumber that was the best he could expect.

In his excellent novel *Rogue Male*, Geoffrey Household wrote of the dawn that although it was the hour of the outlawed, the persecuted and the damned, yet no one could ever fail to feel some hope anew with the sun about to rise over him. It certainly brought a peace of sorts to my pain-wracked father. I, too, in later life, following hours of sleeplessness when the world seemed bleak and the mistakes and follies of my past life would rise to haunt the dead hours of night, I, too, could not fail to feel some stirrings of hope when that same dawn light put the dread and dismay to flight. I was many miles away from St Leonard's by then, but the memory of that first commuter train of the day comforting my father still thumped loudly in my mind's-ear, easing me, just as it had brought a kind of peace to him all those years before.

Indeed, dad's generally deteriorating health meant he never saw much of the town or what it had to offer either in the context of a place to live or a seaside resort, but the rest of the family did. Our first experience of Hastings and St Leonard's had been as the latter during the previous summer when mum had brought us down to the coast for a holiday while she was actually house-hunting in the town. Then, my sister and I had had eyes, ears and noses only for the beach. It had been an adventure not without its typically Wellsian problems but we'll come to those a little later . . . In those early, freezing days of 1971, that sunny sojourn seemed more like a pleasant dream. However, it wasn't long before we started to explore the other attractions the town had to offer. Easter came in the second week of April that year and it wasn't a desperately warm one, either. The newspapers were reporting heavy snowfalls in Yorkshire as late as the last week of the month. Nonetheless, we learned that Easter was the time when Hastings woke from its winter slumbers, waiting anxiously for the dominant grey hues of sea and sky to brighten to the deepening blue that told traders and townsfolk alike that spring had sprung. Then, striped awnings would start to appear and the sharp tang of salt and vinegar would compete with the thick, sweet scent of candyfloss across the Old Town. The council's parks, gardens and flower borders would explode with geometric colour while the over-arching sky rang with the calls of swooping, circling seagulls in their thousands. So it was during that first spring and early summer that we started to explore those places that the official guidebooks earnestly assured us were 'must-see attractions' – the beached fishing boats, the narrow lanes and stairways of the Old Town, the Pier, the Caves and the funicular railways running up both the West and East Hills.

First on the list, though, had to be the castle; for me, it was already a personal icon of the town not least because its illuminated ruins had been framed by one of the tiny windows of the attic bedroom in which I had slept during those wonderful two weeks spent with Aunty Joyce the previous summer. Poor old Hastings Castle! It must have been magnificent; an all but impregnable, high-tech fortress high on the cliffs above the surly Saxon fishermen in their cottages huddled between the West and East Hills. But Hastings fell out of favour; the fabric was not maintained while wind and wave kept up their indefatigable assault on the soft sandstone on which the castle stood. It degenerated into a formless ruin which flatters to deceive when seen from ground level and, particularly, when illuminated after dark.

Dad, as a history teacher, could never quite come to terms with the apparent lack of respect that his new home town seemed to attract. In the context of the battle of 1066 and the Norman Invasion, he once described Hastings as 'the birthplace of the English-speaking peoples'. Whether he thought that one up himself or borrowed it from someone else, I don't know; but in the light of the near-millennium of history that followed that momentous October day, I don't think he was too far wide of the mark. That crumbled, neglected and redundant castle seemed to him a symbol of the wanton neglect the nation afforded the cradle of its origins. It was a high-visibility abandonment of a town whose name, he felt, should be at the very heart of every Englishman's consciousness.

Many, many years after my first and only visit to the castle (and let's face it, most people only ever go inside it once), I took a stroll over the grassy humps and through the solitary archway that decorates every postcard ever printed of the place. I sighed. Hastings Castle may dominate the town's skyline and it may have a pleasing effect on the eye when illuminated on a summer's evening but the truth is inescapable: Hastings Castle is rubbish.

It's rubbish as a castle and it's rubbish as a tourist attraction. If you're going to be a ruin, you have to be a quality ruin and Hastings Castle has neither echoes of the architectural magnificence of, say, Fountains Abbey nor the mystery of deep antiquity that Stonehenge offers. It's a hopeless pile of stones and without a map or guidebook it's all but impossible to work out what was what and which bit had what function when it was in its original state of repair. Insult is added to injury by the proximity of the magnificent Bodiam Castle which, although a shell today, is, externally at least, not so very different to the fortress that our forebears would have seen emerging from the mists curling off the Rother meadows 700 years ago.

On the West Hill, I allowed my mind to wander into a world of imagination and I sat on a rock and spent a physically idle ten minutes inventing a little scenario in my head. I imagined a smart and enthusiastic young man (whom I named Mr Blenkinsop – I've no idea why) being sent on a special mission by the big-wigs of the borough council. That mission – should Blenkinsop have chosen to accept it, which he did – was to meet with the boss of Turret Tours, a company which specialised in running coach trips to the most famous of the nation's castles, mostly for elderly Americans on the Grand Tour of the Old Country. Turret Tours used executive coaches to bus its wealthy patrons to the likes of Corfe, Windsor and, of course, that ancient and dread symbol of royal authority . . . armoury, treasury, fortress and top people's prison – the Tower of London.

Young Blenkinsop's job was to convince Old Man Turret that Hastings Castle was a worthy addition to the existing itinerary and I imagined the two of them meeting in Mr Turret's cluttered office, seated at a desk which, for some reason, featured a small model of the Eiffel Tower. (Again, don't ask me why; it's just the way my brain worked, I suppose.) We join the pair as Mr Turret picks up his pen and addresses his visitor.

'Right then, Mr Blenkinsop. Just a few questions to help us establish just how historically important your castle . . . let me see, it's at Hastings, I note . . . might be to the nation. Ready?'

'Yes, indeed. Fire away.'

'Good. Now, this castle of yours . . . is it an old one?'

'Ooh yes, very old. Built in 1070 – the first example of a permanent, stone-built Norman castle in England.'

'Excellent! We're off to a good start. Now, did any mighty army ever lay siege to a small but valiant group of defenders inside the castle until they were forced to eat their own cats and dogs – I'm seeing marauding French raiders here or evil Swiss mercenaries, perhaps, during the civil war between Stephen and Matilda?'

'No.'

'Hmm, pity. Did it see any military action at all?'

'Well, there were anti-aircraft people there during the Second World War, apparently.'

'That's what we want! Battle of Britain and all that. How many guns in the battery?'

'Just the one.'

'Oh dear. Well, never mind. Let's try going back a little further. Did any captured kings meet a grisly end in the dungeons of Hastings Castle?'

'Not as such.'

'Not even one of the rubbish kings that no one was likely to miss like Edward II or Richard III?'

'We don't think so.'

'I know! What about the Gunpowder Plot? Did any of the conspirators ever meet there in secret or store their barrels of gunpowder there before moving them up to London?'

'No.'

'Well, was Charles I imprisoned there? Must have been, surely. There's barely a castle in Britain where Charles wasn't shut up for a few months while the Parliamentary forces tried to decide what to do with him.'

'Well, there's a story that it was rumoured at the time . . .'

'He never went anywhere near Hastings Castle, did he, Mr Blenkinsop?'

'No. No, he didn't.'

'Oh dear, we are struggling rather, aren't we. What about nobility generally? Was the castle ever the ancestral seat of one of the nation's great families; you know, like the Dukes of Norfolk at Arundel?'

'Well, it was owned by the Sixth Earl of Chichester and it stayed in his family for some time.'

'Splendid! And then . . . ?'

'They sold it to the local council for £3,000 in 1951.'

'That's not a lot.'

'There wasn't a lot to sell. The castle had suffered rather badly during the famously furious storms of the thirteenth century, you see, and some of it had fallen into the sea.'

'How much of it?'

'About half, I should say.'

'Well, Mr Blenkinsop. I think the most important thing about this castle is that you clearly love it very much and, after all, that's what really matters, isn't it. Be so good as to close the door on your way out.'

There's a saying known the world over: 'An Englishman's home is his castle'. In Hastings this is particularly true for there are a large number of Englishmen whose homes really are their castle. Their ancestors ransacked the tumbled masonry piling up at the foot of the cliffs and even headed up to the top of West Hill and bodily carted back as much of the stonework as they could knock off – in both senses of the phrase. They used it for the construction of their own homes, creating a spreading town beneath the ruins of the all but impregnable fort which, in its brief heyday, had kept a vigilant eye both over them – and on them.

But if the castle was a one-off visit and something of a disappointment, there were plenty of other things to entertain us. We may have become residents but we were happy to be 'Grockles' – as Hastings people referred to holiday-makers and trippers in those days – as we worked our way through the guidebook, sallying forth into the town via the curiosity of Bottle Alley.

Bottle Alley was one of those oddities that one heard about rather than read about. It was not in the first tranche of tourist attractions with the West and East Hill lifts, the castle and the caves, but it was an anecdotal draw in its own right. I still encounter people who, when told I hail from Hastings, say, 'Isn't that the place where they've got that tunnel decorated with bits of broken bottle?'

The glassy phenomenon was created as part of the second promenade – the lower or covered promenade – which ran from Warrior Square Gardens to the pier directly underneath the top prom. It was the work of an extraordinary individual named Sidney Little. His title of Borough Engineer belied this man's vision and passion for bravura building – and he just loved concrete. Even today, he is remembered in the town as 'King Concrete'. He was also responsible for the massive underground car park – the first of its kind in the country – and the bathing pool in West St Leonard's complete with its Olympic-size swimming pool and fantastic Art Deco surrounds – in glorious concrete, of course.

Bottle Alley was, in its own right, a unique and stylish addendum to the seaside heritage of both the town and the nation and was one of the features designed to propel Hastings and St Leonard's out of its Victorian somnambulism and into the twentieth century proper. It was constructed – like all the great man's works – in the 1930s and originally had shutters to protect those who came to see it from the wilder elements – and it drew a lot of people. Legend has it that Concrete Sid actually had the idea for the glass decoration after discovering a vast horde of discarded bottles on a rubbish dump. How's that for recycling vision years ahead of the pack? Unfortunately, in recent times the people Bottle Alley has drawn have been those in pursuit of Class A drugs and people looking for somewhere to drink that will ensure their cans of Special Brew remain both undiluted by downpours and out of view of the CCTV cameras. Thus, there are not many now who would elect to walk the length of Bottle Alley after dark even if it does mean being able to get from the pier to Warrior Square without a wind-blown soaking. Personally, I've always seen this architectural by-the-by as a little gem. It's a warmer spot out of the wind when the sun struggles low in the winter sky; a cool colonnade in the summer when the sun bakes the sea front and bastes it with diesel fumes. And it's all backed by a wonderful mural of silicone-based detritus; a fancy weskit; a glittering undercoat-of-many-colours hidden to all but the eyes with time to pause and ponder its fantastically intricate construction. I have lost count of the number of times that I lost count of the individual mortared sections of glass pieces: it's quite impossible to tally them up with any accuracy although I tried regularly through my teen years. Neither have I ever even been able to count the number of different colours featured in the alley. Am I drifting towards hyperbole? Maybe, but I think Bottle Alley is another of those half-hidden metaphors for the town's irritating lack of self-esteem: half-heartedly maintaining what it instinctively knows are its assets while consistently under-selling and under-using them. I think it's a problem common to so many of the British seaside resorts which lost their way and their confidence with the advent of the foreign package-holiday.

The eastern end of Bottle Alley was hard by one of our favourite visits – the model village at White Rock. It's long gone now, replaced by the successful Clambers play park. The model village fascinated us because no matter how often we visited it, we always found something that we hadn't noticed before. Unfortunately, as time went on the main feature that we noticed on each visit was that yet another section of the little town had been smashed to matchwood by vandals. The model village had been there since 1955 and featured a castle, a watermill, a high street with shops and cleverly designed 'Sussex-style' houses. The miniature community finally vanished from the micro-map in 1972 after those vandals' damage had totted up a wreckage bill of £5,000 – a pretty hefty sum today, a seriously substantial wedge then. It sticks in my mind not simply because it was a miniature work of art which had been destroyed for ever but because, unlike the imponderable cataclysms of Mother Nature's earthquakes and tsunamis, this destruction was contrived and controlled by a malign and nihilistic thuggery which destroyed for the pure pleasure of destruction and deprivation. Yes, it happened then, too.

It was 'kids', of course, who had been responsible for the model village massacre, said the grown-ups. They always said, 'It was kids', and I was a kid. For the first time in my life I felt a sense of shame that my peers and contemporaries had been responsible for the destruction and disappointment caused by so few to so many. Seventeen years of loving work gone. I felt it very sharply and saw, clearly, the difference between this sort of violence and the almost good-natured mischief that saw the occasional bottle of washing up liquid surreptitiously dumped into the water to 'froth up' the fountain at the end of Castle Street. Equally amusing to the juvenile mind – and equally non-permanent – were the traffic cones regularly placed on the head of the statue of Queen Victoria at Warrior Square. Indeed, the poor old girl had to put up with a lot. On one occasion some wag painted footprints on the pavement leading from the statue's plinth to the public loos and back again. The adults may have tut-tutted at such puerile antics but they smiled in private at them, too; but the model village? Perhaps I was starting to grow up; I certainly experienced similar emotions over the destruction of the Albert Memorial.

Ah, the Albert Memorial. There's something that will really date a resident of Hastings. To this day, I still occasionally

take a bus into town and absent-mindedly ask the driver
for, 'Memorial return, please.' Strangely enough, all the bus
drivers know what and where I mean – even the younger
ones. The Memorial was a Victorian edifice – not surprising,
really, when one remembers that it was erected by public
subscription to the memory of Queen Victoria's adored
husband, Prince Albert, who died in 1861. Gone now, of
course, but for more than a century it stood as a clock tower
of Victorian Gothic chutzpah right in the centre of the town
where Queens Road, Havelock Road, Cambridge Road,
Robertson Street and York Buildings converge.

It was demolished in the late 1970s after another attack
of vandalism during which the perpetrators got inside and
managed to set fire to the edifice. Deemed too unsafe to be
left standing, it was dismantled – rather than demolished
– and the pieces put into storage at the Town Hall. For me,
the town centre has never looked so well since. For a start,
the Memorial actually defined the centre of the town; all
Hastings seemed to revolve around that sturdy monument.
Today, the town centre, in its confusingly semi-pedestrianised
state, seems to lack a certain 'something'. Personally, I think
it lacks the Albert Memorial but, oddly enough, even those
too young to remember it frequently say that the open-plan
town centre would benefit from some sort of structure.
Opinion divides on precisely what would be best suited to the
location and I've heard numerous suggestions – including a
purposefully-oversized statue of the late Princess of Wales; a
life-size fishing smack cast in bronze; serial art installations;
traditional plinth-based statues of Sir Winston Churchill,
John Logie Baird and, interestingly, William the Conqueror.
I say 'interestingly' because even today the general sympathy
of the average Hastings resident tends to be with William's
Saxon adversary Harold rather than with the Norman
invader. Harold would probably be a popular choice if only
the statue maker could refrain from putting that wretched

arrow in the poor man's eye – something for which there is, apparently, no sound historical evidence anyway.

Slightly more 'fringe' suggestions? A multi-image 'big screen' showing all the town's CCTV pictures 'live' at any one time; a bank of recycling bins; an open-air police point with stationed officers and more statues – everything from polystyrene coffee cups to empty mussel shells from the beach, everyone and everything from iguanodons known to have inhabited the area 80 million years ago to Jimi Hendrix (no, I've no idea why, either . . .). Another rock 'n' roll legend with slightly more claim to a local connection who gets suggested is Syd Barrett, the flawed genius and founder member of rock band Pink Floyd. It's widely believed locally that Barrett's last performance – or at least his last appearance on stage – with that band was in January 1968 on Hastings Pier. Apparently, his bizarre and unpredictable behaviour had reached such intolerable levels by the time the group reached the town that, following the gig, the other band members simply didn't bother to pick him up when they left for the next show on the tour itinerary at Southampton University. I like that story – even if it does turn out to be apocryphal. I have a sneaking suspicion that Syd would have appreciated Hastings Logic and that he might have lived very happily somewhere in the Old Town.

But if the Albert Memorial is no more, the other famous edifices which we explored remain. Still my favourite after all these years is 'The Piece of Cheese', that tiny, yellow-washed, wedged–shaped cottage abutting Starr's Passage, off All Saints Street. We all liked that, I remember, and enjoyed the obvious jokes, no doubt convinced we were the first to think of them.

'Piece of Cheese? You'd have to be crackers to live there.'

'If it's only eight feet wide, are they cheesy feet?'

'If that's the cheese, I don't want to meet the mouse!'

'I don't want to meet the cat!'

And talking of cats, just up the road from the 'The Piece of Cheese' was something I very much did want to see but was not allowed to view. The Stag pub, in All Saints Street, had for many years on display two mummified cats. This rather grotesque and slightly sinister exhibition was not purely gratuitous. Its origins are in the old tradition that a dead cat – sometimes preserved, sometimes not – was frequently secreted in the fabric of buildings under construction or renovation. The practice was a superstitious attempt at warding-off bad luck, deflecting malicious intent and even barring demons and evil spirits from the premises. I desperately wanted to see those talisman cats but back then pubs had a total ban on children in the bars and that was that. By the time I was old enough to blag my way into the old town pubs I was on the lookout for things that intrigued me far more than mummified cats.

We had a good time being tourists within the borough boundary and there was no shortage of things to do and see whatever the time of year and whatever the weather. But Hastings was a town beyond the vestiges of both its historical and watering-hole origins. Not all the entertainments on offer, therefore, depended on the resort tradition. Our first trip to the cinema was an entertainment in its own right. In London, we had seen our films in the huge Odeons and Regals at Uxbridge, Southall and Ealing. They were palatial places, grand movie theatres built to accommodate four-figure audience numbers. They had stalls, balconied circles, dress circles and an army of short-skirted, uniformed usherettes who escorted customers to their seats with smiles brighter than the beams from their regulation-issue torches. Of course, cinema-going has changed dramatically (and not for the better in my humble opinion). For a start, back then you got two films for your money. The main feature would be preceded in turn by a string of trailers advertising forthcoming blockbusters and then the 'B' movie – a full-

length feature which, on occasions, turned out to be better
entertainment than the big-name feature that one had
actually come to see. Then there would be an intermission
whereupon the lights would go up, the beaming usherettes
would reappear with illuminated trays of choc ices, Kia-Ora
orange drinks and packets of cigarettes. The lights would dim
again to the famous 'Pah-Pah-Pah-Pah' Pearl & Dean theme
music heralding the advertisements and then, at last, our
anticipation sharpened, the big picture would begin. In those
days, too, the whole programme ran as a cycle so it was quite
possible to take a seat half-way through the main feature and
stay on until the combined programme had returned to the
point at which one had joined it. As a child, of course, the
whole thing was a major adventure, especially if mum could
be persuaded to splash out for choc ices – something we were
only likely to get in a cinema.

Our first trip to the pictures – or 'the flicks' as we called
them – after moving to St Leonard's was a short walk down
to Norman Road to the old Curzon Cinema, now long-gone,
the premises today occupied by Bookers, the DIY store and
builders' merchants. I don't remember the film we went to see
but it would have been something suitably gentle – a Disney
cartoon like *101 Dalmatians* or *The Aristocats*; perhaps a live
action kiddy-flick like *Bedknobs and Broomsticks* or *Chitty
Chitty Bang Bang*.

The first thing that struck us was the size of the place; we
felt like we'd accidentally strayed into someone's front room
as we bought our tickets at a tiny kiosk from a lady who kept
the takings in a shortbread tin with 'A Present from Scotland'
on the lid. The next thing that we noticed was the distinct
lack of children in the audience. Everyone about us seemed
to be at least ninety years old and most of them were busy
trying – and failing – to prop sticks and crutches against the
curved backs of the cinema seats. Mum looked about her
thoughtfully and then approached a man with blue overalls

and a broom which he was using in an attempt to retrieve something that had clearly fallen under one of the seats. She waited patiently until he got up, using the broom as a prop to help restore him to the perpendicular.

'There you go, missus,' he said in triumph to a tiny, silver-haired crone in an adjacent seat as he handed her back the top set of her false teeth. 'Couldn't quite reach the toffee – though I don't suppose you'll be wanting that back,' he chuckled. Then he leaned closer to her and whispered confidentially, 'In here, you'd be better off sticking with the Murray Mints, Betty, love.' Betty was clearly overwhelmed by the actions of her blue-overalled white knight and patted his hand in mute gratitude.

'Now love,' said Mr Overalls, turning to mum, 'what can I do for you?'

'Ah, well,' said mum in a lowered voice. 'I was just wondering whether I'd got the dates right. It's supposed to be a children's film this week . . . today, I mean.'

'That's right, missus,' said Mr Overalls. 'But it's raining outside this afternoon, innit.'

'Yes, but I don't see . . .'

He lowered his voice and nodded at the chattering collection of geriatrics, some of whom were already producing knitting needles and balls of wool. 'We always get the coffin-dodgers in when it's raining. After all, they don't want to sit in the seafront shelters when it's piss . . . err . . . pouring down outside now, do they? So they come in here for a chat and a cup of tea.' Then he squinted at his watch and said, 'Film'll be starting soon, love. Get yourselves sat down.' And, shouldering his broom like a sentry on duty, he marched back up the aisle to many admiring glances.

There was no 'cup of tea' in evidence but there was plenty of 'chat'. The lights went down, the programme commenced and the old folk all but drowned out the soundtrack with their conversations; a constant hum sporadically penetrated by the whistling shriek of feedback – as huge, Bakelite hearing aids were adjusted – and the occasional loud 'Cooo-eee!' as someone spotted a friend or acquaintance a few rows ahead or behind.

'Ooh-ooh! Is that you, Norma?'

'Ooh, hello, Glad. You got Ron with you today?'

'No, dear. He's still poorly.'

'Yes, of course. Stroke, wasn't it?'

'Stroke of good luck. He's tucked up in a nice, warm hospital bed with a telly while I've had to come down here. Do you know they charged me three bob to get in today? It's disgusting!'

The furious rattle of knitting needles made us feel like we were sheltering from a rain storm in a tin shack. The cup-of-tea reference was at last explained when the film reached its intermission. The lights went up and an excited buzz ran around the theatre. There was a loud bang as the doors were flung open and a hugely fat woman appeared. She was gamely manoeuvring a rattling trolley the size of a small armoured car that contained a huge tea-urn and piles of white china teacups. Dressed in a blue floral housecoat and a frilly white apron, the tea lady sported a little white cap on top of her head that looked like a polystyrene coffee cup that had been sat on – probably by the person who was currently wearing it. We stared at her in astonishment.

'Here you are, my lovelies,' she sang as she bullied the trolley across the threadbare carpet to a spot in front of the stalls. Sticks and crutches were hastily retrieved as the audience members shuffled expectantly towards the aisles in pursuit of their amber elixir. We continued to stare in astonishment. Was this a cinema or was it a day centre that happened to be showing a film on a wet Wednesday afternoon? The intermission seemed endless but no one seemed to mind and mum, ever the pragmatist, adopted the policy of if-you-can't-beat-them-join-them and made sure she had a cuppa, too. We even got our choc ices although we had to go to the foyer to get them. The second part of the film was much more enjoyable; we were among the approximate ten per cent of the audience who remained awake to see it.

There didn't seem to be any shortage of cinemas in the town. Apart from the Curzon, which was our 'local', there was the Classic in Queens Road, the town's premier picture house and first with the major releases; the ABC, an imposing edifice of rather faded glory in Cambridge Road, which became first an in-town Sainsbury's supermarket and then the ESK discount store which is with us today. There was also a curious, narrow-fronted movie theatre at the very bottom of Cambridge Road which was, as I recall, the Orion. This was the town's acknowledged flea pit. I remember sitting on the bus that was taking me home from school one day and idly pondering on the nature of the films that were showed within. They all had titles such as *The Erotic Adventures of Siegfried*. Who was 'Siegfried' and what did 'erotic' mean? I decided it was a cinema given over to those dense and wordy films made from the very thick novels written by Russian people that swots had to read to get A-Levels. I couldn't have been more wrong, of course, although it is interesting to note that the Orion occupied the premises of the former Hastings Music Hall – a theatre in which the great Charles Dickens himself had taken to the stage in 1861 to give readings from his own *The Pickwick Papers*. Isn't life deliciously ironic?

3

Invitations Go Out

We anticipated the first two weeks of August 1971 with a sense of great expectation and excitement. That fortnight was reserved for our first invited visitors – mum and dad's oldest friends, Ken and Inge Britte Smith.

Dad had met Ken when they both took jobs as teachers at Rutland House in the late 1950s. They immediately hit it off and the wives followed suit, so much so that Ken and Aunty Britty – as our young tongues could best articulate her name – became my godparents. Ken was the sort of small man of quick movements that people call 'dapper'. He had lively brown eyes, a razor-sharp mind and a general animation and energy that belied his voice which mum once described as 'slowly flowing liquid chocolate with a hint of tobacco'. He was a born story-teller and a brilliant raconteur who could have an assembled company in stitches within minutes. Physically, Inge Britte was his complete antithesis, a languid, blonde Swedish girl, silent and shy, she had met and fallen for the beguiling maths teacher while working as a secretary in Ealing. Even if she hadn't had those classic Scandinavian looks she would have revealed her roots by her English – she spoke it far too well to have been born here! They were generous hosts, unfailing friends and permanently available babysitters. On top of that, Ken had a roguish schoolboy charm that would see him hiding bangers and squibs in a 5th November bonfire before I'd even thought of the idea. At his baby son's christening party, on a summer's afternoon in his tiny Hillingdon back garden, he opened a row of champagne bottles arranged like a mini-battery of howitzers and fired the corks into the air for us children to chase and claim for prizes from his pocket. It was only fitting that they should be our first guests and, at the start of the long summer holiday of 1971, we were eagerly anticipating their arrival, excited at the prospect of showing them everything we had discovered and to boast how their two-week holiday by the sea was now our everyday existence.

Their stay with us started with our waving frantically at them as the train they had caught from Charing Cross accelerated out of Warrior Square station. We saw their bewildered faces looking for us from that blasted rear carriage! Yes, we'd forgotten to tell them about the mismatched trains and platforms. We waited twenty minutes and they duly disembarked from the same train as it headed back to London on the opposite platform. Back at the house, mum and dad, in the ways common to their genders, displayed our new home. Mum led Inge Britte through the various rooms, talking rapidly about carpets and curtains and punctuating her descriptions with expansive hand gestures. Meanwhile, dad and Ken stood in front of various doors and fences examining wood grain and angles. One or the other would occasionally step forward to shake a fence post or step back to fetch a kick to a door frame or skirting board. Both would then grunt, nod their heads and move on. My sister and I followed the grown-ups over the house and garden repeatedly asking when it was going to be time for tea.

My bedroom was at the back of the house and I was woken very early next morning by the sound of low voices talking outside my window. I peered between the curtains and saw Ken and Inge Britte standing on the patio. They were still in their night attire, barefooted and with Ken, as ever, clutching his packet of twenty Guards. Unusually, though, he didn't have one lit. They were looking at the view down to the sea and I saw them pointing to various things in the distance. They then strolled down onto the lawn and simply stood still, looking about them, taking in the air of a brilliant, fresh, August sunrise.

I caught something of their mood then; they were breathing that pristine morning air, drawing its pureness into their lungs while savouring that slight but unmistakable mystery of the sea on their lips. I knew that they were bathing their feet in the sparkling dew. I knew that they were listening to that peculiar and awesome silence that shrouds the world at sunrise until the birds greet the glory of the golden light with voices exhilarated by the new life flaring on the rim of the world. My heart leapt and I sprang from my bed to drag on my clothes. Excitement gripped me as realisation dawned and I raced from my room.

'Come on!' I shouted to my sister. 'We got guests. Mum always does BACON when we got people staying – BACON! I'm gonna eat yours!'

A wail of dismay and a series of shuffling thumps told me my sister was only seconds behind me.

That morning, we decided to walk Ken and Inge Britte down to the town via Bottle Alley. For that reason, dad excused himself from the excursion and the five of us set out, we children chattering non-stop to our guests about what we were going to show them. I remember they loved the Old Town, its narrow streets and the crooked houses with their overhangs. Ken was fascinated by the Stade and the fishing boats drawn up on the beach. It may sound strange but this visit was the first time that the Wells family had, itself, explored this ancient heart of Hastings from any vantage point closer than Rock-a-Nore Road. We saw that it was not just a picture-postcard tableau complete with salty dogs sitting atop old tar barrels and mending nets, periodically spitting the evil juice from the quids they were chewing. This was industry; this was organic; this was a vital working organ of the body Hastings. And, boy, did it stink! There were odd bits and pieces of sundry sea creatures lying discarded on the oil-streaked shingle and by the middle of a summer morning they were combining with the dust and diesel fumes to produce a heady aroma that I always think of as the marine equivalent of a farm yard. We watched as an asthmatic old engine encased in a small shed coughed into life. There was a shout and immediately a steel hawser, lying all but hidden under the sand and shingle, leapt up and quivered in the air. We followed it with our eyes to the prow of one of the landing boats. The line tautened as the old engine laboured and the boat inched its way out of the water and up the beach, two young lads laying short planks of wood beneath the keel as it crept forward. I thought they looked like devoted servants casting rose petals beneath the feet of an arriving emperor. It was an amazing sight then and I still think it is now. It's classic Hastings Logic; quite bizarre to see seamen dragging their craft from the water. Why? Surely, that's the whole point of boats; they live in water. But not in Hastings: proud to boast what is still the largest beach-launched fishing fleet in Europe. That was how it had been done since before anyone could remember anything and that's how it's done today.

Of course, there is no harbour at Hastings, natural or otherwise. The Harbour Arm, started in 1897, was never completed and what was constructed was partially destroyed during the Second World War to discourage any passing Nazis who might have fancied stopping off for chips or candyfloss. About the best thing that can be said for it is that it did prevent the shingle from cluttering up the fisherman's beach. The fishermen themselves saw it all come and go; the big ideas, the brilliant plans, the 'new starts' designed to propel the town into the vanguard of whatever was desirable or fashionable at the time. All those plans are long gone but the fishermen are still there, plying their trade in pretty much the same way and from the same place as their forefathers back for nigh on half a millennium.

Boats aside, the most striking feature of the Stade is the collection of net shops – that cluster of curious, black, weather-boarded huts, some 25ft tall. We were fascinated by them when we first saw them because they looked like attenuated versions of our bottom garden shed.

'What are they, mum?'

'I don't know. Go and ask that man . . . and be polite!'

We approached an old boy busy nailing a plank back into place at the foot of the nearest hut.

'Excuse me, sir. Who lives in those tall, thin houses?'

The old boy peered up at the hut, 'Them houses? Who lives in 'em? Well, these tall, thin houses are special homes for tall, thin people.'

His response was so deadpan we never thought to question it until we'd reported the answer back to mum.

'Well, there you are,' said mum, the corners of her mouth twitching.

But suspicion had cast a shadow in my mind and, emboldened by mum's presence, as we passed the old boy I said, 'If they are for tall, thin people, where do they sleep? They must need long beds and they wouldn't fit.'

The old man never wavered. 'Know anything about horses?' he asked. 'Well, they sleep standing up because they're too big to lie down. Same as the folk as live in them tall, thin houses.'

My sister, pony-mad like most girls of her age, had heard that horses can sleep standing up and her fragmentary knowledge was the indisputable proof of the old boy's answer. We went on our way, my mind not satisfied by this explanation and further troubled by the smiles I saw exchanged between the adults. At the same time, I was keeping half-an-eye open in case I spotted a sleepy-looking, 20ft tall fisherman on his way home for a nice lie-down . . . or, rather, a nice stand-up.

It was a wonderful day throughout which we proudly displayed our new home town to a genuinely impressed audience while actually seeing a number of things properly for the first time ourselves – a close-up of the Fishermen's Beach being one of them. So entrancing did Ken and Inge Britte find it that they insisted on buying a large crab, ready cooked, to take home and dress for the evening meal. As Ken said, 'If you live in a fishing town, you're going to have the freshest fish available every day.'

My sister and I were fascinated by the purchase. We'd never eaten crab in any shape or form and thought it only came in tins, anyway. We could not, for the life of us, work out which bits of the crab one ate – it all looked thoroughly indigestible. Where was the crab meat? Did you get served a pincer like you got served a leg when chicken was on the menu? Back at home, Ken and dad went into the kitchen with the crab while mum and Inge Britte settled into armchairs with liberally-poured glasses of sherry. My sister stayed with them while I headed for the kitchen to join the men. I couldn't remember ever having seen dad in any kitchen in the role of food-preparer so I instinctively knew that what was happening in there was likely to be highly entertaining.

'How's it going?' called mum from the dining room after twenty minutes.

'It's going OK, love,' dad called back.

'Good. Don't forget to get rid of the dead-man's fingers!'

'We know what we're doing,' answered dad in his long-suffering patience voice before hissing at Uncle Ken, 'What the hell are dead-men's wossnames?'

'Hmm,' mused Uncle Ken thoughtfully as he picked up one of the crab's pincers and peered at it. 'Rings a bell. I think there is some part of a crab that's poisonous . . . the brain or its stomach or something like that.'

Then he put his head close to dad's and muttered something I didn't catch. Both of them were immediately convulsed with silent mirth. I jumped up straightaway.

'What did you say, Uncle Ken? Dad! Dad! I didn't hear what Uncle Ken said,' I pleaded, desperate to be part of this group of real men in their exciting hunter-gatherer mode. There is a primeval streak just beneath the surface of even the most domesticated urban man. It's most frequent manifestation comes with the lighting of fires – especially the barbecue which no man worth his salt will allow his female to oversee. Dad and Uncle Ken were not rubbing sticks together in the depths of some ancient forest but they were busily attempting to provide a meal for the assembled family group by dismembering a dead animal. The task had clearly ignited that very primeval streak – largely because the animal concerned was not shrink-wrapped in polythene with cooking instructions printed on a label. They were having a great time and tearing the bloody guts out of it while the women twittered safely by the fire (although there was no fire) and looked after the babies (although the only baby to look after was my sister who was, in my opinion, 'a big baby' but hardly an infant). The whole thing had a wonderful 'caveman' feel to it and had excited me to the point at which I was frantic to be part of it, to be one of those hunter-gatherers. But whatever atavistic memories lingered in their instinctive subconscious, they were too deeply buried to be of any use to 1970s-Man that day. For the best part of two hours dad and Uncle Ken prodded, poked, prised, pulled, stretched, bent, sawed, hacked and whacked at the stubborn crustacean in their hunt for the infamous dead-man's fingers. They seemed to think they were looking for small, human-like digits complete with proto-fingernails. My eager contribution was to dance about the kitchen pleading and imploring to be allowed to 'have a go'. Finally, when I had made a grab for a large crosshead screwdriver – Uncle Ken's preferred kitchen utensil for the preparation of dressed crab – and narrowly avoided losing my own fingers as dad brought down a meat cleaver on one of the wretched creature's claws,

I was ordered out of the kitchen with one highly brusque and brief command. By this time, about two-thirds of the crab's interior had been discarded as 'looking a bit iffy' and a heated debate began over whether the dark meat was better than the light meat, assuming that the dark meat wasn't a close ally of the elusive dead-man's fingers and liable to lay us all low with ptomaine poisoning. Things were getting serious; there wasn't a huge amount of meat left – dark or light – bearing in mind the crab had been intended to form the basis of a salad tea for six.

In the meantime, banished from the kitchen, I was forced to join the women-folk who were chatting happily. I stalked into the dining room and attempted to sit on the edge of the dining room table; a site and a pose which I knew would signal my deep unhappiness and draw out the sympathy I wanted. Unfortunately, as I lifted my leg to perch on the edge I inadvertently let go with a particularly rasping and rather wet fart. Even more unfortunately, my sister immediately guffawed and started to roll about on the floor in highly exaggerated amusement at my Trumpet Involuntary. Mum looked up sharply, convinced that I had engineered my flatulent outburst on purpose, and ensured my cup of humiliation flowed over by snapping, 'If you're going to do that you can go back out to the kitchen. I'm sure those two will find it highly amusing.' And, as I slunk from the room with a hard look at the sherry bottle, she added, 'And go and change your pants. I've had enough skids to wash out this week to last me a lifetime!'

Mum and Inge Britte, encouraged by more sherry, finally allowed their curiosity – and their growing hunger – to get the better of them and crept to the kitchen to see how the meal was progressing. There were immediate shouts of laughter and I heard mum's voice say, 'Now we know why it's called dressed crab! You two are wearing it!' The two women doubled up while the two men sheepishly picked crab meat out of their eyebrows and off their shoes. The sorry remains were consigned to the bin and that ubiquitous standby, the tin of pilchards in tomato sauce, was pressed into service. I never did see those mysterious dead-man's fingers.

That same evening, our guests were honoured by the throwing open of the front room (which was at the back, remember). No evening spent slumped in front of the TV that day; it was the best china for the tea and coffee, more sherry and an old-fashioned evening of 'socialising' which probably would have gone off very nicely, indeed, had not someone (who never subsequently owned up to it) uttered that fateful question, 'What about a game of Monopoly?' Had we paused to think about the likely prognosis of that suggestion we might well have passed on the game, but we'd had a good day and we all, I think, wanted to go on in the warm spirit of camaraderie and friendship that we had enjoyed thus far.

One of mum's shrewd and pithy observations on the human condition was that you never tested your friendship with someone until you went on holiday with them. True enough. I'd add that you never really test your relationships with your family members until you play Monopoly with them. That's true, too; I had seen the evidence. The Wells family playing Monopoly invariably started with tension and suspicion, passed through factionalism, tantrums, and sulks and ended with someone hurling board, cards, playing-pieces and the contents of the bank across the room.

By the time my sister and I were packed off to bed, dad and Uncle Ken had gone into the garden for cigarettes – although one had opted for the back garden while the other pointedly chose the front. Inge Britte was sobbing quietly in the toilet and mum, with lips compressed to a liver-coloured line, was staring fixedly into space as she stood by the boiling kettle. As I quickly and quietly poured myself a glass of milk and ducked out of the kitchen, I heard her muttering to herself, 'I don't care if the blue ones aren't worth very much . . . I like that colour . . . And why shouldn't Inge Britte have a hotel on Liverpool Street station? All the big London stations have hotels on them.'

○ ○ ○

By the high summer of our first calendar year in Boscobel Road North we felt that we had just about been accepted. Indeed, the spotlight of collective anxiety that the street's residents had trained on us had wavered midway through 1971 when (Horrors!) another family with children moved in.

As a retired 'professional' and a man who was known to have devoted much of his spare time to the Conservative Party's cause in local politics, my father was held in high esteem, albeit notionally because he went largely unseen and was known to be less than enthusiastic about visitors regardless of whether they were family, friends, neighbours or distraction burglars. He said once, 'The Chinese have a saying . . . "House guests are like fish; after three days they stink".' I know now that his reticence was as much borne of embarrassment and humiliation from the knowledge that he was rapidly becoming crippled by his arthritis. That year mum and the doctor persuaded him to accept a wheelchair in the hope that it would encourage him to get out of the confines of the house for mental stimulation, at least. It didn't work. No. 17 seemed to have been designed by an architect who had feared his home was likely to be assailed and invaded by a small army of murderous paraplegics. The place was a cunningly contrived collection of steep slopes, steps and right-angled corners – each and every one of them perfectly placed to thwart any attempts at manoeuvring a wheelchair up, over or around them. Even the road itself, in its unadopted state, riddled with potholes and fissures and without any conventional pavements, seemed part of the anti-wheelchair plot. Mum didn't press the point. Realistically, where could she take him anyway? There were the cussed St Leonard's hills in all directions and she knew she hadn't the strength to bring dad and the chair back up any of them. Dad remained indoors but he did take an interest in what was going on in the town.

In the autumn of 1966 he had decided it would be a good idea if I started a stamp collection. Guess what the first set of stamps he bought for me was? That's right – the Battle of Hastings 900th anniversary commemorative set. Five years later we were residents of the town and my stamp collection was languishing, unloved and unsupplemented, at the bottom of a box somewhere in the attic. Dad remembered it, though, and was looking forward to the 905th anniversary of this historically seismic and nation-creating event. After all, we were at the very heart of things here. I think he was a little bit disappointed with the celebrations. They did exist but if you blinked, you missed them. Ironically, it had been in 1966 itself that the good burghers of the town had decided that, henceforth, 14 October would officially become Hastings Day and would host a selection of events – albeit the rather dignified and understated civic sort of events which the municipal masters of the time thought appropriate. But a good idea tends to develop wings of its own: by 1976 the Hastings Day commemoration had become a four-day event and, by 1980, it was a week. Sadly, dad had departed while it was still the one-dayer and I often think it is a shame he was never able to see the torchlight procession, the massive bonfire and the spectacular fireworks that we enjoy today at the culmination of what is now Hastings Week. He always felt that the English never really pulled out the stops for national celebrations of their history and identity and I think he, like me, would have been quietly thrilled by the dark, rather pagan and slightly menacing costumes and characters which appear in the night streets to drop those noisy firecrackers under the flickering torchlight.

In the early 1970s, though, the major date of the festive year was still the carnival. Today, of course, when we talk about the carnival we're talking about the Old Town Carnival. Back then, it was the Hastings and St Leonard's Carnival organised, I seem to recall, by the local Round Table. It was worth seeing too, comprising, as it did, three major events. There was the carnival procession itself, of course, but there was also a fair on the Oval and a visit from the Red Arrows. You knew the carnival was imminent when the normally devoid grass of the Oval suddenly, seemingly overnight, sprouted Henry Bottom's Mammoth Carnival Fair. To us kids it was a week of magic and a visit to the fair was anticipated almost to the same degree as birthdays and Christmas. The memories are very much of the senses: the din of the generators which powered the rides and the blaring pop music played from them; the colours by day and the flashing lights by night; the smell of candyfloss, fried onions, diesel oil and summer-dew on the turf. You spent a month's pocket money in an hour, saw all your mates from school looking odd in their own clothes and ended up being sick from too many sweets and one more ride on the Waltzer than your stomach could handle. It was one of the highlights of the year. On carnival day itself, the procession was preceded by a visit from the Red Arrows, the RAF's spectacular aerobatic team, and thousands would pack onto the Promenade, crowd the balconies of the seafront properties and even climb onto the roofs of the seafront shelters to get a good view. A maroon would sound the fact that the procession was starting its journey from the bathing pool to Alexandra Park and we'd wait expectantly for the floats.

The carnival notably missed out the Old Town – it always had – so back in 1968 the Old Towners rather sniffily decided to create their own carnival. It went from strength to strength and, as the two were separated by a good few weeks, we got two bites of the cherry. The Old Town

Carnival was an altogether racier, boozier and generally more chaotic affair and was great fun, too. Ironically, it was the newcomer carnival that triumphed in the end. The main town carnival started to wither: the Red Arrows were lost, the fairs were smaller and the floats in the procession began to have a rather threadbare and even an impoverished look. It fizzled out completely in the 1980s but, on its deathbed, it bequeathed the right and the title of 'Miss Hastings' to the Old Town Carnival to turn into the formal position of 'Old Town Carnival Queen'. In the modern, equality-conscious and politically correct world of today the idea of beauty queens and girls parading in swimsuits and evening dress sits uncomfortably – but in the carnival world it's an absolute must. I remember mum looking forward with great relish each year to the announcement of the next Old Town Carnival Queen in the *Hastings Observer* because, as she always said, 'Give it a couple of weeks and the girl will be out on her ear when it's discovered she's pregnant, or she's forty-three or she's having an affair with a magistrate!' She wasn't always wrong, either.

But there was one social event that was sacrosanct in the Wells family calendar and which dad, like all boys between nine and ninety, thoroughly enjoyed – Guy Fawkes Night – and if he anticipated it with his typically reserved enthusiasm, his children had always heralded its approach with unbounded glee. Planning for the big night started weeks in advance. The Wells family had celebrated 5th November since my brother was old enough to be entrusted with a sparkler and it was an event in the family calendar only rivalled by Christmas – and moving to St Leonard's wasn't going to break the tradition. And what an opportunity our new home offered! At Hillingdon, our small garden had severely limited both the size of the bonfire and the accompanying firework display: at the bungalow it was different. There was much more space and, better still, with mum having bagged the allotment that lay at the very foot of our back garden, I had the opportunity to build the sort of bonfire that Hastings hadn't seen since the beacons were lit to celebrate the victory at Trafalgar. I was fanatically saving my pocket-money by the end of August while canvassing and soliciting every relative and friend of the family to whom I could gain access: and it wasn't going to stop there. The good people of St Leonard's would be shamelessly importuned for Pennies-for-the-Guy as soon as that Guy could be constructed and transported to a profitable thoroughfare. But as the weeks passed I identified a shadow of doubt hanging over the plans and, strangely, it was emanating from mum. Now, she may not have been the biggest fan of noisy fireworks but, like mothers the world over, she loved anything that brought the family together in peace and harmony. Her contribution was critical, too, for the post-firework supper she served up was almost as good as the fireworks themselves: mugs of tomato soup around the bonfire and then inside for hot sausages, marmite on toast and a whopping chocolate firework cake. In truth, the same chocolate cake appeared on Bonfire Night, Christmas, Easter and family birthdays but it was no less welcome for that.

I discovered the cause for her anxiety one evening when I should have been in bed but was, in fact, in the kitchen stealing digestive biscuits. Mum was talking to dad in the dining room. The doors to the serving hatch which connected the two rooms were not quite closed and I had the perfect opportunity to earwig the conversation without their being aware that I was doing so.

'The neighbours are bound to complain,' I heard her say to dad. 'You know what they're like here. If you mow the lawn before midday there's a letter in the *Hastings Observer* about noise pollution. I don't care so much if they complain afterwards but they'll see the bonfire being piled up and they'll see the kids taking that wretched Guy out and if they start objecting before the event, we'll have to either tone it down or let it go completely. Either way, the kids'll be heartbroken.'

'Who's most likely to kick up about it?' asked dad.

Mum reeled off half-a-dozen names: the usual suspects.

'Invite them all,' said dad simply. 'Send them all formal written invitations.'

'They won't come,' said mum, aghast.

'No, they won't, will they,' dad replied.

I couldn't see mum from where I was lurking but I could hear the smile of comprehension come into her voice as she said, 'And they can hardly complain and try to stop us having a Bonfire Night party when we've invited them to be guests of honour in the first place.'

'No, they can't. They'd look pretty inconsiderate and ill-mannered if they did and aren't those precisely the things they claim to detest the most round here?'

'Jim,' I heard her chuckle. 'You're a genius!'

'I do my best, sweetheart,' he said. 'Now pop the TV on. I'm missing the football.'

I beat a hasty retreat. I'm not sure I quite grasped the full subtlety of the plan but what did register was the tone of relief in mum's voice. The crisis she had feared could clearly be averted. I had no doubts that it would be and if she was happy then all was right with the world.

The invitations (I still have one, dated 21 October 1971) were masterpieces of formal etiquette '. . . request the pleasure of your company . . . delighted to welcome you into our family celebration . . . etc.' They conscientiously suggested pets be kept indoors from 6.30 p.m., confirmed reassuringly that the noisier fireworks would be set off first and that buckets of water were to be stored near the bonfire site. They even informed the invited guests that individual torches would be available for safe passage from house to garden. We received equally polite responses, all variations on the theme of 'prior engagement' but not a peep of complaint was uttered. The only potential clouds on the horizon left to trouble us were the sort that come on strong winds and dump a lot of rain but, like our formally invited guests, they clearly needed to be elsewhere, too, and we were granted a crisp and starry night to stage a Guy Fawkes party that would have had one of today's health and safety officials rolling around the floor and vigorously chewing the carpet.

In the fortnight before 5 November we became a thorough nuisance to everyone as we were constantly hunting both for burnable matter for the bonfire and suitable attire for the Guy. We were very proud of our Guys. Being a history teacher, dad had a fairly accurate idea of what the real Guy Fawkes would have worn and, although we didn't strive for complete sartorial accuracy, we did try to give our Guy a flavour of the period. This normally came in the form of a tall, brimmed hat with a silver buckle on the front made from tin-foil covered cardboard plus a white overlain-collar. It would have been a fair approximation to the dress of the early Stuart period had it not been for the fact that Guy's top half was usually one of dad's old knitted cardigans that had gone through at the elbows while the lower half was a pair of his old trousers which had become so shiny on the backside that mum wouldn't let him wear them.

We usually gave Guy some structure by using a length of wooden pole to fix his head – one of mum's old stockings stuffed with newspaper – to his torso. Strangely, it was always about this time of year that one of her mops or brooms tended to go missing – but life is full of coincidences. Once the Guy had been finished, he had to be taken out so that we could 'Penny-for-the-Guy' from passers-by. This involved transporting the Guy down to London Road to catch the shoppers. Had we attempted it in Boscobel Road North the pickings would have been slim indeed. Passers-by were few and most of them so old, dad said, that they were likely to have been personal friends of Guy Fawkes and thus offended by our attempts to replicate him in shiny trousers and a C&A cardigan.

Here, though, is an interesting insight into my parents' attitude to our new environment and their perceptions of how we were viewed. As far as they were concerned, it was OK to Penny-for-the-Guy in St Leonard's but only if (a) We created a credible and quality-built Guy; (b) We accompanied him in a similarly well-dressed style and (c) Although allowed to accept any pennies proffered, we weren't allowed to ask for them. Our first outing with a Guy in St Leonard's saw us wheeling our creation proudly down Pevensey Road in dad's wheelchair which we had 'borrowed' for the occasion. Mum looked at us doubtfully. I realise now that she felt uncomfortable that the splendid, brand-new wheelchair, obtained for dad on medical loan, was being employed for such a triviality. But she went with it, bless her. Outside the London Road post office she presented us with a washed-out peaches can – minus the label – and dropped a couple of coppers into it.

'That'll get you started,' she said. 'People will be more inclined to contribute if they think other people have already done so. Good luck – and don't move from this spot!'

She disappeared into the post office and left us feeling rather alone and awkward. It wasn't like Hillingdon at all where there had always seemed to be kids everywhere and a gang of our pals would always happen along within a few minutes of being anywhere. St Leonard's seemed bereft of children on that sunny Saturday morning and, strangely, I remember that day more than any other as being one on which I was aware of our new location – despite the fact we'd been in the town for nearly a year. But within a minute of mum's disappearing into the post office, Mrs Eldritch came out. Mrs Eldritch was an extraordinary creature who lived an ascetic life in a large and rather neglected detached house at the very top of Boscobel Road North. Like others of her ilk she made a weekly trip to the post office and, at her slow pace, it was a major excursion. For Mrs Eldritch was old; very, very old. She was so old it was almost painful to look upon her. She had less hair than dad (an achievement for a man, a truly astonishing feat for a woman), was bent almost double and wore a sinister green eye-shade which rested on a pair of spectacles which appeared to have been constructed from two milk bottles and a wire coathanger. She wielded two thick walking sticks like a mountaineer wields ice picks and she came out of the post office to the slow, heavy thump of rubber ferrules.

She turned towards us and paused for what seemed an age before raising her head slightly as she attempted to focus on the indistinct group of two children and the wheelchair-bound Guy – who had now been improved by a pair of wrap-round sunglasses and one of dad's Embassy Number 1s wedged into the mouth slit of his mask. Mrs Eldritch's toothless mouth twitched into a smile as she peered at the figure in the chair and said, 'It's Mr Wells, is it not? How nice to see you out to enjoy this clement weather.'

The Guy sat silently in his chair, looking for all the world like some psychotic Mafia don trying to decide which one of his rivals to have murdered first. But Mrs Eldritch didn't wait around for any reply. 'Good morning,' she said pleasantly and turned away to begin the slow clump up the hill towards Timothy White's and home. We never saw her on a bus. As soon as she had moved away we doubled up with laughter.

'Can I light your fag for you, dad?' I inquired of Guy – and we went into further convulsions. When mum emerged from the post office we told her what had happened. She gave us a thin smile and said, 'Probably best if we don't tell dad about this. Yes, I think so.' Then, more earnestly, 'Now, promise me you won't tell him what Mrs Eldritch said, poor soul.' We promised faithfully that we would keep the exchange with the ancient Eldritch a secret between ourselves . . . .

'She did WHAT?' roared dad as we stood innocently by his chair. 'She said "Good Morning" to that . . . that . . . monstrosity . . . thinking it was me? The old witch!'

'Jim, she's not far off being blind,' said mum trying to be conciliatory.

'She'd have to be brain-dead to think that thing was me,' spluttered dad.

'Well, she's not far off that either,' replied mum shooting my sister and me a venomous look. 'Like you two!' she mouthed at us.

We beat a hasty retreat and kept a low profile for the rest of the day. Mooching about in the front garden later in the day I saw Mrs Eldritch come thumping past on her sticks. It was three hours since we had seen her start her journey back up the hill. I watched her pass as she headed home to the still and solitary existence which she lived in her back parlour, like a mouse in a cathedral.

We were allowed just the one Penny-for-the-Guy outing that year but, as I recall, it did make us enough cash to boost the box of fireworks that we were accumulating in advance of the big day. However, our efforts were thrown into distinctly paltry relief by the blue-skies commercial innovation dreamed up by a group of children which we ran into the following Saturday. Their Guy stopped us dead in our tracks; we'd never seen one so life-like.

I'll call them the Dunlops although that, of course, was not their real name. We knew them vaguely in the same way that everyone in the area knew them. They were a tough, sprawling family who occupied a crumbling place in Carisbrooke Road and seemed to number in the hundreds. Our first introduction to them came when the oldest brother, Ray, was pointed out to us in Gensing Gardens. He was cycling slowly and provocatively around the paths (all marked as 'cycling prohibited') with an empty beer can clamped between his teeth. We became more familiar with the younger scions of the brood although they didn't go to our school. Their mum was almost as well known as her offspring, a high-energy, permanently pregnant and permanently furious woman who screamed at everyone as she lived life at 100 miles per hour. She did her monstrous weekly shop at Tesco, in Wellington Square, just as we did and we would sometimes see her with a gaggle of children carting the groceries home in two babies' prams. But she was kind in her way and would help anyone she could. For example, Mrs Dunlop looked after a neighbour's child when his mother had to go to work – I guess she thought one more wouldn't make much difference. That child was an eight-year-old called Dennis who was what was then termed 'Educationally Sub-normal' (or ESN). The term today would be 'Special Needs', I suppose. With callous efficiency, Dennis had been dubbed 'Divvy Den' by the three Dunlop brothers we knew best – partly to ensure that he wouldn't get confused with any other Dennises of their acquaintance but mostly out of spite because, as they freely admitted, they didn't know anyone else called Dennis. They dreaded the days when Divvy Den was under their mother's charge as they were frequently ordered to include him in their activities and games. However, with 5 November approaching, the Dunlop trio had had an audacious and potentially lucrative brainwave and it began one day with their innocently informing their mum that they wanted to take young Dennis out.

Mrs Dunlop greeted the news by looking at her sons as if she would have quite liked to kill them. She gave an exasperated sigh and shrieked, 'Bloody good idea. It'll get the little sod from under my feet this morning.' She immediately hurled an approximated number of coats and scarves in the general direction of the boys and added in an accusing roar, 'It's fucking freezing out there today so make sure he's wrapped up nice and warm! And if any of you come home with the coppers again, you're dead meat!' She needn't have worried. The Dunlop boys had every intention of making sure Dennis was very well wrapped up and very well protected, indeed.

We encountered them that Saturday morning at the end of Kings Road, near Warrior Square station. At that stage, we were on cautious nodding terms with the Dunlops although we hadn't yet met Dennis. When we passed them that day they were Penny-for-the-Guying and a splendid Guy they had, too. Dressed in modern clothes, true; but they'd done a good job with the Guy Fawkes paper mask and a bright yellow sou'wester pulled down low on the Guy's head. The feet, in Wellingtons, and the hands, in woollen gloves, were brilliantly done. It reclined regally in an old pushchair and we stopped and stared in frank admiration.

'Smart!' I said out loud ('smart' being an expression of the highest admiration and approval; the early 1970s equivalent of 'wicked' in today's youth argot). I gasped in amazement when I looked into the old enamel mug they were using to collect donations. It had silver coins in it!

'Not bad, is he?' said Dunlop senior modestly.

'I want to go wee,' said the Guy.

We looked in astonishment from the Guy to the Dunlops.

'How did you do that?' I asked, scanning their faces for a clue as to which one was the ventriloquist. Then realisation dawned.

'Who is it?' I asked in a whisper.

Dunlop senior sighed. 'It's Dennis – Divvy Den. Our mum looks after him some days when his mum's up the RESH*.'

'I need wee,' said the Guy again with more insistence.

Dunlop senior nodded towards the Guy and said to his younger brother, 'Give him another one.'

Dunlop junior pulled a packet of sweet cigarettes from his pocket, extracted one and carefully inserted it through the mouth-slit of the Guy Fawkes mask.

'Here you go, Den. Have another one of these.'

The sweet cigarette slowly disappeared inwards. The Guy sat in its pushchair, its head nodding gently as Dennis eagerly chewed his sweet cigarette.

---

* The Royal East Sussex Hospital, off Cambridge Road, which served as the district's main hospital until the advent of the Conquest in the early 1990s.

'That'll shut him up for a little while longer but we have to keep moving,' said Dunlop senior. 'Only problem is, bumping him along in the pushchair makes him want to go to the bog. The sweets shut him up but we've already got through three packets. He's eating the profits.'

I last saw them struggling up St John's Road, two Dunlops pushing the chair while the third attempted to stop Divvy Den from getting out of it. He wanted to help push the pushchair, too.

The Dunlops were the first people – old or young – whom we encountered in St Leonard's doing anything that even approached the entrepreneurial. In Hillingdon, Penny-for-the-Guy had been a highly competitive business with the best pitches on Saturday mornings grabbed at an early hour. It was not uncommon for them to be fought over and there were even occasions when sabotage had been the subject of dark hints. In the year before we left, the kids from one of the streets on the other side of the Uxbridge Road ('council houses,' mum would sniff, as if that explained everything) actually operated a Penny-for-the-Guy collective, blitzing the area and covering all three parades of shops with their Guys with a view to pooling the profits afterwards.

Mr Gribalski, the little Ukrainian Jew who ran our Hillingdon corner shop, shook his head when he heard what the kids were doing and said, 'Dis ees how it start – always it start like dis. Big guy collect what der little guy works.' His family had been farmers who had had the wit, the luck and the cash to get out before the lid was nailed down in that particular part of the world. He had strong views on Collectivism in all its guises. It turned out that the idea for the kids to pool their profits had come from a couple of the older brothers and it was in their personal 'pool' that the profits ended up. I can imagine Mr Gribalski being gloomily triumphant at the news. I can still remember his timeless anti-Soviet mantras as mum stood at the counter.

'Vee only eat vot vee hide in hole under barn. Dey collect everyt'ing and vee never see none of it ever again, missus.'

That first autumn in St Leonard's saw dad's physical capabilities so restricted that I proudly took control of the fireworks themselves and was determined to put on a show to remember – a spectacular boosted by my discovery of 'rookies'. Coming from an urban background, I'd never encountered them before but they were readily available in Hastings surrounded, as it was, by an expanse of agricultural land. Rookies were rookscarers, essentially loud fire crackers stapled in series to a piece of thick, sulphured rope. The idea was simple: you hung a string of rookies on a fence pole and lit the end of the rope. It would smoulder away until it reached one of the rookies which would then detonate with a seriously loud report – scaring the thieving birds from the peas, barley, maize, turnips or whatever the feathered fiends were attempting to burgle.

However, with care, the rookies could be removed from the rope and, hey presto, one had a handful of 'firecrackers' which made the boxes of bangers offered by the likes of Standard, Paines-Wessex and Brocks sound like champagne corks popping. I decided to keep my discovery of rookies a secret; some of them I earmarked for 'pepping up' the bonfire while the rest would be used to 'arm' some of the rockets.

The big night arrived. With the assembled spectators huddled together waiting to 'Oooh' and 'Aaah' at the display, I opened proceedings with a fusillade of my 'Rookie Rockets'. Unfortunately, I had overlooked the small matters of power-to-weight ratio, trajectory and general aerodynamics. My overweight projectiles certainly put on a show. They spiralled off in various directions, skimming fences and spectators. One lodged in a neighbour's hedge where the rookie detonated with a deafening bang and a blizzard of privet leaves, leaving a hole the size of a football. Another went through the window of the lower garden shed. Fortunately, it failed to go off where it wedged itself under the makeshift perch on which mum's beloved pet chickens were roosting. Apart from a broken pane of glass, no serious damage was done but it was a fortnight before mum got any more eggs. A third went up, doubled back on the route I had planned for it, fizzed off the chimney stack, disappeared into the road in front of the house and blew up. My first 'set piece' of the evening had ruined a manicured hedge, broken a window, terrified the life out of two chickens and set off a frantic chorus of angry and frightened dogs along the road. Things were looking good for the rest of my display!

Back then of course, fireworks were only available for the few weeks around 5 November and most people had back garden displays. It was the time before restrictions started to be imposed on who could sell and buy fireworks and which fireworks were available anyway. One of my favourites, long since removed from the market because of its unpredictability, was the 'helicopter' – essentially a firework that expelled its sparkling thrust through a hole in one side of its cardboard tube. With that tube stapled slightly off-centre to a cardboard 'wing', the helicopter, when lit, would spin round with the wings enabling it to lift off from any flat surface. The problem was that where it would go when it did lift off could only be guessed at. Jumping jacks or squibs also had that mind-of-their-own which was, for me, what made them so entertaining. It was also what got them banned. My helicopters behaved themselves that night – well, all but one. The last one to launch shot off sideways and went straight into the upper branches of our bay tree dislodging half a dozen roosting blackbirds and pigeons which clattered out of the foliage piping in alarm.

A large catherine-wheel was quickly nailed to the washing-line pole and lit. Unfortunately, it hadn't been nailed as securely as it might have been. It began to spin round for a few seconds in a fiery arc and then, to my alarm, detached itself, leapt from the patio over the rockery, rolled down the lawn, bounced off the raised earth of the rose bed, flew through the air and ricocheted off the back fence to drop neatly into the centre of the garden pond with a bang, a loud hiss and a sorcerous cloud of green smoke and steam. There was a smattering of applause from behind me and a chorus of appreciation.

'I've never seen one of those before,' said mum. 'Is it a new type?'

My furtively ignited squibs hopped about the garden; the bonfire keeled over in a swirling column of sparks with the Rookies secreted therein detonating like an exchange of small-arms fire ... And everyone wrote their names in the air with their sparklers. The silent and deserted row of back gardens was, for one night, illuminated and animated by a barrage of screaming, whistling, crackling and exploding pyrotechnics.

'This is the grand finale,' I shouted above the hubbub as I lit the blue touch-paper on one of my special creations which I had augmented by the gunpowder carefully extracted from two boxes of 'Mighty Atom' bangers. There was a dull yellow flash, an explosion which rattled the lounge windows and a gust of hot air that compelled one or two of the more elderly spectators to sit down rather abruptly. I saw something fly up into the air and disappear over the fence into next-door's back garden. There was a pause among the spectators followed by a smattering of polite but uncertain applause.

'Very good,' said mum, eventually. 'Well done, Jem, love. Bit noisy but a lovely display. Where's the bird table?'

'Let's go and look at the bonfire,' I suggested quickly.

4

Ghosts In Our Machines

've already mentioned 'Hastings Logic' – that bizarre, counter-intuitive, frustrating but entertaining complexity that seemed to inflict itself upon even the most basic aspects of everyday life in our new home town. We'd encountered buses that waited for people, trains that didn't fit the station and fishing boats that lived out of the water; but it was within the realms of technology that the cheerful absurdities of life in Hastings really took flight. Television for instance: it was something that we had always taken for granted in Hillingdon. Now, however, things were not to prove so straightforward. We discovered that a simple aerial on the roof would not suffice because TV transmissions didn't do in Hastings what they did in the rest of the known universe and come soaring through the ether direct to your rooftop. Hastings telly came to the house via the back garden and a long cable attached to what looked like a clockwork egg-timer screwed to the dining room windowsill.

We learned that the geography of the place made beaming direct TV signals, well, nigh impossible, so the TV service provider of the day, Rediffusion, collected the broadcast transmissions at one reception station and 'piped' it to individual homes. The little box on the windowsill clicked from BBC1 through BBC2 to ITV – Channel 4 still a good ten years away. As a bonus, Rediffusion also provided BBC Radio 2 and 4 via the same conduit. In one sense, we were years ahead of the game because we had, in effect, cable TV decades before the digital revolution. All we had to do was get the TV man round to connect us up and install a speaker-box under the set itself. But there was a downside. Rediffusion had the technical capability of overriding whatever was being broadcast with what they considered to be vital public service announcements, and they weren't shy about doing so. The soundtrack to the programme we were watching would be suddenly silenced before a disembodied voice would intone, 'This is a Rediffusion announcement.' My father's fury was a sight to behold as the last five minutes of *The Sweeney* or the subtle denouement of a convoluted spy drama like *Callan* was submerged beneath the adenoidal tones of the man we dubbed 'Reedy' informing us that the police were looking for witnesses to a traffic accident in Mount Pleasant Road earlier that day.

'Why are you asking me?' dad roared at the silent images on our TV set. 'I haven't been out of the bloody house since Christmas!' He seemed to be under the impression that these announcements were being fed through to our TV set alone in the town. In due course, a more conventional TV transmission arrived for the benefit of Hastings and St Leonard's residents; but, to this day, one can find flats and bedsitters in our big old Victorian town houses that still have the old Rediffusion switch-box screwed to a wall or windowsill, a curious relic which never fails to perplex the next generation of tenants.

Incidentally, I hear that 'Reedy' himself is still at large within the borough boundaries, no doubt today in well-earned retirement. I still wonder idly on occasions what life must have been like in his household during the days of his invisible fame. Did he emerge onto the landing of his home every morning at 7.30 and loudly declare, 'This is a family announcement! Corn Flakes, toast and tea are currently being served in the kitchen'?

As for millions of other people up and down the country, watching television was the main entertainment in the evenings and our new greener, airier environment didn't prevent our evening gatherings round the set for the likes of *Upstairs, Downstairs*; *Dad's Army*; *Morecambe and Wise*; *Tomorrow's World*; *Special Branch* and *Sunday Night at the London Palladium*. I've long held to the theory that the TV set has superseded the domestic fire as the nucleus of family security, the hub around which family society revolves in the hours of rest and recreation. Just as our ancestors would cleave to the blaze in the hearth, its warmth and its light, so the 1970s Wells family gathered round its 22-inch Pye. Dancing flames had been replaced by the flickering images of our 625-line miracle of modern technology; but while those ancestors focused their attentions by the fire, we focused our attentions on the TV and sat in our regular places each evening, forbidden to make any noise while 'mum's programme' or 'dad's favourite' was showing. The only time conversation was likely to break out was when the TV unexpectedly offered up something too near the knuckle for my parents' comfort.

The end of the 1960s and the start of the 1970s was a time when the cultural band-width available to the masses broadened dramatically. The phrase 'The Permissive Society' suddenly became the topic of heated debate in the media generally and on late-evening TV talk shows in particular. I remember being bored to tears – and even to bed – by endless programmes featuring earnest and bespectacled young women and laconic and bespectacled young men who constantly talked over each other and smoked liked chimneys. Dad loved those programmes and got thoroughly animated watching them. I couldn't work it out. The angrier the discussion made him, it seemed to me, the more he enjoyed it all.

Meanwhile, the prime-time representation of this new era was a series of TV plays, drama series and adaptations which majored on sex, violence and bad language. I have a very clear recollection of my first taste of this new liberality and it came before we had even arrived in Hastings. I was being babysat one evening and the indulgent sitter, complacent at having got my sister to bed at the first attempt, unwisely allowed me to sit with her while she watched the infamous *Big Breadwinner Hog*. This was a highly controversial eight-part drama serial in which a very youthful Peter Egan played an ambitious and ruthless London gangster. I recall that the very first episode featured some poor unfortunate having his faced doused with hydrochloric acid. I was both appalled and thrilled; my parents were both appalled and furious when I innocently recounted what I'd seen the next day. They were determined, from that point on, to root out all the unsuitable TV offerings and ban them from the house – or at least 'from the house' while my sister and I were still up in the evenings.

Poor dad! It must have been a difficult time. For example, the 1971 dramatisation of *Casanova* was, to all intents and purposes, a legitimate historical story. It even boasted the acclaimed actor Frank Finlay in the lead role; but it proved to be yet another opportunity to trail an endless succession of bare boobs and bums across our screen. And this was from the BBC! Things rapidly reached the point at which any dubious content appearing on the screen provoked a reaction in my parents that was both comical and rather touching. On the occasions that they were ambushed by unexpected nudity or sexual shenanigans their normally silent attention to the box was replaced by a sudden and desperate animation. For example, a rather wordy and intense drama would suddenly become enlivened by the lead actress provocatively removing her blouse while pouting at the leading man in a way that telegraphed, even to an eleven-year-old, what was likely to come next.

'Good lord!' dad would say loudly, swivelling in his chair. 'Was that lightning? Did anyone see lightning?'

Two children, eyes opened as wide as their mouths, didn't reply. The girl on the screen was now attempting, with much wriggling, to get out of her skirt.

Dad, desperation in his voice, said, 'I'm sure that was lightning! Jem, pull back the curtains. We might be getting a storm.'

I had no intention of moving out of sight of the screen while the actress had her hands behind her back in search of her bra catch. At that point, as if alerted by some maternal sixth-sense, mum breezed into the room, caught the look of pleading anxiety in dad's eyes, glanced at the screen and took in the situation immediately.

'Have you two left your toys in the garden?' She demanded.

'You said we could.'

'But if there's a storm coming they'll all get soaked. Better fetch them in quickly,' dad chipped in.

'But if there's a storm coming we might get struck by lightning,' said my sister cunningly, her eyes fixed on the screen where the actress's attempts at undressing had now been transferred to the leading man.

By this time, to our irritation, mum had subtly inserted herself between us and the TV, allowing dad to say, 'No, I think I must have made a mistake about that storm. I don't think I saw any lightning.'

'Then if it's not going to rain, we don't have to bring our stuff in,' we argued knowing that mum could not spend the rest of the evening standing where she was; but we always cracked first.

'Mum, your blocking the telly!' we yelled.

'Sorry, dears,' said mum vaguely. 'What was that?' She was standing all of four feet away from our furious faces.

She kept stealing surreptitious glances at the screen while pretending to be searching for something in the bookcase behind the set until she was finally able to turn her head and raise her eyebrows to dad as a signal of 'all clear'. The sense of relief between them was palpable as dad asked casually, 'Anything else on? This isn't very interesting.'

We felt it would have been very interesting indeed if we'd been able to see it but we knew better than to pick a fight that would end with our being sent to bed and seeing no more TV of any description. We went through this pantomime on many occasions. However, mum wasn't always available to come to dad's assistance and there were times when the poor man had to sit it out. I can see him now, ramrod-straight in his chair, jaw set like granite, only his eyes revealing the agonies he was enduring as he prayed that the images on the screen would change before my sister looked up from her drawings of horses to ask him, 'Dad, why's that man undoing that girl's dress while they're still on the bus?'

Bad language was another problem because mum could not be called upon to screen the screen. Their usual technique, when any effing and blinding started up, was to attempt to distract our attentions by asking us questions about school or homework. If we proved uncommunicative, they would then talk between themselves in over-animated and rather shrill tones about the possibility of a miners' strike or, that good old standby, the weather. On rare occasions dad would even be rescued by his old TV adversary, 'Reedy' the Rediffusion public announcer – with his ability to block out the entire TV soundtrack.

It was all so daft. By the age of eleven, the language of the playground had equipped me with knowledge of just about every half-decent swearword, curse and blasphemy in contemporary circulation – and I could even spell most of them. The supposedly hard-hitting scripts of the TV dramas taught me nothing at all but the old beans were desperate to screen out the ugliness and brutality. We knew they were trying to protect us even if their attempts were awkward and pretty much futile. I might add, too, that having seen the thoroughly nasty content of DVDs and, worse, computer games to which some parents allow their youngsters seemingly free access these days, I rather admire my mum and dad's motives and commitment – even if I laugh now at their clumsy methods.

◉ ◉ ◉

TV could be unpredictable but the telecommunications at no. 17 were just plain bewildering. Mum was a great telephone user, staying in regular contact with her parents, her brother and the many good friends she'd left behind in London while racking up phone bills that used to send dad frantic. Installed in the bungalow that first cold January, it was an exciting day when the man from the GPO turned up to turn on the telephone and tell us our number (yes, it was the jolly old Post Office which had control over the nation's telecommunications back then). If you think I'm going to recall it now, you're wrong; I don't remember it. I do recall, however, that a good few numbers in the district were only three-digits. That seems bizarre in these days of ten- and eleven-digit numbers. The telephone man had barely disappeared through 'the airlock' before mum made herself a cup of tea and pushed the curtains to one side to get the telephone from the windowsill. She had been looking forward to reporting the house-move successful to all concerned. She plonked the heavy, rather old-fashioned, handset on the table before her and opened her well-filled telephone book as we all gathered round her, wanting to be part of the good news.

I saw mum pause and then I looked at her face. She was staring at the telephone in a sort of mute horror, her index finger poised in mid air. It took me a few seconds to identify the problem.

The telephone had no dial.

It was a telephone, to be sure, with a receiver on the cradle and a length of flex connecting the receiver to the body of the apparatus but, indisputably, undeniably, there was no dial! At Hillingdon, we had been possessed of a fine old example of the 300s series handset, a robust Bakelite creation in shiny black with a nifty little drawer at the base for the storing of your favourite phone numbers. That model may have appeared before I was born but at least it came with a dial. Our new portal to the world of telecommunications looked like it had been designed and built by the same company that came up with the Sherman tank. It was the size of the average breadbin and it squatted before us like a locked door, seemingly grinning and mutely taunting us, 'Ahh . . . Weren't expecting ME, were you ..!'

'What do we do now?' I inquired.

'Better phone the operator,' said mum.

'How do you do that?' I asked.

'You dial 100,' said mum distractedly.

'How?' asked my sister. 'We can't dial.'

A tremor of something close to panic seemed to thrill through us as we stared at the phone. Slowly, I took the handset and held it to my ear. There was a deep silence until, suddenly, a sharp pop was followed by a crisp voice which demanded, 'Nember, pleece!' I was so surprised I dropped the handset.

'There's someone on the other end!' I hissed.

We crowded round mum as she took up the phone and put it to her ear. We heard the voice impatiently demanding, 'The nember you require, pleece!'

With a note of desperation in her voice, mum said, 'I want to speak to my mother,' and added helpfully, 'She lives in Southall.'

There was a pause at the other end.

'Have you just moved to the area, caller?' asked the voice.

'Yes,' said mum apologetically.

'Well, you have to tell me the nember of the person to whom you wish to be connected, then you tell me the nember of the telephone apparatus from which you are making your call and I shall then connect you,' said the operator, who sounded very much as if she had a bulldog clip securely clamped over her nose. 'Now, what is your nember, pleece?'

'The number is always written in the middle of the dial,' said my sister helpfully.

'We haven't got a dial, you mong,' I retorted.

None of us could remember what our 'nember' was – despite the man from the GPO having told us just a short while previously. He had, allegedly, written it down on a little card. Everyone thought they remembered seeing the card but then hotly denied having taken the card from him when he left. Now, it's a fact that most of us can pick up a phone and dial the numbers of our friends and relatives without a moment's hesitation. But if someone suddenly asks us to recite any of those numbers, our minds go blank. Some of us, me included, have trouble quoting our own telephone numbers. It's exactly the same with the written word. I will write the words rhythm, diarrhoea, Burkina Faso, accommodation, unsuccessfully and Hezbollah without a thought: ask me to spell them out loud and I'm flummoxed.

Poor mum couldn't remember our new St Leonard's number and she couldn't remember a single number of her nearest and dearest. She apologised humbly to the operator and hung up. Ten minutes later, I saw her pulling on her boots and overcoat. With purse in hand she muttered, 'Just popping to the shop for some milk and bread.'

We let her leave, then quietly followed her – as far as the callbox at the top of the road; a callbox with a dial on its phone.

We got used to our dial-less behemoth and, after a while, even began to enjoy the labour-free phoning out. I would entertain my friends by snatching up the receiver and, when 'Nember-Pleece' answered, I would bark, 'Sell ICI, buy Glaxo . . . and tell Jenkins he's fired!' and bang the phone down. I had to give this up when the operators actually called back one day to complain about my abuse of the network. Unfortunately, dad happened to answer the phone on that occasion.

The Hastings exchange finally welcomed Subscriber Trunk Dialling – or STD – in 1974 and the Wells family managed to secure a telephone complete with the all-important dial – a smart 700 series handset – and we even got to choose the colour with mum daringly opting for bright red. I understand they're highly collectible now. But, by that time, my brother had long since trumped us all by equipping his London flat with a hyper-trendy Trimphone in the famous avocado green. It was the first time I heard a phone that didn't indicate a call by ringing a bell. The Trimphone warbled – and it had a luminous dial! St Leonard's was clearly still in the stone-age, I sadly concluded after viewing this spectacular apparatus for the first time.

What a difference a couple of decades can bring! When we arrived in Hastings there was no such organisation as British Telecom and you had to rent your telephone handset from the very limited range offered by the GPO. Today, when there are fifteen-year-olds out there who change their mobile phones more often than I change my socks, it's probably in telecommunications, and the information technology based on routing via the phone networks, that the most dramatic advances in daily life are apparent. Even the old red call boxes are confined now to the edges of village greens and they only remain because the preservation societies have fought to keep them for aesthetic reasons. I still miss the clunking, mechanical satisfaction of pressing Button A and Button B.

○ ○ ○

So engrossed had we been in the exploration of our new house and garden that it was a little while before I noticed the most ostensibly striking aspect of the location – although it had been, quite literally, under my feet every time we came in and out of the property.

It was the road itself.

Apart from the fact that it had no Tarmac, no white lines and was a cul-de-sac, it had no pavement. The clue to this puzzling state of affairs lay at the top of the road where the street signs proclaimed 'Boscobel Road North' and, in parenthesis, 'Unadopted'. Unadopted? What did that mean? Had this road's mother and father abandoned it? Was it so unattractive that it could find no one to embrace it? At eleven years old, that was my only interpretation of adopted, adoption and unadopted and I thought I must have been on the right track. In a curious way, I was: as dad explained, an unadopted road was one not technically owned by the local council so not kept up by it. The road was owned by the residents and it had to be maintained by them. Similarly, the areas between the front garden boundaries and the kerbsides, which would have been the conventional paved walkways, were also owned by the householders. Ours was laid to lawn, as most of them were. Some had been concreted over and although they were, in later days, to make excellent hardstandings for the occupying families' second cars it was, back then, more for the expediency of sparing ancient and creaky joints the agony of lawnmowing – something that was to become the bane of my life as the spring and summer arrived. We felt doubly proud when we realised we were part of a community that actually owned its own road. It made us feel like part of a small, independent country.

Unfortunately, for every up there is a down and 'down', in this case, was the appropriate word – again quite literally – for just a few months after our arrival a section of the road immediately in front of our house started to sink. Like some sinister tectonic plate movement in miniature, a large area of the concrete surfacing dipped down, leaving the edge of its neighbouring section standing some three inches proud. That may not sound very much but driven over in a 1960s car with 1960s springs and shock absorbers that misalignment caused a loud bang as suspensions grounded, a horrible rasp of metal as exhaust pipes were filed down by the concrete edge and a nasty jolt for unsuspecting drivers – most of them elderly. One of them, a diminutive old lady in a pristine Mark II Cortina, actually suffered a mild stroke after striking the 'tanktrap' and being bounced over the low back of the driver's seat into the rear of the car – the vehicle veering into the kerb and, thankfully, stalling. We all rushed out to find the car intact but the driver with her head jammed between the rear seats and one sensible brown brogue waving feebly out of the driver's window.

Seatbelts? Well, when I was a child, it seemed they were, at best, an unfathomable curiosity and, at worst, an entangling nuisance supplied, according to dad, for the use of cissies, poofs and neurotics. I recall seeing very few drivers wearing them and I never once remember being told to belt-up myself. Seatbelt awareness only really began to make headway when Jimmy Saville appeared on our screens with his 'Clunk, Click, Every Trip' campaign, coincidentally, during the same month that we took up residence in the town.

Mum and dad were highly alarmed at the turn of events. It wasn't the fear of personal injury or legal action that bothered them – our wretched compensation culture was still many years in the future – but the simple prospect of having to fork out for their share of the repair bill. The shift may have been a few inches but the quake in the family finances looked set to be positively seismic. We discovered that it was generally accepted that whenever any one section of the road need attention the four houses adjacent to it (two on either side) would be responsible for the remedial work. That was not something that the Wells family budget had been constructed to accommodate. I often wonder whether the unadopted status of the road with its possible ramifications was highlighted when my parents had the survey carried out prior to purchase – assuming they did have a survey carried out. It's compulsory when buying via a mortgage, of course, but with a cash buy? I guess I'll never know now.

In the end, the financial disaster never happened because the repairs never happened. We weren't the only people who didn't much fancy coughing up for repair work and the raised section of the road obligingly and of its own volition sunk to match its brother, leaving just a shallow dip. As the road was a cul-de-sac, resident motorists soon learnt to slow down when approaching the problem spot; any motorist who did pass over the dip too quickly and grounded their car got what they deserved because, as far as we were concerned, they were either going too fast or they were strangers – in which case they had no business driving up our 'private' road, anyway. In a few months, the grinding of metal on concrete was greeted not with anxious glances exchanged between my parents but with whoops of laughter and my dad exclaiming triumphantly, 'Got you, you reckless road-hog bastard!'

○ ○ ○

With a new home, a new school and new friends, it seemed everything in our lives was changing and, just a few weeks after our arrival, we had new money, too! Decimalisation came to us overnight on 15 February 1971. We went to bed on the 14th knowing that 240 pennies made a pound; when we woke up those 240 pennies had magically become £2.40 or 98p – depending on how you looked at them. Never-before-seen coins were in circulation, old coins were either doing new duty or were earmarked to disappear. The guinea was effectively redundant and dad went into immediate mourning for yet another pusillanimous sacrifice of the national heritage on the altar of Euro-appeasement. To me, of course, it was an exciting day – until I realised I'd spent all my pocket money and wasn't going to enjoy any coins – old or new – for several days to come. Fortunately, a stroll around the shops of London Road and Kings Road provided plenty of entertainment as the older generation attempted to carry out the daily shop, spending their old pounds, shillings and pence and receiving the New Pence as change. I went into the newsagents in Kings Road and spotted a fractious queue headed by a classic St Leonard's crumbly attempting to pay for the magazines she was buying.

'That'll be two-and-a-half pence, deary,' said the shop assistant.

'Tuppence ha'penny?'quavered the crone. 'That can't be right.'

'No, dear. Not tuppence ha'penny. Two-and-a-half pence.'

'Yes, yes, I know,' said the customer rather pugnaciously. 'Two pennies and a ha'penny.'

'No, no,' said the shop assistant, resigning herself to however long this was going to take. 'Not two pennies and a ha'penny. Two-and-a-half pence . . . Two-and-a-half new pence!'

'What's that in real money?'

'That is real money. If you mean, what is it in old money, it's sixpence.'

'Six pence? That's outrageous!'

'No, not six pence . . . I said sixpence . . . a tanner . . . that's what it would have been yesterday. If I was charging you six new pence, that would have been one shilling and tuppence ha'penny.'

'Yes, I've got the tuppence ha'penny bit,' said the old dear thoughtfully. 'But where does this new shilling come into it?'

'Look, love, there is no shilling. It's just two-and-a-half pence today.'

'Ahh, tuppence ha'penny! That's more like it! Are all your prices coming down like that now we've got this foreign money?'

As I left the shop I heard the shop assistant's voice wearily explaining to the next in the line, 'No, Mr Jarvis. I can't accept that. Those ten shilling notes were withdrawn two years ago.'

It must have been a very, very long day for a lot of shop staff. Indeed, there was at least one business (I think it was a wool shop in Kings Road) that actually closed down because its elderly proprietor just couldn't face the aggravation of dealing in decimals with both the clientele and the shop's books.

But, with the help of a seemingly endless TV advertising campaign, we all got there in the end notwithstanding local traders incurring the deep suspicion of having taken advantage of the national confusion and used the currency changeover for a surreptitious price hike. I recall there were similar allegations levelled when the Euro made its appearance in those EU countries which had elected to adopt it. It seems strange that the changeover caused such confusion when it was, in fact, a huge simplification; one hundred pennies equalled one pound. It doesn't get much simpler than that; certainly a lot more logical than declaring twelve pennies to be one shilling and twenty shillings to be a pound. Whatever had been the point of deciding that a pound comprised 240 pennies?

Probably none.

But they were our pennies and our pounds and our coins – coins you could get your fingers round; in those days, a pocketful of change really was a pocket full! The half-crown was my favourite; worth two shillings and sixpence and still, because of the pre-war exchange rate, referred to as 'half-a-dollar' by some of the older folk. There was the bizarre twelve-sided brass threepenny bit, the two-shilling 'florins' and the sixpenny bit 'tanners' as well as chunky pennies and ha'pennies. Even though the farthing had been demonetised in the year of my birth, I still found them rattling around in the sideboard drawers and liked the little picture of the wren on the reverse. All these coins, it seemed to me, were as unique and as separate from the rest of the world as the dank, damp, foggy little islands we had chosen to inhabit. I can't help feeling that just a touch of our native colouring faded to grey on that fateful but sunny February day.

5

Next-Door Neighbours
And Other Eccentrics

t was important to remember that we were now residents of St Leonard's rather than Hastings . . . Excuse me, St Leonard's-on-Sea.

Even then, the more elderly or genteel of the people we met were constantly lamenting the fact that Hastings and St Leonard's 'weren't what they were'. The argument was usually the same: the town had started its list towards decay and degeneration some time after the arrival of whoever happened to be bemoaning the declining standards of resident, youth and bus service to the town centre.

Our next-door neighbour to the left was a fragrant, mature lady with beautifully coiffured snow-white hair and a wardrobe of floral housecoats. She was a woman of flawless etiquette and she hated the very sight of us. Mum had lived all her life in streets where to step out of one door was to be invited in through another for tea and a chat so she was both non-plussed and disturbed at the sub-zero politeness she received from Maisie Neads.

A chat with Mrs Neads had all the warmth and familiarity of a tea party with the Taliban and revolved, for the most part, around her telling mum how quiet Boscobel Road North had always been – 'positively tranquil, Mrs Wells' – as she eyed my sister and I with resentment only thinly veiled. She had a daughter who visited periodically, just as snow-white and beautifully coiffured as herself. They both had toy poodles just as snow-white and beautifully coiffured as their owners. The snow-white Mrs Neads senior also possessed an immaculate but sterile back garden which seemed to exert some bizarre gravitational pull of its own. I could be absolutely certain that if I so much as touched a football, cricket ball, tennis ball, shuttlecock or balsa wood glider, it would loop gracefully over the hedge to be drawn to the centre of that perfect lawn on which it would sit looking for all the world like a particularly virulent boil marring an otherwise flawless complexion. Never was I bold enough to request their return.

So my sister and I transferred our ad hoc sporting adventures out of our back garden and into the road at the front of the house. In Hillingdon, playing football in the street had been almost impossible due to the volume of traffic that tended to invade the pitch. In Boscobel Road North, we could play a full ninety minutes plus extra time plus a full-length replay before having to grant passage to a trundling Morris Traveller. If our parents discouraged the activity, it was for fear of our safety; for Mrs Neads, ball games in the street were a clear sign of incipient anarchy. Our next-door neighbour and guardian of the neighbourhood morals had been, until retirement, the buyer for Philpot's, the gentlewoman's outfitter which nestled with an assured lack of ostentation, beneath the colonnade of Marine Court on the Seafront. It's gone now, one of a series of out-of-time shops in a parade which also featured that most bizarre outlet to the modern eye – a furrier. That was a business that eventually threw in the towel after one final shower of late-night glass in a war waged by the implacably hostile animal rights activists. As I recall there was, until quite recently, a faded sign on the boards announcing spunkily 'business as usual despite the broken windows'.

Mrs Neads, I'm quite sure, would have been utterly unable to comprehend such behaviour . . . the actions of ill-disciplined young people with far too much time on their hands and whose parents probably allowed them to play football in the street. She was, sadly, the one shadow cast on our new life. Her mute disapproval of pretty much everything we did was interspersed with sarcastic sniping over anything and everything that presented her with the opportunity – and she had sharp eyes! The subject matter may have varied but the message was constant; we were lowering the tone. What riled mum the most was not the suggestion that we were one stage removed from riff-raff but that we couldn't possibly have known any better.

Even as a boy, I had a keen eye for the symbolic – as did mum – and the fact that Mrs Neads' semi was built next door 'up the road' and thus on slightly higher ground than our bungalow meant that she could look down on us – literally and metaphorically – even when standing in front of her kitchen sink. The positions of her bloomless windows seemed the product of sinister design. We looked set for many years of living chilly cheek by frosty jowl. The rapprochement was, when it came, as dramatic as it was unexpected and centred on the hedge that divided our back gardens. Mrs Neads had not been slow in pointing out that the hedge in question was considerably better maintained on her side than on ours. After she had endured another impromptu lecture on garden management and the offer of 'her' jobbing gardener that Mrs Neads well knew we could not afford, mum went very quiet . . . too quiet. Desperate times had called for desperate measures.

Woolly Head was summoned.

Woolly Head was a strange, furtive creature; small, wiry, immensely strong and capable of handling any tool offered to him – power or hand. He ostensibly made a living by doing odd jobs for odd people – but not half as odd as the jobs he did for himself, so it was hinted, and which occasionally led to his being 'unavailable' for periods of some months at a time. But when he was around he would tackle anything with a sort of dogged 'orders-is-orders' ruthlessness that would probably have endeared him mightily to King Herod. He was the slightly menacing Cain to the Abel of bumbling buffoonery provided by the hilarious Stanley. He was actually called Woolly Head because he always wore a woolly hat, whatever the season of the year or the temperature, pulled low down over his eyes and highlighting his unshaven face. Mum found him a blend of the comical and the sinister but he came with good recommendation (I suspect the all-seeing and all-knowing Aunty Joyce again) and she quickly trusted him. We kids liked him, I think, because he offered a hint that not everyone in St Leonard's was as old, safe and comfortable as they had hitherto appeared.

Woolly Head appeared in the garden the same day that mum got the hedge lecture. There was a hurried council-of-war between the two of them, some vigorous nodding of the woolly hat – and then its owner went into action.

'Got to sort this here hedge. Stand back, old young'un,' he said to me as he passed by with shears, a saw, a bill hook, a bundle of rags and – excitingly – what looked like a can of petrol. It was amazing. He was like a one-man combine harvester. He cut the hedge, gathered the cuttings and burnt them all in one slow thorough progression down the line of the garden boundary. When Mrs Neads returned home that afternoon she was confronted by a pall of rather fragrant grey smoke above a hedge that looked as if it had received the undivided attention of a man with a flame-thrower.

'Mrs Wells! I really do think you might have . . .'

Mrs Neads never got any further, for mum had been anticipating just this reaction and its utterance was the straw of remonstration that broke the camel's back. Mum, as the youth of today would have it, went off on one big time. Mrs Neads visibly withered in the super-heated blast that was turned on her. Months of humiliation and embarrassment were vented in a roar of verbal Napalm. Our tormentor was vanquished and fled back to her house where she remained invisible for the best part of three days before emerging cautiously to break the ice with some innocuous comment about the weather. Mum, like all good-natured people provoked beyond endurance, had spent those three days feeling mortified and guilty about her outburst, the righteousness of her onslaught evaporating almost immediately to leave a residue of doubt. Consequently, she welcomed that overture and from that moment on things changed between them. They became, if not friends, then courteous and respectful neighbours with Mrs Neads, in the early days at least, going out of her way to indulge my sister and I in a stilted and horribly contrived manner that indicated that she truly had entered new territory. It was, I now realise, a bitter defeat to concede and all the more nobly carried for it. Footballs, cricket balls, tennis balls, shuttlecocks and balsa wood gliders were anonymously lobbed back into Wells territory and there were no further complaints about cat poo in the pelargoniums. She even stopped theatrically slamming her kitchen window when she spotted mum with twists of newspaper and a box of matches on her adjacent allotment. It was a benchmark moment for two reasons. The first because it was a personal victory for mum, a traditionally subordinate wife, unaided or abetted by dad. In fact, I'm not sure he ever met Mrs Neads in the five years he lived at no. 17. He didn't see many people, really, his anti-social inclinations compounded by his poor health and the fact that he was well-nigh housebound from the start. I do remember mum standing in front of him ranting about the 'neighbour from hell' while he subtly shifted his position in his chair so he could see round her to his beloved *ITV Seven* on the telly.

But there was another broader and perhaps more important aspect to the episode. Today, I can see that the row over the hedge was a key moment. Mrs Neads – now 'Maisie' – symbolic guardian of the decent, the right and the proper, had allowed the enemy to secure a foothold on the beaches and, to mix military metaphors, some kind or Rubicon had been crossed. Poor old Maisie was sharp enough to realise that the Wells family, outnumbered as it was by Boscobel Road North's blue-rinsed natives, was but a presage, an advance guard of the invasion that must surely come as the 1970s progressed and the street's elderly owner-occupiers either died or were relocated to nursing homes – or Bexhill. And, in time, like many of her kind, she was forced to concede defeat in the face of a casually brutal onslaught by high-energy young couples with as many cars as children and an arsenal of Sunday-morning power tools.

Mrs Neads sold up and moved to Bexhill. Excuse me, Bexhill-on-Sea.

◎ ◎ ◎

In complete contrast the house on the right, no. 15, was occupied by one Florence Eastgate, whom my father nicknamed 'Digit' because she was … 'a small figure'! She was indeed – and a lot more besides. Digit was five foot nothing of empire bedrock, a bright-eyed, bird-like little woman who exhaled cheery aphorisms such as 'Mustn't grumble' or 'Worse things happen at sea' as naturally as she inhaled oxygen. Hers was the original early 1930s show house and garden of the road although both were deteriorating rapidly by the time we arrived. Digit must have been over eighty when we arrived at Boscobel although she was still spry enough for a cane-assisted march to the London Road post office once a week. She adopted the non-interventionist approach to sounding out her new neighbours. That first Easter not a word was said but a box of Milk Tray chocolates appeared hanging over our shared fence. She loomed larger in our daily lives after that opener, a smiling, bobbing face at a window, the shy waves and then the gifts of sweets to us kids.

She watched us stumble into our teen years, always keenly aware of our birthdays and, for a while, it was as if we had a gentle, country grandmother on site. She seemed to glow briefly with a light that looked as if it might fuse us together permanently before she suddenly started to crumble with the same cheerfulness that she applied to everything else she did.

The closeness that mum and Digit ultimately enjoyed stemmed from an incident in which the old lady, sitting too close to her electric bar fire, burned her legs quite badly. Her doctor, one of two retired lady GPs who happened to live next door at no. 13, wanted her in a home for proper care and attention; but the small figure had no intention of being prised out of her own home. She knew all about those places; very nice – but once in, never out – other than 'feet first'. She dug herself in like a curmudgeonly old badger, confining herself to one room equipped with bed, chair, table, commode and a transistor radio played at ear-shattering volume to counter her deafness. A war of attrition should have followed but it didn't, largely because Digit was far too cute to think she could win one. She had another idea and put it to mum. A deal was struck. Mum agreed to get her up in the morning with tea and the paper and to put her to bed at night as well as providing her with a hot meal in the evening.

In return, Digit instructed mum to collect her weekly pension, use it to pay her household expenses and spend what ever was left on keeping the hard-pressed Wells family on track. Thus, the threat of the dreaded 'home' was lifted. When I asked mum why she was prepared to take on the extra work when she was 'always moaning' about looking after the existing family, she said simply if forcefully, 'Because she asked me to and it's just so nice to do something for someone who's actually grateful.' I was sensible enough to drop the subject at that point.

So the daily routine began. In the morning, mum would help Digit into her chair at the back window (no. 15's view of the distant beach at Bulverhythe, of Glyne Gap and Eastbourne was even better than ours), provide a small pot of tea, a couple of biscuits along with the previous day's *Daily Express*. At six o'clock she would take in a plated hot meal and, around nine, she would tuck the old lady into her bed, say goodnight and turn off the light. When mum, for whatever reason, wasn't around, the duties fell to me. My sister refused point-blank. 'She's as deaf as a post and it stinks of wee in there.' I must say I rather enjoyed it – not the 'wee' bit, of course, but I did quickly see what mum had meant. Digit was grateful for everything but it was a gratitude born of the meeting, the moment and the service in hand rather than a fearful need to ingratiate herself with the family who, by withdrawing its daily help, could condemn her to an institution overnight.

She had nothing to fear and I think she knew it. The little creature was the proverbial tonic. In all the time I knew her – even when she was in pain – not a word of complaint passed her lips. Once, she asked mum to get her a bottle of orange drink but a couple of weeks later declined the offer of a second because she thought it 'a little too sweet' for her. So as not to cause offence she had sipped her way though the whole bottle quite unaware that it was a concentrate and needed to be diluted with water before drinking. Where some would have had mum running in circles, Digit asked for nothing, expected nothing and was consumed by delight at the mere sight or sound of any one of us. I can still see her now, gurgling with flattered glee, when our first pet cat, the haughty Timothy, stalked into her room behind me one day, jumped on her bed and immediately settled down to lick his anal zone. He stared at Digit in surprise, his ears flattening against his head in feline irritation as she shrieked, 'Hello there, Jimmy!' in a voice to wake the dead.

In the spring of 1976, mum had a spell in hospital and I had to cook the meal as well as serve it. As a spotty sixteen-year-old with fingernails permanently loaded with oil from constant tinkering with my newly acquired moped, I was hardly the Galloping Gourmet. My first attempt was frozen beef burgers, instant mash and a tin of baked beans. On delivery, the hairy chin twitched as the toothless mouth began to work in anticipation.

'Here you go, Mrs Eastgate,' I roared. 'Dinner time.'
'How lovely,' she shrieked back at me. 'Home-made beef patties.'

What more can you say? To the world and his brother they were frozen beef burgers from Tesco; to Digit they were home-made beef patties. She made me feel like a culinary master. Years later, in seemingly less simple times, mum would reminisce and sigh and say, 'I never went into that house without coming out again feeling enriched.'

Digit's material generosity was warm and pertinent. Towards the end of our first year at no. 17, I got my first paper round. When Digit was told, she slipped a pound note to mum and told her to make sure I had my own alarm clock. It was a responsible undertaking and the boy must make sure he wasn't late. There were occasional gifts for mum, 'Mrs Wells, I'm too old to change my will now but I wanted you to have this.'

She did become the unofficial fifth member of the family, watching our Bonfire Night fireworks from her window with specially delivered soup and sausages, joining us in next-door absentia for Christmases, birthdays and Sunday lunches. Every evening when mum put her to bed she would insist they both had a glass of sherry. Mum would grit her teeth, pick up the sticky glass and knock back its contents, trying hard not to look at the amber liquid with its film of dust.

'Very nice,' she said on one occasion and quickly turned away so that the old lady wouldn't see her picking the dead silverfish from under her tongue. When I took on the duty in mum's absence I would avoid the sherry by telling Digit, rather piously, that 'I never touched alcohol' knowing full well that she was far too deaf to have heard the occasions on which I returned home from a session of under-age drinking in the Silverhill Tavern to fall over the front gate while singing at the top of my voice.

Towards the end, when she forewent even her bed and spent all her time in her armchair, she would say, 'Sitting here is fine. I've had my time and now I have my memories. They're good memories.' Mum found her one morning in January 1982, cold, still and tiny in her chair. Interestingly, she had refused her meal on the previous evening and had said 'goodbye' to mum rather than the usual 'goodnight'. Mum had thought little of it at the time. She didn't want to believe what she knew to be the fact so she made her old friend a hot water bottle, tucked it under the chilly eiderdown that covered her and took the dog for a walk just to give Digit 'a little more time'. Then she went back into that house next door, hoping. She called her friend from no. 35, the ever-steady Alice Batterham, who offered to come down 'just to check'.

They stood together for a while in the icy room, dimly lit by the grey winter clouds, then kissed the cold cheek and went to call Digit's doctor so the mechanics of legal-requirement could begin. When there was no one and nowhere left to absorb the vestiges of her home, mum and I burned the residue on a still, damp and sullen morning. I remember feeling a curiously fierce anger that the unwanted letters and papers, the photographs of formally posed and long-dead strangers were much more her life than the 'nice bits of stuff' that had already disappeared up the A21 with the distant relatives who suddenly materialised after the old lady's death. Among those papers was a liver-spotted sepia photograph of a young man – boy, really – in the rough serge uniform of the First World War. Overly romantic I might tend to be but I knew this was a photograph of the great love of Florence's young life; the lad to whom she had been engaged. He didn't make it home; life went on. But she never forgot him and kept his picture among her private things for the rest of her life – even after her marriage – a marriage of convenience, we gathered – to a ne'er-do-well in middle age.

For a moment I felt awful that this image, one that had endured for so long after the mortal coils had vanished, was set for the fire but, as I held it in my hand, I had a strange sensation (I'm not usually given to them) that we were doing the right thing. The last manifest images of Florence Eastgate and her young man would take the same route to the clay – finally. I hope the pair of them have forgiven the contrivance. We never knew his name.

I can still see the surly orange flame and its growing umbra spreading over the image and the sundry paperwork that accompanied it. There were little books of household accounts which featured Digit's immaculate and studied handwriting. I had a flash then of a pinafored girl hunched over her copybook, the light in her hair, as she practised that writing with ink and nib in the way that children did then but do no longer. Even then, through the media of discipline and practice, she would have known the simple commitment to the obedience and duty that, spread through the nation, maintained the thunderous pistons of a proud empire. It was what had driven the gift of the alarm clock. The boy who delivered the newspaper was as vital as the journalist who wrote it and the proprietor who caused it to be published. None could function without the others so all could take equal pride in their roles – however humble. The chasm between them was the divide of class, both natural and essential. It was a philosophy of simple honesty for a woman of honest simplicity, devoted to the monarchy, deferential to the gentry and uncomplaining when the boy who touched her passion was squandered in the trenches of Passchendaele.

❂ ❂ ❂

My father was not a gregarious man and that fact, coupled with the chronic arthritis that was slowly tightening the joints in his legs, meant that mum effectively did everything: shopping, taking us to and from school as well as holding down a part-time job and seeing to it that Miranda and I went on some trips and excursions, especially during the school holidays. She was aided in her endeavours by Alice Batterham, another minute human dynamo crackling with energy, fortitude and good humour. She lived up the road from us in the last bungalow on our side of the street – no. 35. Leaving her house one day soon after our arrival, she slowed her antiquated Renault with its air-cooled engine as she saw mum bringing us back from school. We all, I think, braced ourselves for another cutting comment but all Alice said was that it was really nice to see some children in the street at last. After the cool reception the Wells family had received in some quarters, mum was both surprised and delighted at the simple vote of confidence and, soon after, asked Alice to help with my sister's impending birthday party. She did and, in the process, had bestowed upon her the honorary title of 'Aunty' thus becoming, until her death in 1998, Aunty Alice. She was referred to thus by mum right up to her own death in 2002.

Alice had been a nurse before retirement and had that sort of brisk, no-nonsense attitude to life that such people seem to have. She openly admitted that she voted Liberal at every election and said, 'Oh, balls!' to anything she considered to be flummery. She possessed a wonderfully dry sense of humour that was, of course, far above the slapstick-ceiling of children. She was beautifully spoken, possessed just a hint of snobbery and a far more generous allocation of nervous tick which made her flick her head to the right several times a minute. What really endeared her to us children was the fact that she seemed to find the old folk of the street just as amusing as we did despite the fact that she was – officially, at least – one of them herself. Miranda and I were aghast that any living person could have so many wrinkles and still function normally. We wondered whether her penchant for sea-bathing – in all weathers and seasons – had anything to do with them.

Alice's husband we saw little of unless we visited their bungalow. I think we liked going there and I think now that what was so attractive was that the house contained a sort of old-world ambience without being terribly old-fashioned. The smell was intriguing, too. We soon learned that old people's houses have two types of smell – old people 'posh' which was a blend of furniture polish, pipe smoke and fresh flowers (Alice and Arthur Batterham) and old people 'common' which was essentially urine (Digit). Arthur Batterham was one of those languid, genteel men with a temperament as sweet and mellow as the cloud of pipe smoke that permanently enveloped him. He reminded me always of Sergeant Wilson from TV's *Dad's Army*. He seemed a permanent fixture in his burnished leather armchair. From it, armed with pipe and a small bag of Mint Imperials, he would regale us with tall tales recounted with such dignity, sincerity and brilliant under-statement that he never failed to dupe us – right up to the punch-line. Arthur it was who said that he liked St Leonard's because 'people were allowed to be a little odd'. It was a house that possessed the sort of stillness only found in one inhabited by a solitary but devoted couple; everything set to their needs and requirements. There, for the first and last time, I saw a Christmas tree with real candles on it; little red ones set in holders with lead weights beneath them to ensure the candles were permanently upright. It was inconceivable to me that those candles would ever be so vulgar as to ignite the pine needles about them and inconvenience the Batterhams.

But it was Alice of whom we saw most. As our family had never owned a car, the transport Alice provided opened up our options considerably. Those first two summers in

St Leonard's were enlivened by many trips and excursions with Alice functioning as tour guide and chauffeur. She introduced us to the cobbles of Rye and the castle at Bodiam; the Romney, Hythe and Dymchurch Railway; Beachy Head; High and Over and many others all of which have become as familiar to me today as my own back garden was becoming then.

When a trip was in the offing my sister and I would become quite excited. We would hop about the house, waiting for our driver to arrive in her rattling old car. Miranda, who always said Aunty Alice reminded her of a tortoise because of the wrinkles, would pull her head into her shoulders and try to create as many creases as possible in her flawless child's complexion.

'If a tortoise owned a car, this is what it would look like,' she'd sing.

'If a tortoise owned a car, that's how it would drive,' I would say as Alice lurched to a bouncing halt outside our house. Cackling with delight at our witticisms, we would then hurtle about the hall holding imaginary steering wheels and emulating Alice's nervous twitch with jerks of our heads that all but dislocated our necks. We were nonchalantly cruel but there was no malice in it. We were very fond of Aunty Alice. For one thing, she never treated us in the patronising manner adopted by so many of our neighbours from the seen-and-not-heard generation; for another, I think that I, at least, sensed how fond mum became of her. It was only later that I learned just what an inexhaustible fount of reassurance, commonsense and sound advice she had been to mum when things were difficult – specially in the period immediately after the death of my father. She stayed a close friend to all of us and was one of the few non-family guests at my wedding in 1988.

But even the turbocharged tortoise had to bow to age in the end. Finally, after joining the ranks of the road's widows, she sold her bungalow and left the town, going into a home in the Welsh Marches in order to be nearer her daughter. Towards the end she became very frail and vague but kept writing to mum. Her death cast a pall over the Wells family and for me, by that time a parent myself, it seemed as if the last nail had been driven into the coffin of my childhood. For mum, it was the passing of a woman who had redefined the expression 'best friend'. Truly, the end of an era.

Of our other neighbours, some we got to know almost immediately; others took longer to embrace us if, indeed, they ever did. The thing the vast majority had in common, of course, was age; after all, Boscobel Road North had been carved into rough pasture on the edge of St Leonard's at the start of the 1930s to create homes for the well-earned retirement of professional people – and, boy, were some of our neighbours retired.

Miranda and I had never seen such a vast collection of old people in one place. In Hillingdon, our road of semis had been a fizzing pint-pot of busy working couples with children, topped off with a frothy head of wailing babies, colourfully-clad Asians and hale OAPs. In St Leonard's, by contrast, the whole pace of life seemed to run at half-speed while eccentricity was so prevalent that, very soon, nothing surprised us. As Arthur Batterham once observed, 'People come to St Leonard's to die but seem to end up living forever.'

Not all of them were old, of course, even if the most memorable were and there were a few other brave and youthful pioneers attempting to establish themselves. I recall, for example, Jo and David Sear who arrived at no. 4 with their three children some time after we moved into no. 17. They were the sort of people who were termed 'a nice young couple'. I think they were ambitious – certainly courageous – and soon after decided to take advantage of the old '£10 ticket' and emigrate to Australia where his plumbing skills were in demand. We were intrigued to learn that they had come back, surprised to hear that they had gone to Australia a second time and astonished when they returned to England yet again. Almost unbelievably, we learned they were planning to set off for Oz a third time. They never made it. The oldest boy revolted, said he was captain of his school football team and wasn't budging again. Then, I thought him crazy to turn down the adventure; now, I realise the importance of stability, routine and regularity in children's lives and I rather admire the youngster's resolve. I hope his football career prospered.

Elizabeth and Graham Willey, originally from Wales, might have been the subject of a David Hockney painting had the great man ever sought the muse on the South Coast. He was a lecturer at the then Hastings College of Further Education, academic and intellectual. She was a teacher at The Grove, elegant and intellectual. They had two young sons for whom mum regularly babysat, taking my sister and me with her. It was a popular way to spend an evening with us because Elizabeth – ever the hostess even in her absence – would leave us a buffet supper that wouldn't have disgraced a civic reception. To cap everything, they had a colour TV! We'd never seen a colour TV before except on television which, as we only had black and white, didn't really count. We sat in awe and gazed at it relentlessly, too terrified to touch the controls and alter the contrast, brightness or colour despite the fact that the late-lamented Reginald Bosanquet's face, although fairly florid at the best of times, positively pulsated with crapulent carmine on that set as he lurched through *News at Ten*. Even the likes of the saintly Michael Aspel looked suspiciously radioactive. Mum was very nervous of that set. I think she felt that all those colours could only have come from some volatile ingredient that must be inherently unstable. Tinkering with the controls could only lead to trouble if not an immediate explosion. My experimental fingers were immediately swatted away. But that was not the limit of the Willeys' technocratic domain. They also had a VCR. It actually belonged to the college but Graham brought it home so that he could tape TV programmes out of hours for the benefit of his classes. It would be a full fifteen years before I had one of my own. He once demonstrated it to me by taping and immediately replaying a snatch of *Blue Peter*. I was astonished. This was *Tomorrow's World* today. Blow landing men on the Moon, I thought. This was technology that you could actually use day to day – the sort of sentiment I now realise was broadly shared by the world and which had condemned Neil Armstrong and Edwin 'Buzz' Aldrin to the title of Mankind's Most Underestimated, Underappreciated and Undercelebrated Achievers. Perhaps such a lack of breadth in imagination can be forgiven in an eleven-year-old boy.

Babysitting at no. 37 was something else, then. With the immaculately presented supper, the sophisticated surroundings and the staggering technology on offer, the three of us frequently forgot why we were there – momentarily perplexed to see a forgotten toddler rubbing his eyes at the foot of the stairs.

At the other end of the spectrum I can remember Mr and Mrs Taylor who lived at no. 21. I recall little of her other than the fact that mum didn't like her (and I later found out when my girlfriends came under her study that, more often than not, she was right in her unarticulated prejudices). Mr Taylor drove a Jaguar complete with leather and burr walnut and owned the toy shop, Hammonds, which was, like Mrs Neads' Philpot's, a major feature of the Marine Court colonnade back then. He had one of those deep voices that are only achieved after marinating vocal chords for years in single malt Scotch and cigar smoke. He had, apparently, in years before, managed several big-name football clubs but no one was ever sure quite which teams he had commanded. I heard, variously, Everton, Preston North End, Manchester United, West Ham and Spurs. Dad certainly gave the stories no credit although he could be rather biased against anybody who had done something he hadn't – specially if, like Mr Taylor, they drove a Jaguar and came from 'Up North'.

'Football manager? Cut up the half-time oranges, maybe . . . Pah!' End of subject.

On one occasion, when my brother was paying us a visit, he indulged me with a kick-about in the back garden. Big bruv managed to hoof the ball over the hedge so that it cleared Mrs Neads' garden completely and dropped into the Taylors'. With his footballing past, I thought, he couldn't possibly object to my retrieving the ball: might even offer us a spot of impromptu coaching. I knocked on Mr Taylor's door and told him what had happened. He thanked me for the information and assured me that he would keep an eye out for the football the next time he happened to be in the garden. He wasn't joking. At least Maisie Neads had one next-door neighbour of whom she could approve.

Mr Coates was a gentle Yorkshireman who lived at no. 38, the distinctive, flat-roofed and very modern bungalow which was known in the street as 'The Chocolate Box'. Mr Coates was one of the men who operated the West Hill Lift and on many occasions he waved us through for a free ride up to the castle. Again, mum didn't like the wife. She said Mrs Coates was ashamed of her husband's job. I used to wonder whether Mrs Coates would be happier if her husband could work the East Hill Lift – far more exciting and apparent to the tourists for not having to pass ninety per cent of its journey through a brick-lined tunnel. The East Hill Lift blended the funfair with sterling British engineering. It was surely the pride of the fleet. I used to hope that generous Mr Coates would be promoted.

At no. 42, the Revd Canon A.H. Cleaver leant the road some formal gravitas. He was – or had been – assistant parish priest at the church of St Mary Magdalene, that striking edifice at the corner of Church Road and St Margaret's Road, which is now the town's official Greek Orthodox church. I got a right rollicking for asking my parents whether 'Canon

Fodder' was a better nickname than 'Meaty Cleaver' for the old boy. The church still commanded some respect back then.

But our elderly friends and neighbours were beginning to fire a fascination in me over and above the enjoyable anticipation of their odd words and actions and it was at about this time that I made the quantum leap of relating people to history and the world at large. As a child, the fact that my father had been a combatant during the Second World War was a great source of pride to me but my perception of his role was rather insular. It was a case of the war belonging to my father rather than my father belonging to the war. Two incidents of which I have very clear memories illustrate the transition I made then from my perception of old people as people who were old (and basically useless) to the realisation that they were, in fact, the first step of the journey into history – each one a mosaic piece which went to make up the picture of what had gone before. It was a mental and intellectual development triggered not by a teacher, but by the environment in which we had come to live.

The first occasion featured my grandfather who came to see us for the day one Sunday. The news was not intelligence I had greeted with any great enthusiasm. From my youngest days, I disliked Sunday at the best of times, wracked as it was by the spectre of a return to school the next day, bath and an early night. There was one bright spot, though; *Stingray*. Gerry Anderson's masterpiece of 'super-marionation' featured handsome Troy Tempest, the mute but beautiful Marina and the guttural and gurglingly-evil fishmen whose fish-shaped submarine exploded so gratifyingly when hit by one of Troy's well-aimed torpedoes. It was, to me, the acme of TV entertainment. But grandpa was there for the day and he liked to watch *Songs of Praise* on BBC 1. It was unfortunate that someone was going to have to miss out on their preferred viewing but I was sure he wouldn't mind. As he was old he would probably have fallen asleep anyway. Stunningly, the court of TV arbitration did not find in my favour. I sat ram-rod straight at the tea table with pilchards on my plate, tears in my eyes and murder in my heart. Grandpa died in 1972 having survived his wife (as is so often the case) by just a few short months. It was a long time after his death that I started to appreciate the man he had been and that typically English modesty that had cloaked his heroic exploits in the First World War. Today, I would give a lot to be able to talk to him, man to man. When I think of the indulgent way in which I have lived my life and compare it with his steadfast, uncomplaining resilience, his two world wars, his dignified poverty and his quietly ferocious determination to do whatever was necessary to provide for his family, I feel rather embarrassed. The *Stingray* episode (or lack of it) demonstrated to me that old people were still sufficiently vital to have their TV preferences respected and, thus, that they mattered. It began to dawn on me that when my parents used expressions like 'Well, she's getting on now' or 'He's had a good innings' and 'Poor souls get a bit confused at that age' they were actually speaking in a sort of admiration and not using the words as justification for ignoring, over-riding or denying the wishes or desires of the elderly of whom they spoke. It was my first introduction to the concept of subjective respect; respect for achievement rather that the automatic respect children give to parents and teachers and police officers all of whom are immediate and indisputable authority figures with the power of sanction.

The second incident took me a stage further in that it provided some form to that nebulous idea of 'achievement' by colouring it with something I had not previously associated with old people – passion.

Americans were something of a rarity – especially vituperative, nonagenarian unreconstructed rebels. Somewhere along the line – I don't know how or when – mum made friends with an American woman named Miss Beale. She must have been in her early sixties and she lived in a house on the outskirts of Crowhurst village with her ancient aunt. The Misses Beale seemed to live an isolated, self-sufficient life redolent of the Great Plains homestead from which they originated. How or why they came to such a homely little corner of cultivated Sussex, I don't know but they had brought something of their native land with them. The elder Miss Beale was confined to a chair and her memories – most of which centred on her father who had been, she told me, a cavalry captain in the Confederacy during the American Civil War. It may have been a conflict now confined to the history books – although the first to be comprehensively recorded in photographs – and one which did not really touch the British, but to Miss Beale senior it was one which lived on. The energy and the righteousness of her father's campaign coursed through her dark blue veins as soon as she could steer a conversation to include it.

One day she called me in to her shaded room – I can still see the curtains drawn over the brilliant square of light that was the window and hear the birds in full song outside – and told me she had something to show me. With a slowness born of reverence rather than age, the old lady produced the remains of a cavalry sabre, the blade snapped about nine inches below the hilt, a pair of leather gauntlets and a pair of spurs which looked like large metal wishbones from a large metal chicken. I was disappointed. The gloves should have been yellow and supple; the spurs should have had flashing, revolving stars at their tips and the sword should have been a glittering arc of polished, bitter steel with ornate guard and the dandy tassels of the dashing hussar. In fact, I thought the artefacts looked mean and crude and dirty. Politely, I handled them as I was offered to do while the old lady's high-pitched voice hardened as she talked of what she called 'The War of Northern Aggression' and her father's role in the desperate and hopeless fight. And for a moment, she was my father sitting on the edge of his desk at Rutland House as the

Indian Bean Tree dappled the sunlight across the classroom and he told us of the murder of Edward II, Wat Tyler and the Peasants' Revolt, the desperate flight of Becket's assassins or the betrayal of the Gunpowder Plot conspirators. Only, this time, I was holding in my hands items that had been present at the event. Suddenly, I realised that this was a sword that had been drawn in anger; the spurs had urged the captain's horse forward in a cavalry charge. I could see the gloves being drawn on to the hands that would grip that sword. Did those palms sweat with the fear of imminent conflict? I heard the voices of men and the jangle of harness, smelled the scent of horses and felt a thrill of fear pass through me. The old lady was lost in her tale. Her father, too, had been in a war but a war that was only in history books; the subject of black and white films on the TV, maybe, but a war for which there were no Airfix kits, no Action Man outfits, no points of reference at all – until now. Yet it had been – and was – real. I was listening to someone who had seen it with their own eyes. It was in the depths of time and it was yesterday. It was history and it was alive.

Thus my attitude to the elderly changed. In the company of my sister or the small group of friends I collected in the immediate period after moving to the Sussex coast I, naturally enough, continued to ape their stilted gait and snigger at the farting that they could neither hear nor control. I was still driven to distraction by their gummy, methodical chewing and the snail's pace at which they walked; but I also started to listen to their reminiscences and to try to marry them as people to the text book incidents and adventures of the past. My concept of time was still very limited and there was a bit of a grey area between a great-great grandfather who may have been at Waterloo and those of his forbears who may have seen the last of the woolly mammoths. Nevertheless, it was a start and I spent a lot of time pondering the concepts of age and the passage of time. I would try to calculate how many dreaded Sunday evenings I would have to endure if I was going to live to be a hundred and how I would feel when I was as bald as my father or as poor as my brother. I began to have a sneaking suspicion that life wasn't the doddle that childhood had hitherto suggested it might be. In fact, it began to look like bloody hard work.

Thus it was that in sleepy St Leonard's, at the ripe old age of eleven, I realised Arthur Batterham's implied assertion that longevity bestowed the right to go a little loopy had a feeling of natural justice about it and was, I now see, his typically understated rationale of tolerance. I learned also that from tolerance comes compassion and so the laughter and enjoyment we had from the geriatric antics around us came naturally and was never spiteful. Indeed, the highly individual nature of the perpetrators seemed almost a metaphor for our new life by the sea and its sense, somehow, of being suddenly unconfined. The world was, indeed, a stage and I welcomed the entrance of a cavalcade of colourful extras and bit-part players.

There was, for example, Blind Millicent, as we knew her. Blind Millicent was the sad owner of probably the world's most useless guide dog. Gareth the Labrador was, in fairness, efficient enough at his job – right up to the moment he caught the slightest whiff of anything to eat. From that point he was lost to himself and to the world. I remember I was playing some ball game in Gensing Gardens when I heard a cry and turned round to see the genteel and elderly Millicent galloping through the flowerbeds, tulip heads flying up like the spray from a powerboat. Gareth had spotted some children throwing bread to the ducks.

On numerous occasions we would find a solitary elderly woman, always beautifully turned-out complete with pill-box hat, sitting on the low brick wall at the front of our garden. If she wasn't sitting on our front wall the chances were that she would be sitting on someone else's – especially if the weather was fine. We nicknamed her, in a flash of inspiration, Sit-on-the-wall. Sit-on-the-wall sat on walls all over Upper St Leonard's causing varying degrees of irritation, curiosity and amusement among homeowners. She continued to sit on walls for some length of time. Finally, after she had disappeared and seemed to be sitting on no walls at all, we learned that she had been 'taken away'. Apparently, after a busy but satisfying day of wall-sitting, she would return to her home each evening, put on her night attire, lock up the house and get into bed beside her husband who, when the police and social workers finally got to him, was – quite literally – a heaving sea of maggots under a freshly laundered counterpane. This was, perhaps, the darker side of Arthur Batterham's implied right-of-passage to Loopydom but I don't recall feeling disturbed by the news. Rights were rights; freedom was freedom.

We liked Peg-Leg. She was a dapper little woman given to tweeds and a beret. The sobriquet, of course, came from the polished black pole, complete with stout rubber ferrule, which had substituted her left leg. She strode about St Leonard's at five times the speed of most of her contemporaries and we would sometimes find her taking a breather on her favourite seafront bench at Warrior Square. She looked like a one-woman coastal defence battery, her peg-leg pointing out to sea like the barrel of a mini-howitzer. Mum felt that such a crude prosthesis, while suitable for an old fisherman, scarcely became a respectable woman. 'She might give it a coat of white paint for the summer,' she would sniff.

From Peg-Leg to Red-Legs – the man at no. 16 was another classic odd-ball. We called him Red-Legs because he would don a pair of ridiculously short shorts at the beginning of the summer and stay in them till the autumn. His barrel-like top half made the sight of him all the more comical. He would start the year with legs as white as over-cooked spaghetti and finish it with the limbs in question the colour of chip shop saveloys. He had served in the Royal Navy during the war and decorated his front garden by picking out HMS *Ajax* in huge letters with white stones at the front of his rockery. Then, for good measure, he painted all the brickwork blood red and strung fairy lights along the eaves of the bungalow. On one occasion, mum got invited in to see his considerable collection of naval memorabilia but was a little dubious over the way he had left a certificate confirming the success of his vasectomy rather prominently displayed on the coffee table. She spoke to him from the road from then on. It seemed, though, that Red-Legs missed his sea legs. He left the street to take up the position of guide-yeoman aboard the floating museum of HMS *Belfast* in London.

The word 'stomp' might have been invented to describe the purposeful gait of Miss Clegg who lived at no. 5. A spinster, she had a face so brown and hair so white that she looked like a photographic negative. She always appeared in sensible tweeds and sturdy Wellington boots and boasted a fine moustache. I can see her now talking to mum over the low front garden wall, bouncing on the balls of her feet with her hands clasped behind her back and looking like a regimental colonel offering a pep talk to his men on the eve of a major offensive. She was another epitome of British sterling stuff, but the 'officer class' compared with Digit's 'other ranks'. It was only in the reminiscences and the jigsaw pieces of information that emerged after her death and at her funeral that we learnt more of her early life. She had, apparently, been something of a demon on the dance floor, no less consummate on the tennis court and had elected to remain single after falling in love with a man already committed. Her personal code of ethics forbade her from making any attempt to steal him away so she remained alone. She had devoted her life to missionary and school teaching work in far-flung corners of the empire returning, as they all did, to pass her declining years in cooler climes with less expansive vistas.

Her home, I recall, was littered with trophies and souvenirs of her life; strange, stylised statuettes in ebony, ivory and dark, alien woods too bizarre to fire my, as then, limited curiosity of the geographical world. Miss Clegg was really rather intimidating reminding me, as she did, of a tyrannical headmaster I had known; but she was kind to us children and took us, on one occasion, to the old ABC Cinema. The film was *The Tales of Beatrix Potter* which featured the old animal stories set to music and performed wordlessly by ballet dancers in animal costumes. Miss Clegg swayed in her seat, hummed the tunes and gently tapped the rhythms of the music throughout. Miranda and I thought it boring beyond belief and were thoroughly embarrassed by our companion. We didn't want to go; we didn't want to go with Miss Clegg and we didn't stop moaning about it for days afterwards. Mum was, justifiably, disappointed in us. But such velitation was rare. For the most part, the gentle eccentricity all around us provided us kids with seemingly endless hours of amusement although the idiosyncrasies of our neighbours weren't always quite so harmless when they were combined with motor vehicles.

The rather cadaverous-looking Mrs Grange, who lived directly opposite Digit, took out her Mini just once a week. At the sight of her closing her front door and tottering towards her garage, Miranda and I would hurry out to our garden gate to make sure we had a good vantage point for the 'show'. Mrs Grange would get into the car and start the engine. Our excitement mounted as we waited for her to adjust her hat in the driving mirror, examine her bag to make sure she had everything required and shift into reverse gear. With clutch screaming in agony, the Mini would edge backwards and start the long, steep descent to the road. Gathering speed, the car would reach the bottom of the drive, pass into the road, across the road, over the opposite kerb, through Digit's garden wall and onto her lawn where it would come to a halt in a cloud of brick dust. It was a regular occurrence and we never got tired of it. Sometimes, when bored, my sister and I would sneak into Digit's garden and pan the grass for the pieces of red and orange glass, remnants of the rear light lenses from Mrs Grange's car, which sparkled in the sunshine. Even when we had all but exhausted the seam and the fragments were becoming as rare as real jewels, we knew we wouldn't have to wait long for the supply to be replenished. As for the adults concerned, there was never any fuss. Mrs Grange would send over a hand-written note of apology and a cheque: Digit would respond with her own note thanking Mrs Grange for her offer and adding that 'worse things happened at sea'. A couple of days later the builder would appear, the wall would be remade and we would all settle down to wait for the whole thing to start again – which it invariably did until even Mrs Grange conceded that she had grown too old to manage a vehicle.

Mind you, almost as dangerous was Aunty Alice Batterham. The last in her series of cars was a vermillion Ford Escort – a distinctive colour for a distinctive driver. In fact, Alice kept a small pot of model-maker's paint in her kitchen and pretty much the first job after any outing was touching up the scuffs and scratches incurred while on the road. Bearing in mind that Alice seemed to think that the broken white lines down the centre of the road were there to mark out her route – much like a pair of scissors cutting out a newspaper coupon – I'm amazed that the occasional altercations with traffic islands, lampposts and other parked vehicles were the only accidents she had, especially in her later years when her nervous twitch had intensified and she seemed to have shrunk to such a diminutive form that she drove by looking through the steering wheel rather than over it. Looking back, it can only have been the limited traffic on the roads back then that saved her life. Imagining Alice trying to negotiate the Seafront or Old London Road as they are today is the stuff of nightmares.

The two doctors at no. 13 were also well known for their less than consummate skills at the controls of a car. Theirs was a forgiving Morris 1100 which, at the start of each outing, was forced to endure a fifteen-minute nine-point turn, the engine revving to the limits of physics before the good doctors finally kangaroo-hopped round the bend in the road, a thin blue haze and the faint smell of something burning left hanging in the air as silence reclaimed the street.

None of these people, of course, had ever passed a driving test: no such thing had existed when they had ventured on to the King's Highway.

'Quick! Everyone stand in the middle of the road!'

'Why?'

'I've just seen Mrs Grange getting the car out! It's the safest place to be!'

Mind you, as far as the menace of the motor car was concerned, the elderly were the victims of far more calamities than they perpetrated. Mum was constantly returning home with reports of cheerful ambulancemen tending crones at the roadside after they had misjudged the speed of an oncoming milk float. Then, it was sympathy, apologies and a reviving cup of tea from whichever householder had an adjacent front door. Now, the milkman would be sacked, the stricken 'victim' would instigate a no-win, no-fee multi-million pound lawsuit, the householder would stay indoors because they 'didn't want to get involved' and everyone even close by to the incident would be booked in for trauma counselling. 'It's not like it used to be' is a sentiment that takes on profound significance when one hears oneself uttering the words instead of hearing them from the lips of the older generation. The world has, indeed, changed and it seems to me that no one – except possibly youth – welcomes and celebrates the individuality of the eccentric and then only under the label of 'nutter'. The rest of the community views them with suspicion and alarm. In the days of our move to St Leonard's no one would have dreamed of suggesting that the two doctors who lived together at no. 13 were anything other than retired lady companions. Today the very mention of two people of the same sex setting up home together is enough for knowing nods and winks regardless of whether anything is 'known' or not. And what chances would you give to a gentle, elderly man who likes to sit on a park bench and watch the children playing in the sandpit because his own grandchildren are at the other end of the country, dragged hundreds of miles away by their father's relentless pursuit of career? Today, the old boy must, of necessity, be a pervert.

The passing years have imposed a uniformity of convenience and comfort but one from which we dare not now stray. We all drive the same car (regardless of the maker's badge), we all buy our food and just about everything else from the same half-dozen supermarkets, we all wear jeans and we all live in terror of global warming, cholesterol, burglars and even more global warming. Grammar schools are undesirable because they dare to suggest that our children might just possess different levels of ability and there is still an educationist lobby which frowns on school sports because they place emphasis on competition and encourage individuals to best their peers. Pardon the political homily, but it grieves me to think of the drab chain-gang that society has become in little more than two generations. My sister and I – mum and dad, too – may have laughed at the 'old farts' we encountered. Yes, they were variously intimidating, crotchety, bizarrely attired, vague, cheerful, splendidly generous, appallingly mean-spirited and sometimes, behind the wheel of a car, downright dangerous; but they almost all had fascinating stories to tell of their early lives. Some had been privileged, others had endured privations hard to imagine in these days of state-handouts and home-helps.

Frank Hopper was a horny-handed son of the soil if ever there was one. He would be on his allotment from dawn to dusk tending magnificent vegetables which he would promptly give away to anyone at hand. I can see him now, whistling melodiously as he wheeled his ancient bicycle through a green and pungent gloaming, a man who had created an almost biblical cornucopia, satisfied that he was heading for home empty-handed after his days of labour. Who could ever have guessed the pain and anguish that splendid, rubicund face had seen and endured for four years as a prisoner of the Japanese in Burma?

Digit, Alice, Frank Hopper . . . and there were many others we knew or encountered as we settled into our new environment. I'm glad I had the chance to meet them fading, as they were, by the time we arrived. They were the last of the bootstrap generation who made of themselves what they could within their imposed limits and were content to do so. They were not tormented by the lure of material goods, impatience to own them or resentment when they couldn't. They believed in the individual's duty and responsibility to the community, respected the property and privacy of others and would have nothing to do with credit cards. They taught me much about the value of dignity, integrity and taking responsibility for one's own actions. That lesson might not have prevented me from making periodic balls-ups of my own life; but it did stop me from blaming anyone else.

6

Restless Natives

Who were the original inhabitants of this enduring town by the sea? What was the origin of those tough, sea-faring folk who found this abrupt combe at the mouth of the Bourne, huddled their simple homes in the shadows of towering sandstone cliffs and wrested a bare living from the treacherous waters?

Absolutely no idea. I never gave it a second thought and I'm not going to start now. I certainly have no intention of boring anyone with a social or demographic history of the town; there are far more competent authorities on that subject than I could ever be and readers who want to inquire will do no better than J. Mainwaring-Baines' definitive tome *Historic Hastings* which was published in 1955 and is still freely available today.

As a 'Hastinger' by adoption – if not birth – I subscribe to the conventional wisdom that English History started in 1066 with the Battle of Hastings so it's the place and not the people who are significant in the wider scheme of things. However, I do want to mention one long-established resident of the town who undoubtedly can claim to have been in Hastings for as long as Hastings has been here itself: *Larus Argentatus* – the herring gull. Love them or loathe them – and they do excite those extremes of emotion in people – they really are an integral part of the town's abstract.

I must confess that I'm an admirer; in fact, I think they're rather magnificent. They're large birds with startlingly contrasting pure-white and blue-grey plumage, slightly hooked yellow bills marked with those curious orange dots upon them and beady but intelligent eyes. They have a stern, proud, almost predatory look about them and, for me, the only thing that lets them down are their webbed feet. I always think such an adaptive, adoptive and enduring bird should have been equipped with fish-grabbing talons like an eagle or an osprey. Instead, their longish legs end in what appear to be down-at-heel slippers or oversized frogmen's flippers. But it's when in flight that they become truly impressive. It's said that Reginald Mitchell was inspired to design the Spitfire aeroplane after observing gulls in flight and it's easy to believe. They are true masters of their element, catching the slightest current or thermal on summer days or hanging almost motionless against angry winter skies and 'riding the storm'. They use their natural design to achieve magnificent aerial buoyancy, just as the little fishing boats they've followed for centuries do the same on the water far below. And, indeed, the herring gull's relationship with the Old Town fishing fleet is a close one and for more than the obvious reason – but more of that later.

As Londoners, we were naturally aware of gulls as an essential part of the seaside town. After all, what holiday on the coast would be complete without waking in the morning to sun streaming into the bedroom and the salt-tang on a breeze that carried the soaring, unmistakable cries of seagulls already hard at the business of the day? We were not aware that they had another side to their picture-postcard image and we had never heard them referred to as 'flying rats' until we came to live in the town. Now, in fairness, the rubbish-raiding that has become such a nuisance in recent times only really boomed with the advent of the bin-liner. We didn't use bin-liners back then; we used bins – great big galvanised steel or tough plastic dustbins with close fitting lids that no beak was ever going to pierce. The birds would scavenge, of course, if there was anything worth scavenging for, but stinking garbage strewn over road and pavement was not something we saw often. Indeed, defenders of the gulls would point out that they were, in a sense, one of nature's 'dustmen' and actually cleared as much detritus as they created. They don't seem to be clearing much of it these days but we'll let that pass.

What was disconcerting, though, was the sheer number of the things that suddenly appeared in the early spring when the breeding season began. Suddenly, the charming cry of the 'gull on the wing' became a strident, endless, baying of birds' voices that rang and echoed round the clock as they squabbled over mates and nest sites. When they started to sit on their eggs they became surly, watchful and faintly menacing: when the chicks were hatched and fledging the adult birds became downright aggressive and even violent. I remember a shirt-sleeved neighbour in Boscobel Road North running at a grounded baby gull trying to panic it into instinctive flight and get it out of the road. It worked but not before the furious parents, assuming their pride and joy had been earmarked as his next meal, dive-bombed the poor man. A wing dealt him a blow on the shoulder with the force of a punch and a bill drew blood from the back of his head. That incident sticks in my mind particularly because, two days later, the Good Samaritan ran over another baby gull in Bexhill while driving home. He still had sticking plaster on his head but was quite distraught at what he'd done.

Still, we were highly amused at seeing the gulls at their 'rain dance'; stamping on the short grass of a wind-swept and empty Warrior Square putting green to bring earthworms to the surface by duping them into thinking it was raining. The birds had another amusing habit that caught the eye – quite literally for the unfavoured few. It wasn't so much amusing as blatantly funny – provided one had the right sense of humour and wasn't the victim.

Someone once calculated that, during the reign of Queen Victoria, if all the horse dung dropped in the streets had been allowed to lie there, London would be six feet beneath it today. As with horses, so with seagulls – and a lot of gulls produce a lot of droppings. And drop it does – from a great height sometimes. If you are the unintentional target and the bird scores a direct hit it can be shocking, embarrassing, dirty, unpleasant and bloody painful.

But it's lucky, too!

Quite why that should be I've never been able to discover but we learnt, soon after our arrival, that being dumped-on by a seagull was considered a sign of good fortune to come. The first time I encountered this curious idea it didn't really register. It was a school day and we had been bussed down from Mercatoria to the playing fields at South Saxons for our afternoon games session. Filsham Valley secondary school wasn't even a gleam in the LEA's eye back then and that vast expanse of grass – frequently waterlogged – backed by scrubland played sporting host to the local primary schools not possessed of their own playing fields during weekday afternoons. For the rest of the time it was deserted but for occasional dog-walkers and vast numbers of gulls who rested on the short grass – probably because it was quiet, reasonably sheltered from wind and gave them a wide view all around with plenty of notice should anything threatening be heading towards them.

We finished our games and came up the footpath to where the school bus was parked waiting for us in Filsham Road. I remember teacher Mr Russell, in his uniform sports jacket with leather cuffs and patches on the elbows, talking to the bus driver in his lop-sided peak-cap and with a roll-up cigarette dangling from the corner of his mouth. One of my classmates came panting up the slope and appealed to the adults.

'Sir, sir! A seagull's done shit down Trevor's jumper!'

Before Mr Russell could say anything a crestfallen Trevor appeared before him, his dark-blue regulation v-neck decorated on the chest with what looked like an underdone fried egg with a small side-order of mushy peas. Mr Russell's eyes rolled heavenwards but the bus driver, fag still glued to his lip, took a step back and guffawed generously.

'That's lucky for you, boy,' he laughed and broke into a fit of phlegmy coughing as he pointed at the soiled jumper and its red-eared occupant.

The reference to 'luck' I thought just a joke and joined in with the general celebration of Trevor's misfortune. However, just a couple of weeks later mum, Miranda and I were walking back home from a shopping expedition to the town. The pavement close to Palace Chambers, near White Rock, was fairly congested and I was forced to step off the kerb to allow a large, smartly-dressed woman in a beige, belted raincoat and silk headscarf to pass. As she came level with me there was a loud, snap-like sound and, out of the corner of my eye, I saw something drop into her wicker shopping basket. The woman stopped dead, squinted at the shoulder of her coat and then peered into the basket. The splattering down her arm was an all too obvious clue to what had happened. She'd been 'got' by a gull and the larger part of the deposit had gone straight into the basket.

A short, fat man coming up beside her gave a loud chuckle and said as he passed:

'Ho Ho! Lucky for someone, I think, love.'

The woman stood still, her lips compressed into a single dark line. 'Not for the person who will now have to clean my cauliflower,' she muttered.

I ran on, trying to put distance between me and the shopper before the laughter broke out of me. But that was the second time that I had heard someone who had been dumped-on by a seagull being told they were lucky. Later that day, I asked one of the old boys on the allotments why it should be considered good fortune to be struck by a flying bowel movement.

'Don't know, lad. Why is it unlucky to walk under a ladder?'

'In case the man up the ladder drops his paint on you?'

'That would be unlucky. So, if it's unlucky to take the risk, maybe if you are unlucky and get the paint, it brings you luck – sort of consolation prize.'

'How's that work, Mr Fuller?'

'Dunno. Maybe it's just lucky because bird shit is easier to get out than gloss white.' He gave me a broad grin and turned his attention back to potato chitting.

We all got hit sooner or later with varying degrees of fortune – good, bad or indifferent – trailing in the wake of the excremental impacts. Dad got off more lightly than the rest of us being a victim only once and then suffering only collateral damage to his shoes in what was, technically, more of a 'near-miss'. He stared down at his highly polished brown brogues with that look of grim self-control which we knew meant he was seething inside. Mum touched him on the arm.

'Do you want me to fetch a bit of toilet paper, love?'

Dad was straight-faced, 'I wouldn't bother, Peg. The bird will be miles away by now.'

The pair of them sniggered together while I looked on, puzzled. Surely, mum had meant get the toilet paper to clean off his shoes? But that was dad; unpredictable, rather eclectic but excellent in the delivery.

The herring gull became part of the backdrop to our lives, then, a distinctive, handsome, flying muck-machine ready to attack us if we threatened its chicks or scatter our streets with rubbish if there was a chance of an easy meal. And yet, to my mind, there was something about this commonplace marine bird that leant it a touch of something . . . not different but somehow extraordinary. It belonged to the seashore in the same way that pigeons belonged to Trafalgar Square and the blackbird belonged to the hedgerow, and yet its presence seemed something more than just the convenience of habitat. The herring gull seemed – to me, at least – to be wrapped in a mystery; it was symbolic of something more than just the foreshore, the cliff-tops and the fishing boats. The longer I lived with them the more significant they seemed to be although I couldn't have told anyone precisely why I thought that way.

It took many years, but I finally unpicked the mysterious tapestry that had seen the herring gull woven inextricably, inexplicably, into the very fabric of the Hastings heritage – or, at least, my perception of that heritage. Oddly enough, the key to my understanding of just why this bird loomed so large in my concept of our island-based, seafaring tradition lay not in the word gull but in the word herring. I had, by chance, discovered a book; a little-known and seldom consulted work of reference by Arthur S. Murray entitled *The Herring: Its Effect on the History of Britain*.

No, I'm not pulling your leg; it really does exist and, what's more, it tells a fascinating story that finally explained to me why it was that the herring gull had loomed so large in my imagination and why the image of the bird had taken on the same faintly mystical connotations as the lion, the leopard and the eagle as they appeared through history in conventional heraldry. I shall explain. The herring – at least, the Atlantic version known to Mr Murray and the marine biologists as *Clupea Harengus* – is, by all accounts, a fickle and temperamental creature. (I've often thought that if fish wrote poetry most of the good stuff would have been done by the herrings; the mackerel would just pen dirty limericks). For time immemorial, then, the herring have lived in their countless millions in that deep, cold cul-de-sac of the Atlantic Ocean we call the North Sea. For most of recorded history, though, for reasons known only to themselves, the herring chose to live in the waters on the Eastern side of the North Sea hard-by the Scandinavian landmass and a long, treacherous voyage from the British Isles. Suddenly, in the sixteenth century and, again, for reasons not known by any except the fish themselves, the herring hordes decamped en masse. The shoals simply left their established territories and relocated to the western side of that same sea. Suddenly, the waters off Yorkshire, Lincolnshire, East Anglia and Kent were boiling with herring.

The Dutch were the first people of Northern Europe to realise the significance of this bizarre migration and to attempt to exploit the possibilities it offered. In short order, the Netherlands – a country for whom sea-faring looms as large in the national culture, history and heritage as it does for us – was getting busy with specially constructed fishing fleets to cash in on this lucrative and accessible bounty beneath the waves. In England, Elizabeth was on the throne and her top ministers were not slow to appreciate just what the rival Dutch were up to. In those days, meat was expensive and only the wealthy ate it in any quantity (as dad had previously explained); but fish was another matter. We were, after all, an island nation surrounded by waters full of fish – nutritious, far cheaper than meat and, importantly, easy to preserve for relatively long periods thanks, largely, to a new method of curing developed by those enterprising Dutchmen just across the Channel.

As in Holland, the Government envisioned a specially constructed national fishing fleet – 400 ships of 70 tons minimum, each employing a ship's master, twelve mariners and twelve deckhands. The new fleet and its ancillary industries would provide work for upwards of 10,000 people at a time when unemployment was a serious concern; it would also provide a cheap, nutritious and preservable foodstuff for the people and, so bountiful was the potential harvest, it would earn valuable export cash, too. And there would be a further benefit not, perhaps, immediately apparent but, in its way, more significant over time than all the others. For this fishing fleet, this standardised, disciplined, merchant marine would be the essential ingredient for a proper military version of itself – a navy. England, a rich prize for any would-be invader, had an oceanic first line of defence and to man it the nation needed a pool of skilled, experienced and disciplined mariners who knew their home waters and crewed technologically sound warships. So this advanced fishing fleet, spawned by the herrings' sudden and mysterious migration, would set the foundations for those twin pillars of English defence and expansion – skilled sailors and good ships.

Of course, all this is by way of serious simplification and, ultimately, the vision did not materialise anyway. It was just too big. Elizabeth's ministers – in particular William Cecil – had the innate conservatism of their race and were, in any event, instinctively cautious when it came to 'Big Government'. Better to leave such things to the natural dynamism and minimal bureaucracy of private enterprise and entrepreneurial initiative. It tended to get the same results, they knew, more quickly and at considerably less expense to the public purse. England's fishing ports and their shrewd, commercially minded inhabitants were not found wanting and, although there were to be many setbacks and neglects over subsequent centuries, English seafaring had learned the flexibility and adaptability that was to serve the nation so well in times of doubt and crisis. Vitally, the impetus of the ideas, the formal acknowledgement that the nation's fishermen were important people making an important contribution trickled down to even the smallest of harbours, the most modest of fleets and the smallest of smacks.

Thus the seafaring tradition of our country is an immensely powerful one and it permeates into many aspects of our native thinking and attitudes. (The Wells family, with no maritime traditions at all, still prized its print of Millais' *The Boyhood of Raleigh* that hung in the 'Front Room' with its panoramic view of the seashore at Bulverhythe). The sea, the Royal Navy, the Merchant Marine, the fishing fleet, the herring and the herring gull – and where English fishermen cast their nets and where English sailors kept vigil on our land, the herring gull would be nearby. The birds even had a mystical quality to them, too. It was said by sailors that three seagulls seen flying together was a sign of an impending death. No fisherman would kill a seagull; that was seriously bad luck – even if it had defecated upon them beforehand. Curiously, the old idea of the gull being sacrosanct was boosted in relatively recent times by a strange and sinister event that, allegedly at least, took place just along the coast at Rye. Local legend has it that a coastguardsman, for reasons best known to himself, shot one of the birds close to his home one day. He was immediately surrounded by a flock of circling, screaming gulls. He was so unnerved that he fled back to his house and locked himself inside. But that was not the end of the incident because, the next morning, the man was found lying in a hollow of the nearby dunes, dead and with his throat cut from ear to ear. Surrounding the body were hundreds of silent watching seagulls.

And that was my explanation of the bird's importance, the significance of its enduring presence in the town. It was a highly visible symbol, somehow, of continuity and embracement. The generations of fishermen pass away and their boats ultimately rot; but the gull we see today is identical to the bird that Sir Francis Drake, Sir Richard Grenville and Sir Walter Raleigh would have seen wheeling and swooping fore and aft of the mast as their little ships braved the choppy waters of the English Channel, setting forth for the far oceans of the world almost exactly four centuries before a Wells set foot in the fishing town of Hastings.

I've often thought that, should the town take an official flag or emblem, it should feature the herring gull as a token of longevity, constancy and endurance. To me, the figure of the gull is a metaphor for that unbroken line of local fishermen who daily risked their lives on the open seas – in peace-time for a bare living in their tiny open boats and, in times of conflict, for the Crown in the Royal Navy's ships-of-the-line.

7
The Wild Side Of Life

Our bungalow and garden backed on to the Marina Estate allotments. They provided a semi-rural backdrop to our new home and a fantastic environment of adventure and exploration for the new children in the road. The allotments, cultivated or otherwise, sloped down from our back garden fence, bounded on the south by Tudor and Cavendish Avenues and to the north and west by Collinswood Drive and a rough grass meadow that ran down almost to the western portal of Bo Peep Tunnel.

Nearly forty years on it all seems a lot smaller. I get the impression that the peripheral scrub between the allotments and the gardens has somehow diminished, as if eroded or nibbled away; and yet it's pretty much as it was – with one major exception. The meadow has gone. That land was used as the site of the new St Leonard's Church of England Primary School while the old school, at the junction of Mercatoria and Stanhope Place in the heart of Burton's St Leonard's, subsequently became a mosque and the headquarters of the East Sussex Islamic Association. It was at Mercatoria that I spent the spring and summer terms of 1971 before going to the grammar school.

The new school not only took out the meadow but gobbled up an unofficial rubbish tip below the houses of Cavendish Avenue. My sister and I mourned the loss of the meadow much less than we lamented the passing of that tip. We spent many happy hours rummaging through the detritus of West St Leonard's life down there. My mother would become totally exasperated by the huge quantities of stuff that I would attempt to sneak through the back gate and into the house. There were buckled bicycle wheels that I intended to hammer back into perfect circles, granite-hard tubes of artists' oil paints ready to be revitalised with the aid of dad's white spirit and a tennis racquet I just knew I could restring if I could just find out what cat-gut actually was, where one bought it and how it was fed through the holes and tied so tightly. My experiments with garden twine were not promising.

I once found an entire collection of mathematical textbooks including a slim volume dedicated to the baffling language of logarithms. I still have it somewhere. I had no knowledge of logarithms – indeed, I still don't – but, because of the books' completeness and condition, I regarded it as a major trophy of the rubbish-sifting expeditions. The greatest find, though, was a pair or well worn but still wearable winkle-picker boots discarded, clearly, because of the broken zip on one of them. I was convinced that if I could just find the patience to mend that zip and stuff the shoes with enough newspaper, I would be the proverbial 'wow' at school. I was sullenly resistant to mum's pleas to bin them; but she used blitzkrieg tactics to win in the end. She said nothing about my boots for days and then struck savagely while I was at school, waiting for dustbin day and throwing them, personally, into the back of the dustcart.

Despite parental reservations about having the garden shed filled with other people's refuse, mum and dad had no fundamental objection to our playing in the tip. Who would consciously allow their children to do that today? One thinks automatically not in terms of old winkle-pickers and logarithmic textbooks but of bio-hazardous waste dumped surreptitiously in the dead of night by cheapskate companies, of the unsaleable siftings of burglary and discarded hypodermic syringes. Well, I do anyway.

During the long summer holidays, my sister and I would leave the house after breakfast and drift through the allotments. Sometimes we'd stop to see whether the model engineers were running their tiny scale-model steam locomotives on the circle of permanent track that was set up within a hedged space at the corner of Essenden Road and Welbeck Avenue. Like eager terriers, the locos, hissing and chuffing, would haul their boiler-suited, pipe-smoking creators around the circuit before they were halted for another eternity of tinkering. That hedged circuit is long gone, replaced by the smart, affordable housing of the Essenden Road extension. Where did the patrons of Lilliput State Railways take those exquisite facsimiles in miniature after that? I wonder how many still remain under canvas in garden sheds or attics, dusted periodically by widows who could never understand why their men couldn't summon the same energy, diligence and artistry for wall-papering the back bedroom that they could always find for their 'toy trains'. Leaving the old boys and their bored grandchildren to their dreams of steam, Miranda and I would gallop along the footpath that passed over the entrance to Bo Peep Tunnel, behind the houses of Collinswood Drive, to the white, weather boarded West St Leonard's station. We would hurtle over the footbridge, its stone steps worn into foot-shaped depressions by a century of rail travellers, and past the old station house that perched on the spur of land between the Charing Cross tracks and the line to Bexhill. I remember it as a fine piece of Victoriana destined to be demolished and replaced by those icons of the modern age – a car park and a mobile phone mast.

From there, it was up Saint Vincent's Road, across Filsham Road and down to South Saxons, an expanse of land that doubled as both our school playing fields and wilderness to be explored by any who had the pioneering spirit! A footpath ran beside the railway embankment to Harley Shute but we would always pause at the foot-crossing to put pennies on the track and watch the train flatten them before running on into the scrub beyond Harley Shute Road – rolling acres of gorse and bramble, bog and brier that stretched in an unguessable wilderness to the village of Crowhurst. Sometimes we came back at lunchtimes; mostly we didn't. Through the long, free, solitary days those two guileless, unguarded children never once ran into any situation or any person in the least bit menacing or frightening.

The bogeymen of my childhood were hereditary, passed down by a mother who, even as a mature woman, could not quite keep the white of her eye subdued when she warned us of gypsies, tramps and wandering sailors. They were the figurative monsters under the bed; they were the evil-spinning familiars that would 'get us' if we wandered too far, stayed out too late or were generally disobedient. Today, of course, the notion is risible but, as a child, particularly a young child, one is a vessel filled with whatever your parents choose to pour in. In my parents' day, there were still true Romany gypsies of horse and caravan fame although they were less interested in kidnapping badly-behaved, middle-class kids than they were in earning a peripatetic living with a bit of poaching on the side. Even by my time, gypsies were mechanised and inhabited vans and caravans. Their beloved horses had been yielded up to a quicker and more immediate age. This I know today even if I didn't know it then. To be honest, I don't think I ever saw a gypsy in the flesh before they were reclassified as travellers and became a middle-class hate-symbol behind which all rural Britain – and a large part of suburban Britain – could unite in its antipathy. I had no real fear of gypsies.

Tramps were another matter, though. If gypsies carried on a normal life on a nomadic basis, they were still subject to most of the basic rules. They lived in family units and had children; they earned a living as and where and when they could and wore proper clothes which they washed. But tramps were different. They were beyond the pale; they had turned their backs completely on the agreed conventions and were unpredictable, beyond the law and outside society. But we didn't see many of them either. There have been a couple of tramps or 'gentlemen of the road' – even the odd 'gentlewoman of the road' – who have made minor footnotes in the social history of the town over the years but they were few and far between. My only encounter with a true tramp – a real rural anchorite – came when I was about thirteen and was exploring the scrubland at the north-western end of South Saxons with a school friend. We burst through a thicket to discover a small clearing that contained a structure that looked like a partially collapsed wigwam. We stole cautiously round it and saw that one side was open to the air. In the centre of this improvised boscage-bivouac sat a bearded figure in an old RAF great coat, turned down wellies and a red-and-white stripped football bobble hat. We kept our distance and observed the old man, trying to appear nonchalant as we traced patterns in the decaying leaves with the sticks we were carrying. (Boys are incapable of going any distance in woodland without cutting, breaking off or picking up sticks to wield in the wilderness!) We thought at first the old man was singing to himself and, in a sense, he was – carrying on a curious, anticipatory chant as he slowly turned the key round a tin of corned beef.

'Corned beef . . . Bully beef . . . Corned beef . . . Bully beef,' he crooned expectantly as he prepared his midday meal. I was fascinated. What strange, feral creature was this living – as near as made no difference – in our ordered midst? What powers had he acquired through the years of silent watching and seeing in the humanless habitats he had chosen to occupy? We stood still and stared. Suddenly, he stopped his key-turning and slowly lifted his gaze. Eyes dark as woodland pools fixed us.

'Well, you two can fuck off for a start,' he barked.

We fled. Although I hadn't expected to be addressed with, 'Ah, Grasshopper' by an opaque-eyed hierophant, I had rather expected some sagacity, at least – even if not a revelation. In the event, he sounded like a cockney park keeper chasing the 'young varmints' off his rose beds. Oh dear. In later years I often wondered what became of him. I suspect well-intentioned social workers finally hounded him to an exhausted 'kill' after which he was placed in a home where he was encouraged to listen to Radio 2 and play dominos with his fellow inmates. Personally, I like to think of him living in freedom and expiring after a heart attack, departing this earth with the scent of burning hawthorn in his nose, wheeling stars filling his eyes and the awesome silence of a clear autumn night rushing in his ears as he set out on the last great journey he would make.

We don't have tramps anymore. We have winos and nutters instead, their incarnadined features housing beady eyes always alert for the right person to tap up for a 'couple of bob'. It's a shame; just as society's tolerance of vagrancy has broadened, so the vagrants' ambitions have diminished. Pull a meagre meal from the roots, berries and herbs of the hedgerow? No, far easier to panhandle the returned-coin slots in the town's phone boxes. Go at it long enough and there will be enough for another can of super-strength cheap cider.

As for the third element in the unholy trinity – the wandering sailor – well, that was plainly absurd and even from an early age my instincts revolted. Wandering sailors were dangerous, in theory, because sailors should be on the sea and not on the land. If a sailor was on the land it was because he'd either jumped ship – and was therefore a fugitive and thus capable of anything – or he was blind drunk and thus capable of anything. But, for me, they could never work as agents of death and disaster. Sailors were fierce men, true, but they were jolly and, more importantly, they were patriots – good Englishmen, all. From the Armada to Jutland, the sailor had been our first line of defence. I thought of them always as heroes rather than villains – even the dodgy ones I'd encountered in *Treasure Island* such as Billy Bones and Long John Silver. Not Blind Pew, though. That scene in the book where Jim Hawkins hears the sightless psychopath's stick tapping through the darkening mist as he comes creeping back to the Admiral Benbow wrung my dreams with the spectre of strange, lawless men of the open ocean for weeks. But even Blind Pew wasn't a sailor; not a proper salty seadog sailor like Long John. In truth, then, there were no horrors to be actively avoided other than those few afflicted souls whom we actively manufactured into terrors to spice up our mundane walks to school or our shopping trips into Hastings. On seeing one of them we would clutch one another in theatrical agony and scan the terrain for alternative routes, fleeing while giggling breathlessly with excitement. A classic example was someone we dubbed the Bogie Shouter. She was a well-spoken woman in late middle-age who, I realise now, suffered from some form of Tourette's Syndrome although we'd never heard of it back then. She would march briskly along the road muttering to herself through gritted teeth, 'No . . . No . . . Breathe . . . Hold on' before roaring to the skies, 'RABBITS ARE OUT, DAD' or 'NO! NOT THE POPE!' We thought her behaviour terrifyingly hilarious, decided she had to be a witch and would even follow her about (as long as we were comfortably close to home). We would then return and gabble a giggling report of her verbal pyrotechnics to mum, frequently ending up quite annoyed because, however entertaining we made the stories, mum would just give us a thin smile and look slightly sad. However, there was one individual who did bring a shade of something approaching adult anxiety into my life and whose behaviour I could not compartmentalise into that charming local loopiness that we had so far enjoyed.

It was a sunny but freezing cold day of early March on which we encountered our first-ever transvestite. We kids were astonished, appalled, disturbed and thoroughly fascinated by the sight of a man in the street dressed in women's clothing. He was very tall and his hairy arms ended in hands the size of hams with blunt, florin-sized fingernails painted crudely with vermillion varnish.

Looking back, I realise now that the gentleman concerned must have been something of a novice as he had made the same error that so many of those tremulous, Sunday-best, cross-dressers make, donning the things that are feminine rather than female (there's a big difference, there) regardless of any external influences or practicalities such as the fashions of the day or the weather. On this particular afternoon of sub-zero temperature all the real women were wrapped in trousers, scarves, padded jackets, overcoats, thick gloves and a variety of woolly or fur hats. They certainly were not parading the streets in floral-print sun dresses, Jesus creepers, strings of pearls and straw hats decorated with jaunty fabric cherries. It was the sort of day on which the only way you could tell the sex of any one individual for sure was to follow them until they needed to use a public toilet.

We stood still and gawped in utter disbelief at the man/ woman as he peered intently through the window of the lingerie shop in lower Norman Road. We immediately started tugging at mum's sleeve and hissing in theatrical whispers.

'Why, mum?'

'What's he doing?'

'Why has he got a summer dress on when it's winter?' my sister's voice piped up. As a practical female, I think her curiosity over the choice of outfit slightly exceeded her puzzlement at the person inside it. Mum looked embarrassed, tried to shush us and hurry us past as the 'lady' concerned – all six-foot-three of him – carried on perusing the collection of Playtex 24-Hour girdles taking pride of place in the window display. To our delight, a man smoking a pipe and towing an ancient and overweight Black Labrador ambled past, nodded at the she-man and said, 'All right, Clive?'

'Not so bad,' said the TV in a rich baritone.

We went on our way, my sister and I almost dislocating our necks to observe 'Clive' while mum hissed at us to 'stop it!' As we turned the corner into Warrior Square and headed for the seafront mum began to chatter brightly about nothing in particular – but we had no intention of letting her off the hook that easily. My sister skipped along firing questions and comments at her while I followed on, trying to adopt a superior, knowing air but just as keen to have the questions answered as my sister.

'Why was he wearing women's clothes, mum?'

'Yeah. He was wearing a dress!'

'Do you think he was wearing his wife's clothes? What if he stretches them or they tear?'

'Maybe they're his mum's,' I suggested.

'Mum! Mum!' A new thought had obviously struck Miranda. 'Do you think he wears a bra?'

'No, of course not,' said mum shortly.

'Then why was he looking at all those ladies' undies in that shop?'

'I know,' said mum brightly. 'Let's get some chips.'

'Cor, yes please! Do you think he wears girls' pants?'

'Who?' said mum clearly hoping that some deliberate obtuseness (plus the promise of chips) would weary our curiosity.

'Clive,' said my sister impatiently.

'Who's Clive?' asked mum.

'The pervert looking at all the knickers, of course!' my sister shouted.

Mum stopped dead and turned to her. 'Pervert? Where on earth did you get that word from?'

'The man with the fat dog.'

Mum was genuinely bewildered now. 'What man with what dog?'

'The man with the fat dog who said hello to Clive,' explained my sister patiently. 'He said hello to Clive and then, when he'd gone past, he looked back and said: "Pervert".'

'Out of the mouths of babes and sucklings', as we say. It's entertaining enough as an anecdote now but this was charming Hastings Logic with a darker edge; an iceberg of eccentricity with two-thirds of its substance hidden from view beneath decidedly murky waters and it left 'Clive' the single most disturbing individual I had personally encountered in the town. The burned airman who terrified me at Aunty Joyce's flat was, in my mind, confined to the bowels of Helena Court while, deep down, I knew that my fear was irrational and that he posed no threat to me. Clive was someone – something – different; I might encounter him anywhere at any time – alone. My sister had found the whole episode hilariously entertaining but I, just that couple of years older, knew that what we had seen was more than just a bizarre pantomime performance of individuality for the streets. I knew that somehow, somewhere, this all had to do with sex. It was a subject I knew nothing about but which had, nonetheless, started to form the shadowy shape of something of immense proportions in my mind. It was during my short time at Mercatoria primary school (of which more later) that I first became aware of girls and my comprehension of the subject began the long, slow journey into focus and sharp relief. At the time of our encounter with Clive I knew only that sex was not something that one talked about and it certainly wasn't something to be made the subject of gratuitous displays. A man dressed as a woman and looking at a shop full of women's underwear was just that.

Of course, on the day, I enjoyed the bizarre apparition with my sister – enjoying it all the more for the way it had flustered our normally unflappable mother. But of all the people I had thus far encountered in our new home town, Clive was the only one I genuinely feared running into for a second time. Clive himself clearly had no intention of haunting me personally for I never set eyes on him again or, at least, if I did set eyes on him again it must have been in a more conventional guise that ensured I didn't recognise him as the individual who, on that cold afternoon, had unwittingly forced a door that was already opening in my mind just that inch or so wider.

So I grew while gypsies, tramps and sailors – along with Father Christmas and Clive – failed to keep pace and dropped by the way side while the real horrors of the world remained beyond my comprehension – even if I was beginning to suspect that they were there. Had we stayed in London it would have been the random violence of the council estates and the more organised 'bother' on the terraces at our local football grounds – Loftus Road or Stamford Bridge – that would have caused concerns to my parents while drawing me towards urban adolescence. But in leafy upper St Leonard's skinheads, burglars, street bullies and other urban ogres where in short supply and our days coursed with a freedom of body, mind and spirit that we had not previously known.

We embraced that freedom by wandering far and wide but that's not to say that there wasn't any fun to be had without even leaving sight of the house. The allotments, many of which were not rented, offered all the raw materials required for swings, seesaws, slides (the muddier the better) and any number of hunting, seeking, chasing games that went on until the dusk made weird shapes from bushes and trees and drove us reluctantly back towards the lights of home. They also provided a haven for wildlife in an enclave which hosted only limited and seasonal human activity back then. Consequently, for my sister and me, the animals and birds we discovered and learnt about came in the sort of volumes one would normally have had to go to a wildlife park or zoo to experience. It was a far cry from the alley cats, opportunistic sparrows and spivvy starlings quarrelling over the bacon rind mum threw out of the backdoor in Hillingdon.

I can still remember, in our first spring in St Leonard's, mum excitedly rousing my sister and I from our beds late one night and shepherding us into the front garden to see three small, snuffling hedgehogs waddling along the flower border beneath the kitchen window. Half asleep though we were, mum remembers us both highly enamoured of the sight – the first of the animals we had ever seen. Not so on another occasion when she turned us out of bed before six on a brilliant summer morning to see a buddleia bush sprinkled, confetti-like, with hundreds of butterflies. We were, apparently, furious and immediately stumbled back to bed leaving mum alone in the garden lost in rapture at the sight before her. Ironically, I now recall the image of the butterflies with far greater clarity than I recall the sight of the hedgehogs – the green of the leaves, the purple of the flowers and the white of the insects. It was – and remains – an impressionistic, almost pointillist, picture in my mind's eye.

Frogs, toads, slow worms and tiny little brown lizards, which I had no idea were to be found in wet and chilly England, peppered the summer days – the more so after dad relented on his pet-ban and we acquired our first cat, Timothy. He was constantly catching the lizards. I remember a scream from my sister as she came upon the cat casually torturing one of the tiny reptiles on the patio at the back of the house. The screams came when she saw the lizard's tail come free. The creature then scuttled quietly away while the cat's attention stayed focused on the still-twitching tail before it. Someone told us that slow worms have the same trick; by shedding their tails they fool their predators and save their lives – growing a new rear-end in due course. I was mesmerised by the very idea and told everyone I met for days afterwards. It was the same delighted thrill that I'd felt when

I learnt the reason behind the herring gulls' comical foot-stamping on the putting green at Warrior Square. I began to have a sneaking respect for dumb animals.

We became familiar with creatures we had only ever seen on TV and in books – more often than not through the predatory assistance of the cats. Truffles, our second cat, a tortoiseshell half-wit with a permanently weeping eye, came over the fence one day wearing what looked like a Saracen's turban. It was a young grass snake which, caught in her mouth, had retaliated by wrapping itself round her head. When I prised her jaws open the snake shot off so fast it literally seemed to vanish into thin air! Truffles was nowhere near as adept a hunter as Timothy but she didn't lack ambition! Returning home late one spring night from West St Leonard's station we surprised our first badger. It stopped dead, considered us for a full sixty seconds, then turned and ambled away, its long digging-claws rattling and clattering on the concrete pavement. We watched it depart, feeling strangely privileged. For the first time we saw jays, woodpeckers and kestrels. We watched for the pair of mallards which came each spring for several years to nest on the pond at the north-west corner of the allotments. To lie in my bed on summer nights, window open, and listen to the 'hoo-hoo' of a distant owl was the stuff of magic.

Now, nobody would realistically offer up Hastings and St Leonard's as Arcadia, a bucolic paradise in which man can live in harmony with his fellow bird and beast. Yet, it's true to say that, away from the city, close to the sea, we all felt nearer to nature or, at least, more aware of it. One must remember that my parents and their subsequent family were urban-born, 'pea-souper' Londoners. The suburban drift of their married years had brought them more grass and less grime but they still saw canals rather than rivers and playing fields rather than meadows. Theirs had been an environment of solid brickwork and admirable street lighting but it featured precious little in the way of exciting flora and fauna. Thus my

sister and I had never seen a slow worm and the only snakes
we'd encountered were London Zoo's vividly coloured and
monstrously-sized denizens of South American rain forests
and Australian deserts. The day that we learned to tell the
difference between an adder and a grass snake was a proud
one, indeed.

It's hardly surprising that, having discovered the wildlife
that shared our environment, my sister and I quickly started
to hanker for wildlife that could actually share our home.
We'd never had pets in Hillingdon. My mother had a dearly
loved Boxer dog that dad bought her in the early 1950s when
they had failed to produce the second child they desperately
wanted; hardly a substitute for a baby but male readers will
probably catch a glimpse of the way my father's mind was
working at the time. Trudy was a well established member of
the family before I suddenly appeared and when she died in
1967, my surprise sister was on the verge of starting school.
Dad had no intention of providing for another hungry mouth
– even if it did only require dog food!

With cats and dogs of our own vetoed, we were compelled
to indulge our fascination for domestic animals vicariously
through the pets belonging to our neighbours and the
friends we made. One of the first belonged to a character
we nicknamed Long John Silver. It was the perfect sobriquet
for, although the gentleman concerned was not called John,
wasn't very long and was far too young to be anything close
to silver, he did share one characteristic with his fictional
namesake – he went everywhere with a bird on his shoulder.
'Jack' was, predictably enough, a jackdaw – a beady-eyed,
black-plumed creature which Long John had had 'from an
egg' (he claimed) and which he took for a walk and a fly
across the allotments on Sunday evenings – rain or shine.

Long John was clearly devoted to his companion. He would
talk proudly of its intelligence, what it liked for breakfast and
where it liked to roost at night while the bird itself would bob

up and down on Long John's meagre shoulder, gripping the short piece of thick cord which Long John had painstakingly stitched to his jacket for easy gripping by birdy claws. He would include the bird in all conversations and it would join in with rasping croaks and squawks.

Long John: 'We went to a jumble sale this morning.'
Me: 'Oh yes, did you see anything worth having?'
Long John: 'Nah, but there was some old dear there selling chocolate cakes. Jack fancied a piece of one of them, didn't you, mate?'
Jack (excitedly): 'Squawk! Squawk! Piercing whistle.'
Long John: 'I told you why. Too much sugar.'
Jack: (testily): 'Caw! Caw! Caw!'
Long John: 'That's all very well for you to say. You don't have to clean up the sick or pay the vet's bills.'
Jack (resignedly): 'Squawk! Croak .'

But Jack was not above a bit of jackdaw jackanapes and I remember one wonderful occasion when he flew up into a tree near the allotment association's shed/office and refused to come down. It was a winter's evening and I can still see Jack silhouetted against the bare and leafless branches, shuffling up and down above our heads and making little darting jabs with his head as if he was saying 'Yah, boo!' to his owner. Long John got increasingly more irate, quite aware that he was being made to look silly in front of an audience of two amused children while Jack played up his part for precisely the same reason.

'Down here now or you can forget your bedtime biscuit,' hissed Long John. Jack sidled along to the very end of the branch, lifted his tail and dropped something white that missed Long John by inches. 'Right, that's it!' said the furious bird-man. 'I'm off. You can make your own way home – but don't expect me to be waiting up for you.'

He stomped away in high dudgeon. Jack watched him go and I'd swear he winked at us before taking off to flap from tree to tree behind Long John, cackling in delight and making the occasional passing swoop to torment his defeated companion. My last view of them was Long John shaking his fist at a Magnolia tree in one of the Tudor Avenue back gardens as words of choking fury penetrated the dusk. 'Ungrateful bastard . . . Think I'm taking you to Alexandra Park on Wednesday . . . Make me look stupid . . . Say goodbye to digestive biscuits FOREVER!'

Long John wasn't the only person we encountered in possession of an unusual pet. One day, on my way back home from a shopping errand for mum, I got caught in a shower of rain. I took refuge from the downpour at the Christ Church bus shelter in London Road. I found myself standing next to a dour-looking man with a large goat on a lead. I looked in astonishment at the goat, the goat looked at me and the dour man stared at the wet, grey and grubby Victorian buildings opposite us. I followed his gaze to the grimed windows and cracked drainpipes infested with vigorous buddleia saplings as he said, 'I remember it here before they got Capability Brown in to get it looking this good.' I wasn't sure whether to smile, laugh or just agree but the dour man didn't appear to expect or need a response. So we stood in silence. The goat continued to observe the urban vista with caprine indifference while the rain rattled off the roof of the bus shelter. A woman laden with shopping bags joined us breathlessly, set her load down and looked at the goat with great interest.

'Well, well!' she exclaimed. 'Now here's something you don't see every day. What's the animal called?'

'Goat,' said the dour man. He wasn't joking.

The shopping lady was undeterred and turned her attention to me.

'You see, young man,' she began didactically, clearly under the impression that I needed an explanation of a goat in a bus shelter. 'Goats are one of the very few domestic farm animals which don't have any waterproofing in their coats. If they get caught in the rain their fur gets as wet as our hair and heads get.'

She turned her attention to the lonely goat-herd. 'Isn't that right?' she asked him.

'Don't know about that,' he said with a sniff. 'We come down from Hollington and he's too lazy to walk back. We're waiting for a 151.'

He looked at the goat and muttered under his breath, 'Bone-idle bugger.'

And when a 151 bus duly arrived the goat leapt on board before the doors were even fully open. I watched in surprise as the bus driver took the man's money, gave him a ticket and took not a blind bit of notice of the goat which, by that time, was looking interestedly out of the window. I walked back home as the rain lessened to a tolerable drizzle wondering what the chances were of persuading my parents to let us have a goat. At least we had a shed it could live in when it rained.

We declared a war of attrition on mum for an animal of our own – indeed, we could think of nothing but animals. So we badgered her and hounded her; we beavered away doggedly; first like bulls at a gate then adopting the softly-softly-catchee-monkey approach. We rabbited on, pecked away at her and made outrageous offers in the hope we could seal the deal, batting away her reasons for saying no, calling her chicken to her face – and cow behind her back – after she said 'dad would never allow it'. Then, having exhausted all animal puns, we tried again. We cajoled, bribed, bullied, demanded, implored, begged, haggled and pleaded for a pet to share our new home and new life so continuously and so indefatigably that poor mum finally uttered those dangerous words that parents use to buy time but which children invariably interpret as a 'yes'.

She said, 'We'll see.'

Now, as a wife, mum had learned the basic lesson that millions of women through the ages have successfully employed in winning round the men in their lives. She knew full well that if she asked dad whether the children could have a pet of their own he would say 'no'. She also knew that if she subtly placed the seed of the idea into his mind, that, slowly and carefully nurtured, it would, before long, germinate into his idea. However, the really clever part of the scheme would be applied when dad was ninety per cent won over. She would then – by offering token reservations – bring the plan to full bloom by provoking him into dismissing the very arguments against allowing us to have a pet that he would have offered himself.

So it was that in the spring following our arrival, dad grandly told mum that he'd had a really good idea. He thought it would be nice for the children to have a pet – a kitten, in fact – minimum work involved so a good start for teaching them about responsibility. Best of all, it would be cheap to feed, the plentiful supply of mice and birds on the allotments providing the moggy with every opportunity to supplement its own income. Mum looked troubled but dad airily swatted away her expressed reservations – to her complete satisfaction. We may have been astonished and delighted at his volte-face, but we lost no time in seeking out and acquiring a feisty little black and white kitten from an erudite old man of academic pursuits who lived in Fairlight. He had tomato soup on his tie, pipe tobacco in a bushy beard and seven hyperactive kittens that he had named after the world's great explorers. My sister beat me to the choice on the toss of a coin and spent an age trying to decide between Ferdinand Magellan, Marco Polo and Vasco de Gama. It was Marco Polo who left with us that night although, by the time we arrived back home, my sister had renamed him Timothy and I had withdrawn into a mighty sulk feeling that if Miranda had been allowed to choose the actual animal I, at least, should have been allowed to name him.

Timothy spent his first night with us yowling under dad's bed in lament for the rest of the great global pioneers who, even before we had left, had bunked down in an exhausted, silky heap in a nest made from an old Fairisle jumper, about fifty back issues of the *National Geographic* and an equal number of antiquated *Kelly's Street Directory of Hastings and St Leonard's*. Before we left, Marco Polo's 'dad' let us into the secret of making sure a cat really knew where its new home was. He fixed my sister with a serious eye and explained that before we let the cat out alone for the first time we must smear the pads of its paws with butter.

'Would lard do?' asked mum hopefully.

'No,' said the cat man.

He explained to my wide-eyed sister that the cat would set off to explore its new domain but, no matter where or how far it went, it would trace its path back home by following the scent left by its buttered paws.

'It's amazing!' said my sister.

'It's bollocks,' said my dad under his breath.

Miranda was adamant that the butter technique would have to be used and when the day of Timothy's first solo outing arrived she delicately rubbed the butter over his pads with a good measure worked in between his toes as reserve. The cat squirmed, wriggled and shrank into himself, furious at his greased-up feet and stolen dignity. As soon as he was released, he streaked to the backdoor and stood there, ears flattened, his tail lashing from side to side until we let him out. He fled.

'It's OK,' said mum nervously. 'It's a nice sunny day. He'll be back for his dinner.' But he wasn't. Dinner time came and went. The dusk deepened and our moods grew as gloomy as the evening itself as we waited for Timothy to reappear. Our parents kept up the 'don't fret he'll be back soon enough, he's probably having a fantastic time hunting birds and mice on the allotments' line but by eight o'clock no one could pretend anymore and we set off to look for him, stumbling along the allotment paths in the darkness and calling his name. Not a sight nor a sound of the absent animal did we get and, at 11 p.m., defeated, we were sent to bed, assured the back door would be left ajar for the night and leaving my parents undoubtedly discussing the best way to get a quick replacement and prevent my sister seeing the body. With our lights out, Miranda and I called softly from room to room, trying to reassure one another and ourselves. 'Don't forget the butter,' she said imploringly. 'That man said the butter would work. He must know what he's talking about. Remember all those books in his house?'

A replacement, let alone a feline funeral, turned out to be unnecessary. We were wakened by mum's excited calls at six the next morning as she banged on our doors. 'He's back! Timothy's come home, kids! Come and see! He's here!'

My sister burst out of her room in tears of relief and vindication. 'See, I told you!' she shrieked. 'The butter on his paws made sure he could find his way home. The man said it would. Cats love butter.' Timothy certainly did. When we got to the kitchen, he was crouched on the worktop busily licking all the Lurpak off dad's toast.

So, for the first time, we knew what it was to welcome an animal as an integral part of the family; but, as someone once said: 'Cats are absolute individuals with their own ideas about everything – including the people they own'. Timothy was a haughty, fastidious and utterly self-centred animal who was prepared to tolerate the Wells family living in his house; but he didn't do anything and he didn't need anyone. Clearly, my sister and I agreed, we needed a dog; but getting that one past dad was another matter altogether especially as he would often rather shrewdly point out that there must be a stack of elderly people up and down the road who would be only too delighted to have two youngsters give their four-legged companions the sort of exercise the two-legged owners could no longer manage. Our first target was Simon, an elderly and overweight Springer Spaniel who looked to have very little spring left in him. At first, he and his elderly and equally unsprung owner, a canny Yorkshirewoman at no. 8 called Mrs Frame, heard our intentions with cautious interest. The fact that we were offering dog walking for free turned that reserved interest into all-embracing delight. Mrs Frame was the widow of a hell-fire lay-preacher and she always made us join her in a brief prayer before we set off. We would bow our heads in reverence while the Godless Simon raked shamelessly at the door and yapped to be off. But with mum's insistence that we always had on clean underwear 'in case we got run over' and Mrs Frame's incantations bestowed upon us we feared neither beast nor man – especially the ambulanceman.

'Florrie', as we soon knew her, included her departed husband in all aspects of her daily life, referring to him as 'Pastor' and talking about him as if he'd just popped down to the garden shed rather than popping off to lie in a windswept churchyard on the bleak Eastern-side on his native Pennines. One day we begged Simon a bone from Orton's, the obliging butchers in Norman Road. Florrie beamed down at us in pleasure. 'Pastor will be pleased,' she said. We got a lot of freebie bones from Orton's. The shop is still there today and it's still operating the old-fashioned pay kiosk at one side of the shop. The stripey-aproned butcher hands you your meat but you hand the money to the lady in the kiosk. All butchers worked that way in my youth: Orton's is the only one I know of still doing it today.

Sadly, our enthusiasm for taking Simon down to the fields to fetch sticks and chase tennis balls soon outpaced that of the good-natured animal himself – whether we came bearing bones or otherwise. Florrie would open the door to two smiling children while Simon crept quietly behind a large armchair, turning to his owner in dumb supplication, his mournful eyes seeming to plead, 'Tell them I'm out . . . Tell them I'm washing my fur . . . Tell them anything . . . Just get rid of them!'

There was Tessa, too; a lovely old Labrador built like a bulldozer. We didn't take Tessa for a walk; Tessa went for a walk and took us. Even two of us couldn't steer her left or right. When she'd had enough she sedately turned about and towed us back to her home.

Jimmy was a lean, rangy creature that looked to have whippet, greyhound and Ferrari somewhere in his make-up. He was unreliable off the lead because he chased cars. Worryingly, more often than not he caught them. Alarmed motorists would weave over the road as the grinning and excited face of an ugly mongrel repeatedly sprung into view at their driver's door window – and that despite the fact they were doing the best part of 30mph. We exhausted every dog for a radius of half-a-mile but the hankering was not excised: dad was not moved. 'No dog – and that's final.'

But the mounting pressure of our clamour for a dog of our own was putting mum under intolerable pressure. The problem was to be solved suddenly, from a highly unexpected quarter and with disastrous results. It was chance that provided mum with a scheme which was high-risk but which, she later told me, she thought was worth an attempt. It centred on a friend of Aunty Joyce, called Miss Hackshaw, who was going on a three-month visit to her son and daughter-in-law's new home in New Zealand. Miss Hackshaw had a young dog called Basil and, clearly, Basil could not be included in the Hackshaw journey to the other side of the world. Basil needed a foster-home and I think this appealed to mum because she had taken on a little bit of fostering – children rather than animals, I should stress – before we had left Hillingdon and, of course, she could, quite truthfully, tell dad that Basil was simply a short-term house-guest who had nowhere else to go. What would happen when Miss Hackshaw returned and wanted Basil back she would worry about if and when it happened.

Basil was not an aesthetic feast for the eye. He looked like a cross between a Basset Hound, a Dachshund and a

Reticulated Python. He was the lowest and longest dog we'd ever seen and he really did look like he could do with an extra pair of legs halfway along his elongated torso to stop his belly dragging on the ground. Intelligence wise, I'd put him on a par with an amoeba with a GCSE but what really set him apart from any other dog we'd ever encountered was a rather distressing habit which Basil's erstwhile owner had neglected to tell us about. I'm afraid there's no nice way to describe it: Basil ate his own excrement. He didn't just eat; he gobbled, he wolfed – those piles of dog-poo didn't even touch the sides. I remember the day that we collected him from Miss Hackshaw's ground-floor flat in Helena Court, her tearful farewell as we set off with his food bowl and his basket, and our blissful ignorance of what lay ahead. We led the eager Basil towards home part thrilled at having the dog, part appalled at the move we all knew we were putting on dad; but it was all right really, wasn't it? I mean, we were only looking after him, weren't we? Consciences are pretty easy to salve if you try hard enough. We'd travelled about 50 yards when Basil paused, sniffed, squatted, turned round – and the awful truth was revealed. We were all too stunned at what we were seeing to take any action to stop him and, by the time we'd recovered ourselves, Basil had finished his recycled meal and was looking round eagerly for seconds.

'Oh my God!' said mum and sighed deeply. 'When we get back, take him into the back garden and keep him there until I've seen dad.'

We entertained the excited and capering Basil in the back garden until mum came slowly out looking thoughtful and not at all reassuring.

'Did you tell him?'

'Is it all right?'

'What did he say?'

'He didn't say anything because I haven't told him yet,' said mum. 'He didn't have a lot of luck with his horses today so he's not in the best of moods. You'll have to keep Basil in one of your rooms tonight and we'll tell dad tomorrow that we're just looking after him.'

'But you said we were going to keep him,' we wailed.

'I didn't exactly say that,' said mum hastily. 'And, anyway, Miss Hackshaw might want him back when she comes home from her trip.'

'She said she never wanted to set eyes on him again,' retorted my sister.

'When did she say that?' demanded mum sharply.

'When you were in the loo.'

Mum's eyes glittered dangerously. 'Just keep him out of sight until tomorrow,' she said shortly. 'Now I've got to get the potatoes on.'

At dinner time came the first test. Basil had to be left on his own in one of the bedrooms while we were at the dinner table. To our relief, he never made a sound of complaint. We began to have hopes for our half-baked but well-cooked mendacity. As dad was always a late riser due to his arthritis slowing his movements, we had plenty of time to get Basil out of the house for his morning toilet. As on the previous day, he found it delicious. It wasn't that we were happy for him to do it; he was just too quick for us.

'Mum, he's done it again!' we yelled as we ran into the kitchen trying to suppress our giggles.

Mum looked worried but just said for the umpteenth time, 'Keep him out of sight.'

For three days we carried on this pantomime dog-ownership, Basil going out before dad came in and vice-versa. I half expected a chorus of 'Look behind you!' to break out as the daily manoeuvring went on. Basil seemed happy enough except when he was thwarted in his attempts to 'eat between meals'. But we were living on borrowed time and, sure enough, disaster struck when we were least prepared for it. It was a Saturday. Mum was in the kitchen preparing our standard Saturday lunchtime fare of chump ends, mash and cabbage; dad was in his armchair watching the first race of the afternoon. My sister and I were, as I recall, spread over the dining room floor with a variety of drawing books, pencils, crayons and felt pens, absorbed in our art and safe in the knowledge that Basil had been consigned to his scatological dreams in the outside loo (a curiously appropriate kennel for him) after a bracing walk round the allotments.

Or so we thought.

As I was lying on the floor actually facing the window, I saw him first. The sunken, head-clouted nature of our bungalow meant that the front garden was actually on a level with the windows and I had a sudden, broad-side view of Basil stamping heartily through the plants in the nearest flowerbed, his nose twitching in eager anticipation of any recent turds he may have overlooked. I froze. He passed out of sight and I prayed that he would not return by the same route: at the same time, I scrambled for a reason to get up, leave the room and alert mum. I was too late. Basil returned and, having found nothing on which to snack, decided to provide his own instant provender.

I put my head down and furiously started to colour in my latest Spitfire, my ears feeling as if they were on fire. I didn't dare look up and prayed anew for Basil to disappear from immediate view before . . . before . . . the unthinkable. So I didn't see the exact moment that dad first set eyes on Basil. An age seemed to pass and I'd almost convinced myself that the wretched dog had passed from view when dad spoke. His voice was quiet, as if he was trying to convince himself that he was actually seeing what he thought he was seeing, when he said, 'There's a dog eating its own shit in our front garden.'

Dad may have been fooled but he was far from stupid and, of course, our reactions immediately gave the game away. Instead of shrieking with excitement and clambering all over the dining room table to get a view of this bizarre apparition, we put our heads down, continued to colour in furiously and pretended we hadn't heard what he'd said – proving immediately and conclusively that we had to be complicit in the presence of the animal.

'You two stay right where you are,' he hissed and then, in a voice that all but cracked the walls and shattered the windows, 'PEGGY!'

Mum later admitted she should just have gritted her teeth and told dad that we were 'dog sitting' for an unspecified period of time. He probably wouldn't have believed her and he wouldn't have liked it but his pride would not have been injured by having his direct instructions flagrantly ignored. After a while, Basil would have just been absorbed into the household – the proverbial guest who never went home. Basil did go home. Marched back to Miss Hackshaw's flat and the bewildered flat-sitter she had neglected to tell us about when she off loaded Basil onto us. The dog was led home by our grim-faced mother followed by two weeping, pleading children. Had it not been for his strange appetites – who knows? We might have won dad round but he was, as I have intimated, a deeply conservative man with an inherent horror of anything he considered 'unnatural' – and poor old Basil was certainly that. To this day, when I hear expressions like 'dog's breath' and 'dog's dinner' my stomach still gives a slight heave.

Our youthful attempts at animal husbandry may not have been riotously successful but they formed a part of an increasing awareness of the natural world. And my appreciation of it expanded dramatically now that we lived in a location where so much more of it could be seen, heard, smelt and touched. As I grew up in a home by the sea I learned that there would come an evening at the fag-end of winter, usually in the earlier part of March, when I would step out of the front door, mentally and physically shrinking into myself for protection against the anticipated blast of icy wind, only to find that everything had changed. Instead of a dry clarity in the air there would be a misty moistness, the flat smell of cold replaced by the sharp tang of the sea.

The first spring: the seemingly overnight explosion of daffodils in the borders and beneath our two ancient apple trees; the cuckoo call floating over the greening allotments; the first bats skimming over the gathering dusk; the glutinous blobs of frog spawn that seemed to fill even the smallest puddle of standing water. . . .

The first summer: the soles of my feet spangled with sand at bedtime – however thoroughly I shook my socks after a day on the beach; the liquid green afterglow in an untrammelled, uninterrupted western sky; the astonishing stillness of the air, saturated with insects and silence, as August thunder storms approached, flickering into view above the distant downland; the sheer eye-watering brilliance of sun and sky which, it seemed to me, had chosen our modest home and garden on which to blaze down with unblinking intensity.

One day mum said from her deckchair, 'Listen.'

'What, mum?'

'Listen!'

'I can't hear anything.'

'Yes, you can ...Insects.'

And she was right. Providing a blanket backdrop to the twittering of birds and the distant purr of a lawnmower there was a pulsating, throbbing and unbroken hum. When I had fully tuned my ears to it I realised, with astonishment, that what I was hearing was the combined beating of millions – probably billions – of insect wings. It had been there all the time but, until I focused my hearing on it, it was just one of the disparate sounds that go to make up what someone once called 'the roar of silence'. It was a curiously humbling moment. Even today, it thrills me to point it out to visitors and watch the expression of surprise on their faces as they envision the source of that sound – the energy and industry of countless creatures squeezing every second out of our short and treacherous summer; one musical note from the soundtrack to the circle of life.

The first autumn: trees and bushes floating in a sea of morning mist, a profusion of perfect spiders' webs strung with pearls of moisture; agitated swifts, swallows and house martins, peeping endlessly and gathering in readiness to obey the migratory call; silent Saturday afternoons when the chill sea mists would roll in, shrouding the view and killing all sound other than the mournful lowing of 'Moaning Minnie' that mother-of-all fog-horns aboard the old *Royal Sovereign* light ship; and after dark, the clear air revealing the constellation of Orion rising in the east earlier and earlier, warning us, as it has warned sky-watchers for millennia, that winter was creeping behind it.

I started at the grammar school in September 1971 and, with the travelling, my school day was lengthened considerably. But autumn was the season of bonfires on the allotments and, like all boys, I had a fascination with fire and would rush home as fast as possible to see if there was anyone 'having a burn' whom I could help. How many times did I step off Maidstone and District's no. 74 bus outside Highlands Mansions and hurry round the corner from Pevensey Road into Boscobel Road North to see a haze of bonfire smoke hanging over the allotments? The smell of it – sharp, mellow or even sweet – was almost intoxicating and I soon learned to recognise which wood was at the base of a fire – apple, hawthorn, cherry, ash . . . I would pause at the top of the road to watch the columns of blue smoke standing pillar-like in the still air over flickering orange flames, the whole scene bathed in the peculiarly golden sunlight that falls at that time of year. In truth, there must have been as many – probably more – days of September and October when I rounded that same corner under leaden skies to be slapped in the face by a squall of rain, the allotments lying brown and unlovely in the murk, but I remember not a single one.

The first winter: the stars were breathtaking. In Hillingdon, the millions of lights from London had meant the sky was never truly dark. In St Leonard's, on moonless nights, the sheer volume of stars seemed to create a diaphanous gauze between my tiny presence and the unimaginable vault of space. I taught myself the names of the stars, the constellations and how to spot the planets – even the elusive Mercury, so close to the sun that it is rarely visible and then only briefly in the west after sunset or in the east before sunrise. I found it, for the first time, when I stood at the foot of the garden as a December twilight gathered under the hawthorn and wild rose trees of the allotments, a tiny pinkish star hanging low in a gap between the Victorian mansions of Filsham Road. I had a sense of triumph and privilege. I'm sure it would never have been able to fight its way through the rippling evening haze of the capital. I may be wrong in that assertion but I don't want to be.

January heralded mating time for the community of semi-urban foxes that was well established in the area and the animals heralded it, too. In the depths of the night came the vixen's call, an eerie, unearthly sound, a weird gasping, croaking that frightened my sister and I quite badly when we first heard it. Even when we had discovered what it was, the sound of it had me pulling the bedclothes up over my head on a regular basis. On one occasion the call had been relatively faint, sounding from way over the allotments. Suddenly, one of the wretched creatures let fly virtually under my window; I nearly jumped out of my skin and the light stayed on for the rest of the night. I think that was the occasion on which I fully realised that the wildlife around our new house was not an added attraction for the human residents, a sort of three-dimensional TV programme provided for our delight and entertainment, but a world in its own right – an immutable and ageless community that was there before the houses were built and will probably still be there when the houses are no more. The vixen's call was an embodiment of that thought;

there is something both cruel and plaintive about it; its savage noise somehow too ancient and alien to sit comfortably with the benign and unostentatious nature of England's wildlife. It is a languageless utterance yet it is communication, too. Even today, it's a noise I shrink from hearing; back then, it made me realise that, despite our opposable digits and power of reason, only the thinnest of membranes separates us from the violent and fitful lives of the animals.

It was a timely and valuable education. That first spring, dad called us into the garden to listen to a cuckoo's call. We had never heard one before. My sister listened closely and then smiled up at dad.

'It's great, isn't it, dad?' she said. 'It really does sound just like the real thing – mum's cuckoo clock, I mean.'

Dad looked at mum. 'I think we got here just in time,' he said.

8

Old School, New School

Rutland House Preparatory School, in Hillingdon, had closed the doors of its elegant, seventeenth-century, red-brick edifice at the end of the summer term in 1970. The Wells family planned to close the yellow front-door on its 1930s, pebble-dashed semi at the end of December and both children had already been pencilled in for the rather grand-sounding St Leonard's Church of England Primary School. It turned out to be more humble than its name had originally suggested; indeed, it was one of the smallest primary schools in the town. It was housed in a Victorian building which was wedged into the corner of Stanhope Place and Mercatoria, the short street in Burton's St Leonard's which gave the school the name by which it was generally known.

However, between my departure from the one school and my arrival at the next, there rose the problem of my education for the first term of the 70/71 academic year and, logically enough, my parents decided I should do 'a stretch' at Hillingdon primary school – the desirable option because it was, quite literally, at the end of our road. It was slightly less desirable because to get to it I had to cross the busy Uxbridge Road, a 24-hour dual carriageway that had already inflicted one injury on my family when my brother was skittled while crossing it a couple of years before. Fortunately, he suffered nothing worse than a broken collarbone but the prospect of our negotiating this major artery to the capital twice a day filled my parents with anxiety – my father in particular – and it was an anxiety not mitigated by the presence of a fierce Lollipop Lady who marshalled the crossing children with the ferocity of a drill sergeant on a parade ground.

My personal reservations about Hillingdon primary did not centre on road crossings. As a Rutland House pupil, I had had to catch the bus to Hillingdon Hill from a stop which was, uncomfortably, right outside the Hillingdon primary gates, thus running a daily gauntlet of taunts and observations on my perceived social background along the lines of 'toff', 'swot', 'little rich boy', and the favoured 'snot-flobbing toss-pot'. I was convinced that, even out of my Rutland House uniform, I would be recognised by my tormentors and 'scragged' on a daily basis. There was a greater shock in store for me although it was well beyond my anticipation at that time.

One must remember that Rutland House was a highly conventional English preparatory school, big on tradition, respect and discipline. It also maintained the notion – rather quaint and endearing from today's perspective – that school life should try to feature some basics of education. (I hear there are one or two schools today which have persevered with the idea, squeezing some simple tuition in 'reading, writing and 'rithmetic' between sessions designed to get their pupils GCSEs in media studies and woodland management.) By the tender age of nine, therefore, I had a weekly timetable that featured maths, divided into sessions of arithmetic, geometry and algebra; and English, similarly split into individual grammar and composition lessons. There were, also, periods of history, geography, science, art and scripture. We studied two languages – French, naturally enough, and Spanish which had replaced Latin. Then, I thought being able to speak Spanish much more exciting and desirable than fluency in a language that was effectively dead everywhere except the Roman Catholic Church and obscure corners of the legal profession: today, I'm not so sure. One of the least

appreciated by-products of studying a foreign language is that
it teaches one so much more about one's own native tongue.
Even then, and much to my father's frustration, fashions were
changing and there was a loud and well-established lobby
arguing that children should not be bogged-down with the
unpredictable and inconsistent rules of English grammar
when the most important aspect of teaching the language in
schools was encouraging children to 'express themselves'.
Unfortunately, in my roles as journalist and civil servant,
I have seen some of those 'children' expressing themselves in
memoranda and reports which have included such gems as
'I should of mentioned earlier', 'thanks alot' and 'something
to wet your appetite'.

Now, young children have brains like blotting paper and
I don't recall that Rutland House timetable overloading me
or scrambling my grey matter with its intensity even though
every minute in the classroom was driven and those minutes
out of it were spent in highly competitive sports and games –
athletics and cricket in the spring and summer; football and
rugby in autumn and winter. I suppose I must digress briefly
to acknowledge the fact that every generation, on leaving it,
believes that education generally is going down the tubes and
that everything from GCSEs to the honours degree has been
dumbed down so the educational establishments can boast
the results they crave. I'm no different: I firmly believe that
the GCE 'O' Levels that I sat in 1976 were substantially more
taxing than the GCSEs of today; that 'A' Levels are easier
and that the NVQ is the single most useless qualification
known to humanity. My first awareness of feeling this way
came when mum, having discovered the money to be made
by hosting foreign students in the summers, decided to tap
into the home market and took in a sixteen-year-old girl
from an East Sussex village. To spare that student's blushes,
I'll call her Doris. Doris was on a course at nearby Hastings
College but such was the nightmare of travelling to and from

her remote village home that she lodged with us from Sunday night to Thursday night. At the dinner table one evening, she told us how the pub in her village was famous for a large, stuffed carrion crow – a hostelry heirloom which had stood on the bar for generations and which had got the pub into a number of guide books. Unfortunately, Doris reported, the venerable bird had mysteriously disappeared during the Second World War.

'What happened to it?' asked mum. 'Did they ever discover where it went?'

Doris looked thoughtfully at her plate and said, 'No. I expect the Nazis took it.'

I thought it was a good joke and opened my mouth to laugh but shut it again as I saw mum's warning expression. I was astonished. Did this girl seriously believe there had been an SS detachment pillaging the pubs of Sussex to boost Hitler's already unsurpassed collection of the taxidermist's art? How could anyone have such a poor understanding of their own local – and national – history? Sadly, it was a trait I was to see and hear repeated all too often. When I was twenty-one, I briefly went out with a girl of seventeen who thought eggs were vegetables because she'd seen them for sale in a greengrocer's shop. I'm not joking. What can you do about something like that? Not a lot other than to take a quiet oath that any children I might have would be installed in the best schools available – and hang the cost.

Luckily, I had had the good fortune to find myself in a high-quality, fee-paying school until the age of ten: unluckily, I had had the misfortune to find myself in a high-quality, fee-paying school until the age of ten . . . .

So, I finished the summer term of 1970 at Rutland House and looked forward to the weeks of holiday ahead; but the new academic year came upon me with alarming speed and the culture shock that came with my starting the new term at Hillingdon primary was profound. Obligatory full school uniform was an unknown concept there, as were teachers who wore their academic gowns daily, desks in immovable rows and the requirement for the whole class to stand up whenever a member of staff entered or left the room. On the first day of term, I was roared across Uxbridge Road by the day-glo virago with the lollipop and presented myself at my new school in long black trousers – the first day I had ever gone to school wearing anything other than Rutland's regulation brown corduroy shorts – an open-neck white shirt and a dark blue v-neck jumper which I had managed to decorate with egg yolk – and managed to hide from mum. Feeling displaced and very alone, I was led to my new class along what seemed half-a-mile of corridor by the school secretary and handed over to class teacher Miss Davenport who looked about sixteen and had holes in her tights. I looked about me in confusion. Where were the desks? I was confronted by a seemingly haphazard collection of tables and chairs – some facing the teacher, some not – each collection occupied by four children. But what astonished me most was the number of pupils in the room – there were twenty-nine of them and, disconcertingly, at least half of them were girls! Apart from jeering and throwing things at my sister's friends when they came to our house, I don't think I'd ever even had a proper conversation with a girl.

The smiling Miss Davenport, about to start the daily maths lesson, escorted me to a vacant chair and sat me next to an enormous girl with greasy blonde hair and a highly pugnacious expression. I could almost hear my mother whispering 'council estate, you can always tell'. I tentatively took my pencil case out of my satchel and placed it on the table in front of me. The girl picked it up, gave it a cursory examination and dropped it loudly back on to the table. I plucked up the courage to acknowledge her. 'Have you got chewing gum in your mouth?' I asked in a well-practised whisper out of the side of my mouth.

'Yeah. Why? You want one?' she replied loudly.

I flinched instinctively and waited to be bawled out – possibly even thrown out – for talking in class. But Miss Davenport seemed to take no notice of the continuous hum of quiet conversations going on before her. She was busy arranging a large box at the front of her desk. From it, she drew a square of card and held it up to us.

'Now, children,' she said brightly. 'Who can tell me what this is?'

The murmur of conversation petered out to silence as twenty-nine pairs of eyes did their best to avoid meeting those of their teacher.

'Anyone?' she said encouragingly. 'What about our new addition. Jeremy, do you know what I'm holding?'

As I was about to speak directly to a teacher, I stood up automatically. There was a titter of laughter somewhere behind me.

'Well? Surely you can tell me what this is?' coaxed Miss Davenport.

Scarlet to the ears, I braced myself and said, 'It appears to be part of a cornflakes packet with an equilateral triangle drawn on one side with a felt pen.'

Miss Davenport's expression changed not a flicker. 'Thank you, Jeremy. You can sit down now.'

There was another outburst of sniggering and nudging as I sat down, wishing I could continue my descent through the floor and into the basement. I had learned a lesson but it was not the one Miss Davenport had planned. From that day forward I kept my head and my hand down, withdrew into myself and did the bare minimum needed to meet the requirements placed on me. Consequently, by the time the January term of 1971 began and I was installed at Mercatoria – albeit in a much smaller class and with a more experienced and observant teacher – all my academic momentum had been lost. The Rutland House formality and discipline which had provided such security faded to old customs from another time and place. Scalene, isosceles and equilateral triangles became a dim and distant memory while 'parts of speech' were just words. Like a lost homeland, cucumber sandwiches on Sports Day, the burnished, ruby glow of the cricket ball and the end-of-year school play seemed more like something I had dreamed.

Now, I concede that I may well open myself to accusations of snobbery, here, seeming, as I probably am, to be banging on about the superiority of private schools to state schools. That's a can of worms I don't want to open but the fact remains that the culture-shock of being transferred from the prep school to the primary school was profound and, ultimately, I believe, hugely detrimental to my academic career – such as it was. Ironically, I only ever attended Rutland House because dad taught there and thus received a considerable concession on the fees. Whether my brother or I would have been accepted for the school otherwise we'll never know; but we were accepted and we both drew considerable benefits from the experience. Having said that, I realise that, in many ways, comparisons are unfair. Hillingdon primary was a sprawling multi-ethnic metropolis which struggled to cater for a large number of pupils of widely differing backgrounds and abilities. Rutland House both limited its intake and chose carefully the boys it was prepared to accept, considering both background and family status. Consequently, it was a school of boys culled from relatively well-to-do, middle-class families presided over by fathers who were wealthy, traditional and conservative (with both large and small letters 'c'). Whereas the primary pitched always at the lowest common denominator, the prep could give free rein to ability. If boys showed promise they would be advanced to the next year; if they showed real ability in a subject additional tutoring would be arranged to nurture their talents. This was something with which the primary, by definition, could not hope to compete. While the state school worked on the basis that academic cream rises to the surface and can be skimmed off and sent to a grammar school, Rutland sent its boys nowhere else and, even at the ages of thirteen or fourteen, they were being groomed for individual universities.

It was that personal attention that was so valuable to me in that it identified my weaknesses for remedial attention and my strengths for development – and how much easier for the staff to do that when each form contained no more than ten or twelve boys. At the primary, I was one of thirty in my class who ranged from desperate specific needs to frail genius and all instructed by the willing and enthusiastic – if barely pubescent – Miss Davenport. She was expected to cover all the subjects on the timetable in a way that would stimulate and progress all her charges – a well-nigh impossible task.

Like all children, I wanted to be one of the pack: I yearned to be unremarkable; I ached to be average and I lived in dread of being singled out as bright or gifted. It was bad enough that I was the newcomer in a class of kids who had passed through the school together and knew one another well. The last thing I wanted was to be branded 'teacher's pet' or 'swot' and excluded from the gang. I may not have been able to hide my light under a bushel completely, but I worked hard to ensure it burned as dimly as possible. Dad was puzzled and disappointed by the evaporation of my enthusiasm for learning, particularly in English and History which were his subjects and my favourites. In the end, my parents put it down to the loss of my former school chums and consoled themselves that I would only be there for a term and little damage could be done in that short period. They were profoundly wrong. School was never the same for me and from that time onwards I never set foot on school premises without the attendant sense of dread, dismay and a feeling of abandonment.

However, school was necessary and to school my sister and I were sent just a couple of weeks after moving to our new town. Mum and dad had chosen St Leonard's Church of England Primary – Mercatoria – because it avoided crossing or even passing along any major roads. Although mum walked us there on the first few days, we were, thereafter, expected to make the journey to and fro unaccompanied. My initial anxieties at having to join another class part-way through the year and integrate myself into another close-knit classroom community ran high that first day but I was in for a pleasant surprise. If Hillingdon had been that multi-ethnic metropolis, Mercatoria was a home-counties village. The school's roll and staff were as small as the premises. I joined the fourth year (it would be called Year 6 today) in a class of fewer than twenty and presided over by Mr Russell. I remember I liked him immediately. He was, like my dad, one of those anecdotal teachers who imparted information less by reference to text books than by personal description and narration. He also had the endearing habit of lapsing into personal reminiscences of his own school days, sitting easily on the edge of his desk and bantering with his pupils. He was informal rather than casual and that informality, coupled with the limited size of the class, played a major part in slowing my slide into hatred of the whole educational process. That was to resume in earnest when I got to the grammar school but for the Easter and summer terms of 1971 I settled down and turned out work of a sufficient quality to keep me in the 'A' stream.

It wasn't just me who felt the dramatic difference in schools past and present, either. My parents also knew the change. In reality, Rutland House had been a school out of time and it was the Hillingdons and the Mercatorias which were the reality of the norm then. Dad had clung to it as much to retain those standards with which he had grown up because it provided him with his living. He had long thought that comprehensive schools, secondary moderns and the unthinkable abandonment of the 11-plus were further proofs (were they needed) that the nation's intellectual inheritance had been mortgaged to bankrupt Socialist dogma and was heading for hell in a handcart. Now, from his position of retirement, he observed with increasingly acute discomfort long-haired teachers and the steady fading and fraying of the school uniform. That first week I returned from school to be asked where my homework was. I told him I hadn't been given any and that Mr Russell didn't set homework, anyway. Dad was incredulous and ended up by phoning the school. I was extremely upset because, clearly, he didn't believe me and was effectively calling me a liar. I realise today that he didn't suspect me of having thrown my books into a hedge at all but, at the same time, was so uneasy with the idea that he needed to ensure that I hadn't misunderstood the situation. When it was confirmed to him, he was speechless. When I came home later in the year with the pamphlets and information sheets which had been issued to us as part and parcel of our first lessons on sex education, he wouldn't even touch them. When he realised what I was proffering he snapped his attention to the TV (which wasn't actually turned on) and said through clenched teeth, 'Leave them on the table and go and help your mother.'

I opened my mouth to say something but he barked, 'Leave them on the table and go and help your mother!' I retreated swiftly, puzzled and worried that I had somehow let him down – or at least his standards. Poor man! Mixed-class sex education for an eleven-year-old . . . it was beyond his comprehension. Fortunately, that prickly subject did not come up again – not, at least, until I got to the grammar school where I remember in the second year a biology lesson that attempted to move in that direction. It was an almost surreal experience. The teacher set up a projector, dimmed the lights and filled the screen with an enormous black and white close-up image of a bloke with no pants on. There was a hushed pause as we stared at the screen in astonishment (all of us, no doubt, silently making the comparison). Shuffling his notes, the teacher sat down at his desk which was, unfortunately, right in front of the screen. His head fitted perfectly into the space between the model's thighs obscuring his genitals but leaving his pubic hair visible around the top and the sides of the teacher's head. As that particular teacher had a dramatically receding hairline, we were confronted in the darkened room by a bald biology teacher who had seemingly sprouted a pube toupée. He looked like Leo Sayer! A couple of lads starting singing 'The Show Must Go On' in contrived falsetto and the class erupted. The poor, harassed biology buff, already struggling with the prospect of explaining the rudiments of reproduction to thirty thirteen-year-olds, couldn't for the life of him understand what had caused predictable sniggers to turn into gales of laughter. Fortunately, things progressed no further anyway because, as usual, one of the class jokers had opened the top of the tank in which the classroom-lab's locusts lived and all hands were required to capture and return the wretched creatures. Thus, in the end and despite the no doubt sincere efforts of the educational establishment, my knowledge of all matters sexual had to be drawn from the likes of *Knave*, *Mayfair* and *Penthouse* with commentary and explanation supplied by older boys with their extravagant and highly mendacious tales of their best friends' sisters. It was all sufficiently horrific to keep me away from such things for a good few years.

But that's not to say that I was immune to the celebrated 'bat squeak' that awakens the consciousness of even the grubbiest, grazed-kneed, football-obsessed boys to the presence of the opposite sex. At Hillingdon, playtimes had seen me standing shivering on the vast expanse of tarmac watching the estate children – who all seemed to be one another's cousins – playing football; a seething mass of thirty or forty boys all chasing one flabby football up and down the 'pitch' like an angry swarm of bees. The Mercatoria playground, being so much smaller, meant that one could never be alone and, for the first time, I found myself in the company of girls.

I was fascinated by them but wary, too. I soon discovered how capricious they could be – welcoming and friendly one minute; cutting and exclusive the next. They left me tongue-tied, clumsy and permanently red-faced. But not all the boys suffered like I did and there was one lad of whom I stood in complete awe. Roddy clearly 'understood women' in a way that left me feeling wretched in my utter ignorance and I would hang out with him whenever I could, hopelessly unable to join in with his favourite enterprise but happy and grateful to sit at the feet of the master. For Roddy's favourite playground pastime was kiss-chase. Now, I must confess that the first time I heard him suggest it I smiled to myself, inwardly confident that my own rapidly burgeoning knowledge (as I thought it) of females had allowed me to predict with certainty the hoots of derision that his idea was bound to earn. And, indeed, the group of girls to whom he made his pitch was less than enthusiastic. They folded their arms, tossed their heads and told him haughtily they'd rather go inside for an extra geography lesson than play kiss-chase with him. I could see their point. Roddy was a gangling, stick-legged, freckle-face with a shock of unmanageable ginger hair, permanently picked scabs on knees and elbows and a less than convincing glass eye that shifted disconcertingly with a seeming will of its own. But Roddy proved that his lack of physical beauty was more than compensated for by his guile. His initial kiss-chase rejection left him quite undaunted and he continued to hover at the edge of the girls' group. I couldn't catch the comments he was throwing out in a low voice but the girls obviously could and, within a minute, they were gasping and giving little shrieks of appalled (and delighted) outrage.

'Roddy, how could you!'

'You're a beast, you really are – a monster!'

'I've never heard the like. Go away now!'

'You're TERRIBLE!'

And within five minutes the playground was filled with flying skirts and flying hair as Roddy, a huge grin on his face, darted across the tarmac, one eye targeting his next victim while the other one focused on some obscure point in the stratosphere. The girls screamed and fled from him. He chased them all – and they all caught him. I'd never seen anything like it and became fascinated by this new dimension of interaction in which familiarity and contempt were separated by a membrane so thin it was, for a great deal of the time, invisible. The general teasing that went on at school both thrilled and terrified me and it wasn't long before I was introduced to the standard Mercatoria taunt, 'I saw you up the Cobweb with Ann (or Julie, or Ruth)'.

Cobweb? What was the Cobweb? I couldn't ask, of course, because I'd be laughed at for not knowing what the Cobweb was. So I joined in accusing people I didn't really know of going somewhere of which I'd never heard with someone else I didn't really know. The accusation was, in itself, meaningless but that didn't matter because it was only a means to an end. Both boys and girls were keen to draw the attention and, consequently, to fire the interest of the opposite sex and teasing was the perfect way to do it. The taunts said 'I'm aware that you're a girl' and, equally, the response said 'And I'm aware that you're a boy'. It was all silly, innocent stuff, the Cobweb jibe being Mercatoria's version of that age old 'You fancy x, y or z' universally employed by children old enough to appreciate sexual attraction but not old enough to know what to do with their embryonic knowledge. The Cobweb, I finally discovered, was a dance hall on the first floor of Marine Court behind the dramatically curved eastern end and immediately above what is now the HSL furniture store. It even had an image of a spider's web complete with a smiling spider painted onto the glass of one of its massive windows.

It had closed down years before I arrived in St Leonard's and had already become the stuff of local, juvenile legend – the fantasy trysting place for generations of Mercatoria kids. I was, of course, a long way away from my first proper date but it was in the humble surroundings of that primary school that the slumber of innocence was disturbed by its first alarm call. I wasn't fully woken then but the sleep would never be so deep and contented again.

◐ ◑ ◒

I have already intimated that I was a shy and awkward child and things were not made any easier for me when I started at Hastings Grammar School in the September of 1971 – just a couple of months before my twelfth birthday. The size and complexity of the buildings and grounds were beyond anything I had previously experienced and this disorientation was compounded by the army of staff and the hundreds upon hundreds of boys who swarmed like bees through every nook and cranny of the academic hive. I was not finally to escape the Parkstone Road penitentiary until January 1979.

Oh, how little I knew of what had befallen me and of what lay in store for me on that grey, mooching-sort of Saturday back in the spring of 1971 when I noticed mum and dad huddled over one particular item that Whistling Postie had handed over in the morning's budget. I was peremptorily summoned to their conclave; but any anxieties that chased themselves through my brain were immediately dispelled by the expressions on their faces. Mum was beaming while dad, lips pursed, seemed to be nodding in silent approval at whatever he had just read in the letter he was holding. In short, I had been offered a place at the grammar school and was expected to present myself there on the first day of the 71/72 academic year equipped with the one-thousand-and-one items of clothing and equipment that the letter informed us were pre-requisite.

In fact, I was expected to present myself at the school on the day before term started for an induction tour of the buildings, grounds and ancillary facilities. I had to go in uniform – and I had to go alone. To my parents, getting the boy into the local grammar school after just two terms at a local primary school ranked alongside a knighthood for dad or a major win on the pools – the feel-good factor was the same, at least. They spent the next few days alternating between mute and mutual reverie and close-headed huddles in which lists were made, items checked off and calculations made. Today, I realise that their pride and delight at my academic success (as they saw it) was tempered with a degree of anxiety over the expense that it would incur. I have already made reference to the significance of the blazer buttons and that was the attitude that set the tone for the acquisition of everything else that was required. If I was going to Hastings Grammar School, I was going with everything of the best – and new! A trip to Wards, then in Queens Road, supplied us with everything on the list. Mum was in her element, brandishing the family cheque book and sending the shop assistants hither and thither in search of black socks, PE singlets, trousers, shoes, a regulation raincoat, sports shorts, plimsolls, shirts, a school tie – plus, extravagantly, a second one for when I managed to get gravy or baked beans down the front of the first-choice – and, of course, that most wretchedly useless item of school apparel, the cap. And not just any cap, either, for grammar boys were, on reception at the school, allocated to one of six 'houses' within the school. Each house had its own colour and that colour was featured in the form of a broad band around the rear of the cussed caps they had to wear. The houses were Beckett (dark blue); Norman (light blue); Saxon (red); Saunders (green); Wykeham (maroon) and Parker (yellow). I was to be part of Beckett House and thus my cap had to sport a dark blue band. Now, you may wonder why I seem to have such hostile memories of something as innocuous as a school cap; after all, I'd worn one at Rutland House and not given it a second thought. The problem at Hastings Grammar School was that the cap was only compulsory for first and second formers; no one else had to wear one – and it was this seemingly arbitrary edict that gave me my first taste of rebellion in life and introduced me to the novel and heady sensation of revolution.

'Why do I have to wear one when he doesn't?'

'Why should any of us have to wear a cap?'

'If I have to wear one, everyone should have to!'

Puerile polemic, I know, but we all have to start somewhere and my antipathy to the cap proved to be the first twitching of a political and cultural growth-spurt which is about the only positive memory I have of my entire time at the school – and I'll come back to my dreams of putative school cap revolution and where it led me a little later on.

That summer of 1971 seemed to whip past. I remember still that it was particularly warm and wet. In July and August, there were days of baking heat and torrential rain with not a few spectacular thunderstorms. They would tend to come up the Channel from the west as evening fell. The air would grow still and yet alive with flying insects. Small sounds carried and there would be a stuffy, breathless feeling indoors which was, if anything, even more stifling outside. Dim flickers of pinkish light would start to outline the promontory of Eastbourne and Beachy Head, as we saw them from our back garden, and they would be followed by gruff mutterings, as low in frequency as to be almost felt rather than heard.

Through those weeks we had people who came to stay with us in our new home – as already recounted – and we hosted foreign students for the first time – to be recounted shortly. But I couldn't get away from the vague feeling that something had changed; that I had finally (as I was constantly being told) 'grown up' in a way that I didn't quite understand. I veered between clinging to the familiar games played with my sister and dismissing her company altogether. I watched the days slipping past with a growing excitement and an increasing despair. Suddenly, it was September and mum was into back-to-school mode; just as suddenly, I was ready – fully equipped, uniformed and provided with the bus timetable for the no. 74 which would take me pretty much from door to door. The very last thing to be organised was a trip to the barber, Shaw's, in Norman Road – it's still there, today – for the regulation short back and sides that would leave me pristine for the afternoon of induction at the school and the subsequent start of a glittering academic career that my parents were convinced would see me Lucasian Professor of Mathematics at Cambridge by the time I was thirteen.

I chiefly remember that Induction Day as one on which I travelled up and down more stairs in one afternoon than ever before or since. We were a cavalcade of frightened, wide-eyed little boys who wore our new and over-sized blazers as comfortably as if they were made of corrugated cardboard. We were introduced to science labs, metalwork shops, playing fields, changing rooms and a forbidding succession of stairwells, corridors and grim-faced teachers who eyed us up with all the cool and detached professionalism that the slaughterman bestows upon the latest arrival of six-month old lambs. And, of course, there was no way we were going to make it through that day without at least one of the new first-formers managing to disgrace himself. The unfortunate concerned was a lad named Terry Popkin. He turned up for the Induction Day in the company of another nascent grammar scholar selected from his primary school, a small boy with white hair and almost translucent skin, who importantly cleared the way for his companion at each gathering by squeaking at the rest of us, 'Let him through, mate! Don't crowd him . . . He was born with a hole in his heart.'

Whether it was the heat of a glorious September afternoon, the strain of climbing endless staircases in a stiff new blazer or the general pressure of his new found celebrity, poor old Terry managed to throw up all over the floor of one of the top-storey classrooms, depositing a lusty pool of vomit whose major constituent was his lunch-time spaghetti hoops. A fascinated crowd gathered round the whey-faced Terry and his evicted lunch.

'Who done that?' demanded one of the boys, clearly impressed.

'It was the kid with the all the holes in his ticker,' volunteered one of the pipsqueaks eagerly.

'Blimey, he must have done in his heart, for sure, then,' said another impressed youth pointing to the spaghetti hoops, 'Look, he's chucked up all the holes!'

The new term started and I duly turned up on my first day to be buffeted by a remorseless and raging tide of boys charging hither and thither. Having to move from classroom to classroom for each lesson – or period, as we had to call them – was an exhausting and bewildering aspect of the morning broken only by the respite of playtime – or morning break, as we had to call it. Lunch was managed in two sittings and then it was back to the seemingly endless processions of up-stairs and down-stairs to find the rooms for the next period on the timetable. That first confusing and exhausting day finally ended and I was released back to the bosom of my family; but if I thought the day's travails were at an end I was mistaken. My parents were waiting for me expectantly and wanted a full report on my first day as a grammar school boy. Things got off to the worst possible start because the first thing I had to tell mum and dad was that I was now in form 1Z.

Dad's eyebrows arched in surprise. 'Form 1Z?' he asked. 'Why have they put you in a 'z' form? You're better than a place in 1Z – I should know, I bloody taught you for a year!'

I had to explain that my being consigned to form 1Z was not a reflection on my personal abilities but a simple matter of logistics. Previously, each first year intake at Hastings

Grammar School had been split into three forms. Boys with
surnames starting with the letters 'A' to 'H' went into 1H;
the 'I's to 'P's went into 1G and the 'Q's to 'Z's went into 1S.
H – Hastings, G – Grammar, S – School. Nice and easy and all
very democratic. However, by the time I arrived at the school,
the town had grown and its population had, for the 71/72
school year, produced more grammar school candidates than
could be comfortably accommodated in the three first year
forms of tradition. A fourth was required to keep those class
sizes to fewer than thirty boys apiece and someone, somewhere,
decided that the additional first form should be called 1Z.

My father was not impressed: Z – twenty-sixth and final
letter of the alphabet; bottom of the pile; omega; last thing;
the end . . . He looked at me accusingly, 'If they needed
another letter, why not 1B?' he demanded. '1B ... "B" for boy
as in "Hastings Grammar School for Boys!"'

I stood there helplessly, feeling that I had already
disappointed him and, worse, dashed his hopes of the
glittering career that I was scheduled to deliver to the glory
of the family name. He turned back to the TV and I retired to
my room to ponder the homework I had been set and to stand
in front of the mirror to rehearse my telling dad that if he
didn't like the fact that I had been categorised by the twenty-
sixth letter of the alphabet it was partly his fault for dragging
the family through life with a surname beginning with the
twenty-third letter. Mum stuck her head round the door and
heard me delivering a sound ticking-off to my reflection.

'Don't worry, love,' she said kindly. 'I understand what's
happened and I'll make sure he does, too. He's just so proud
of what you've done.'

Her head disappeared but popped back almost
immediately. 'And I am, too,' she whispered and disappeared
again.

I sat on the bed miserably picking at the bedspread,
suddenly overwhelmed with fatigue, uncertainty and a

surging love for her and for dad. I swore then that I would do everything I could to shine in my studies so that my first end-of-term report would positively glow with paeans of praise. Unfortunately, the lure of painting my Airfix model of the *Bismarck* proved more alluring than the finer points of Boyle's Law and the properties of gases generally and, by the time mum called me for dinner, I had resigned myself to a lifetime of emptying other people's dustbins.

But you get used to anything, as they say, and I swung into the rhythm of my new routine so that the mundanities of everyday school life exercised me just as urgently as the more cosmic issues that hovered above them – and one of those mundane things centred on my head. As I said previously, the school cap was mandatory wear only for first and second formers. As soon as one reached the third form – and the start of academic streaming proper – the cap disappeared from the regulation uniform requirements. And it was those third formers, released from subjugation at last, who took the greatest delight in ensuring that the legion of schoolboys tripping after them through the sunlit glades abided by the rules and donned their caps. They knew, from painful experience, just how many eagle-eyed teachers monitored the daily arrivals and departures for bare-headed transgression – whether it was born of surly rebellion, absent-mindedness or high winds. For those third-formers, it was a major entertainment to snatch the caps from the heads of the youngsters still fettered to them and lob them into the front gardens of adjacent houses, flip them on to the branches of trees or even to skim them – frisbee style – on to the backs of passing flat-bed trucks. My introduction to this fine old grammar school tradition was a relatively gentle one. About a week after the start of term, my cap was plucked from my head and tossed to the back of the no. 76 bus – my alternative ride to school – as it was pulling up at the bottom of Parkstone Road. By the time I had reclaimed it, the bus had pulled off and I ended up having to walk back a stop and then up the length of Parkstone Road – which made me even later for registration than I would have been – which earned me fifty lines. On the way home, my tormentors from the early-morning bus-grab struck again, this time hurling my cap into a Parkstone Road front garden where the peak neatly decapitated a rather fine late-blooming rose – somewhat after the manner of Oddjob's lethal bowler in *Goldfinger*. I managed to retrieve the cap and beat a hasty retreat even as the furious householder rapped on his window. The next day, I spent an uncomfortable morning expecting, at any moment, my successive classes to be interrupted by a serious-looking deputy head accompanied by a grim-faced son-of-the-soil pointing earth-stained fingers at me and shouting, 'That's the lad what done it, guv'nor!'

In the third episode of my persecution that week, I was a hundred yards or so from the bus stop when I spotted my tormentors approaching stealthily from behind. Before they could reach me I snatched off the cap myself and crammed it deeply into my blazer pocket. The smirk of victory was promptly wiped from my face as a car came to a sudden halt beside me and Harry Bowman, my history teacher, leaned out of the window and demanded to know where my cap was. Sheepishly, I tugged it out of my pocket and put it back on.

'This isn't the first time, Wells, is it?' he demanded in that curiously humming and high-pitched adenoidal voice that thousands of former pupils will recall. 'Detention tomorrow. Come and see me in Room H after school.'

My persecutors, who had all this time been standing beside me in respectful silence, sadly shook their heads at such flagrant disregard for 'the rules', bid Harry a polite 'good afternoon, sir' and watched him drive away. They then grabbed my cap from my head and threw it into the road where it was promptly run over by the bus I had hoped to catch and was now about to miss. For good measure, I got a professionally-aimed dead-leg which ensured there would be no chance of my redeeming anything from the situation by running for that particular bus anyway. Those buses became almost as much a bane of my life as the blasted cap I had to don before I could even strike forth to catch one. The no. 74 ran from West St Leonard's station, along West Hill Road and up Boscobel Road where I caught it at 8.06 every morning at a cost of 9 pence return. It then went down Pevensey Road and into London Road. It turned into Lower Norman Road, passed between the two sections of Warrior Square Gardens and then headed for the town centre via St Margaret's Road, Falaise Road and Cambridge Road. It went round the Memorial into Queens Road and on to the grammar school via St Helen's Road, Park View and Parkstone Road. It was quite a hike and the bus was heaving by the end of the journey. On those occasions when Maidstone and District Motor Services Ltd could only provide one of its more antiquated models for the school service, it was not unheard of for the vehicle to struggle so badly in its attempts to haul itself up the slopes of Park View and Parkstone Road that the driver would detail anything up to twenty-five boys and order them off the bus to enable his decrepit machine to get up the steepest parts of those hills. It wasn't much fun being one of those kids either, especially in the rain. Sometimes the driver would slow down and pull up where the hills levelled out to let us back on board but there were some drivers who clearly thought, 'What the hell, they're only a couple of hundred yards from their stop and the exercise will do 'em good,' at which point they would accelerate away – much to the delight of those still aboard who would clamour and jostle for a position at the rear window to ensure those of us following on foot got a good view of the two-fingered encouragement they were offering us.

On the occasions when the no. 74 became just too densely packed with squabbling third-formers, mocking fifth-formers and chain-smoking prefects, I would decide to travel on the no. 76. This was always a double-decker and was the circular route travelling from the Seafront to Silverhill via London Road, Pevensey Road and the Green. It then went on to the Briers roundabout before heading down St Helens Road and Queens Road into the town centre. From there, after stopping outside Debenhams it went along Robertson Street and onto the seafront again by the pier. The no. 76 clientele seemed somehow more sophisticated but using that bus meant I had to walk up and down Parkstone Road at the start and end of the school day and, strangely enough, the timings of that bus seemed to have been created for the pure inconvenience of the school. The morning buses either arrived too early or too late and the afternoon buses meant that unless you could get to the bottom of Parkstone Road in less than four minutes, you had another twenty-five to wait. One boy, Malcolm Edmonds, was phenomenal. He shot out of school everyday like a greyhound out of a trap and was halfway down Parkstone Road before the rest of us had collected our raincoats. He always made it to the early no. 76. One day, I decided to try to match him. Malcolm leapt out of school like the proverbial gazelle with me hard on his heels. He had a good 20 yards on me but I was convinced I could catch him. Absent-mindedly, I pulled my cap off my head and crammed it into my pocket to lower my wind resistance. Big mistake. A car pulled up ahead of me and an angry face appeared at the window. Yes, it was Harry Bowman again. I missed the bus and got yet another detention which meant I missed it the next day, too.

Intimidating though I found the grammar school, it was not without its unexpected inspirations. I soon noticed that while I made the daily journey by bus, a large number of my contemporaries were arriving on bicycles. One lad, I didn't know him, caught my eye particularly. He always seemed to arrive at school at the same time as I did – and it was how he arrived that I found so compelling. I used to gaze at his bike with undisguised admiration. It had contrasting red and green metallic paintwork, a racing saddle, five-speed derailleur gears, toe-traps, cotterless chain wheel, split cables, taped drops (believe me, this will mean plenty to the cycling enthusiast of the 1970s) and centre-pull brakes. Centre-pull brakes? The best!

And I wanted one! It was the first time in my life that I recall really wanting something badly; not a wanting with the irritating impatience of the greedy child who can't wait for birthday or Christmas Day (which I certainly was) but a desire, an aspirational desire for something that was more than a diversion or an entertainment; something that would enhance my life and take me forward as a person. I didn't realise it then but this burgeoning desire for a bike of my own was the first time that I was prepared to consider – albeit subconsciously – that I might just be prepared to shuffle out of the shadows of anonymity to declare myself as an individual. In lessons, I still wanted to sit at the back of the class and do everything possible not to draw attention to myself; but in the matter of a bike it was very different. I had fantasies of pedalling through the school gates, casually throwing a leg over the bike to allow one pedal to support my immaculately balanced weight. I would slide to a skilled, almost balletic, halt by the bike sheds to stack my trusty steed in its rack. As I gave it a fond pat on the saddle, a small knot of timorous boys would have gathered outside whispering to each other, 'That's Jeremy Wells, that is . . . Wow, that bike is so cool! Gotta be the fastest racer here.' Like an Olympian bestriding the paucity of human imagination, I would shoulder my bag of books and head for class leaving the admiring group to dream while I remained master of my time, my machine and my destiny.

'No chance,' said dad. 'You're not risking your life on main roads during the rush-hour and we haven't got the money for that sort of thing, anyway.'

'What about Miss Newman down the road?' said mum quickly as she saw my face redden with disappointment. 'She's got a bike and she never rides it now. Perhaps she'd let you use it.'

I looked at her with withering contempt. I'd seen Miss Newman's bike. It was very much of a kidney with Miss Newman herself. Both were about 100 years old; both looked like they'd been manufactured by a company whose principal products were artificial limbs for Boer War veterans and both had a maximum speed of about 2mph. They also shared the need for mass lubrication to all moving parts before there was any chance of even a basic animation. I threw a half-hearted tantrum which gave me the mean-spirited satisfaction of upsetting my parents: mum because, like all mothers, her nature was to provide for her children and make them happy and dad because his inability to buy me a bike made him feel inadequate as a provider for his family. It also made him angry.

'If you want a bike, boy, you get a bloody job and buy yourself one. It's about time you understood that the things you want don't grow on trees,' he lectured.

'Can I have an apple, then, instead?' I shouted from the doorway.

'No, but you'll get a pair in a minute – a pair of thick ears!' he yelled back.

I stormed off to sit in the garden, striking a pose of injured dejection and persecution, positioning myself where, I hoped, my misery could be observed from the dining room. Unfortunately, it started to rain and I wasn't inclined to be hard done-by and wet. I came back inside to be greeted by my jeering father. 'Good job you weren't out on your bike, eh!' I hurled myself on to my bed and wished I'd never been born.

But the seeds of initiative can sprout in even the most unlikely terrain and dad's comment about my getting a job was just such a seed. It did, indeed, inspire me to investigate that very possibility. My progress was slow, tentative. Mum was my ally for it was she who would present my ideas to dad and slowly win him round to them. A few months later, through the good offices of one of mum's friends who knew the proprietor, I had my first paper-round at Hobbs newsagents in Norman Road. I had to get up at 5.30 in the morning and, by 6.15, I was struggling up London Road with a sack of newpapers which weighed little less than I did. It was a monster round, too. I still remember the pain of it! I had papers to deliver in South Street, Cross Street, Silchester Road, Carisbrooke Road, Kenilworth Road, Pevensey Road, Brittany Road, Upper Maze Hill, Albany Road, Pevensey Road (again) and finishing with half-a-dozen papers for the now derelict Winchester House. I could just get it done in time to change into my school uniform, bolt some breakfast and catch the bus – on which I promptly fell asleep and had my school cap stolen and hurled up and down the length of the vehicle to the whoops and cheers of my fellow travellers.

There's a famous quote about schooldays being the best days of our lives. For me, there were only two good things about the school year at Hastings Grammar. They were called July and August. Now, I'd love to be able to tell you, dear reader, that those first days at the grammar school were the glittering atrium under which I found the friends who are still friends to this day and beneath which the buds of a love of learning burst forth and bloomed to guide me through the sunlit glades of Academe all the way to the dreaming spires. But I can't because they weren't. I loathed every second of the seven years, four months and twenty-three days I spent there before I finally got out clutching my brace of mediocre A Levels, still as much at a loss as to what I intended to do with my life as the day I walked in.

9
The Sea! The Sea!

Our introduction to Hastings and St Leonard's had come in the form of a two-week summer holiday hosted by the ever-obliging Joyce McIntyre in her wonderful top-floor flat in Helena Court – a fascinating conglomeration of narrow staircases, gabled-windows and attic-bedrooms with quite the most spectacular views over the town.

In one sense we were lucky that it was two weeks because, just as on the occasion of our permanent move to the town some five months later, the travel arrangements for this particular trip went belly-up from the outset. We didn't seem to be very lucky with travel arrangements – which probably explains the paucity of day-trips we enjoyed as children.

On this occasion, mum left one of the suitcases on the bus that had taken us to Uxbridge Underground station but, as the bus terminated there, it was redeemed with nothing more than a red face. The Piccadilly Line tube train commuted its way across John Betjeman's celebrated Metroland before diving underground and depositing us, after one unnervingly trouble-free change, at the teeming Victoria station. Mum, Miranda and I struggled up stairs and escalators. Heavily laden, we hurried across the massive concourse to be confronted by a suspiciously silent and empty Platform 12. Where was the 10.13 to Hastings? I spotted a telling clue when I noticed the big station clock above our heads. It said 10.18.

Mum clearly had no intention of spending the best part of an hour in the bedlam of Victoria station with two whining children demanding chips, drinks and endless trips to the toilets. She scanned the departure board, noticed that a train was about to leave for Brighton and stormed the gate. It needed storming. The train in question was the prestigious *Brighton Belle*, a sleek Pullman affair with every smudgeless window a framed showcase of tethered curtains, brass table lamps and starched white linen. We bludgeoned our way on to the train as the equally sleek and smudgeless passengers already on board did their best to expand themselves and their possessions in an attempt to 'encourage' us along the gangways.

'This will do,' said mum firmly as we finally found a set of four seats divided into pairs by what looked like a breakfast table straight out of the Ritz. There we sat as the train sped through the Surrey hinterland, pinstriped businessmen picking at bacon and eggs, kedgeree or kippers while the Wells family got stuck into its standard travelling fare – Marmite sandwiches, hard boiled eggs á la hydrogen sulphide and Tupperware containers filled with lukewarm orange squash. I remember feeling uncomfortable for the entire journey on that train, acutely aware of the difference between us and our fellow travellers. I may not have been old enough to be burdened by the English concept of Class but I was old enough to get a sense that somehow we didn't 'belong' in this rarefied travelling environment. Mum was burdened by the English concept of Class; but on that particular day she was a Lower–Middle Class Housewife second and a Mother first and if getting her children to their promised holiday destination meant tossing the Duchess of Albemarle out of a hot-air balloon, she would have done it. She was simply delighted to be on her way; a fact demonstrated by her jovially asking the uniformed penguin on duty in our carriage whether he would be so kind as to dispose of our eggshells. The poor man was so astonished at our presence he took the paper bag without a word and even forgot – or thought better of – asking to see our tickets.

At Brighton, we departed the fleeting luxury of the Belle for a much more humble affair that was ticking over at the far end of the station ready to leave for Eastbourne. It was the second destination of the day that we didn't want but, as far as mum was concerned, Eastbourne was nearer to Hastings than where we presently were so she walloped us on to that train before it could get away. At Eastbourne, we found ourselves on another station platform wondering whether we would actually see Aunty Joyce before nightfall but, encouragingly, we overheard conversations that proved we were in the company of other people heading for Hastings. A train arrived, disgorged its passengers and we got on board. While waiting for it to leave we heard a loud popping sound and felt the whole train shudder. The train popped again, jerked and then all was quiet. Just a little too quiet.

Suddenly, we seemed to be the only people in the carriage until an immensely fat, ebony-skinned woman with a vermillion headscarf and a bouquet of bin liners in her arms appeared at the other end of the carriage and started to collect the assorted litter of journey's end.

'Excuse me,' said mum. 'Do you know when we're going?'

'Dat depend where you goin', ma darlin',' said the cleaning lady beaming at all three of us.

'Hastings.'

'Not on dis train, you ain't.'

'But the board said Platform 3 for Hastings.'

'Platform T'ree, front four coaches, ma darlin'.'

'But these are the front four coaches.'

'No, dey ain't!'

'But they're at the front of the train.'

'Dey was when de train arrive; but after it stop dey's de back four.'

'So where are the front four coaches?' Mum was getting confused.

'Probably Bexhill by now!'

'So we're in the back four coaches,' said mum, the light dawning.

'No, ma darlin'. Now, you in de front four. Dey was only de back until de front go.'

'So these front four coaches will go to Hastings?'

'No, dey goin' to Brighton.'

Mum took a deep breath. 'So where do we need to sit to get to Hastings?'

'You don't.' The cleaner's bulk quivered with mirth. 'You walk! Go over to Platform 1 and get into any one of de eight coaches o' dat train.'

A chubby, bangled arm flapped at the window to indicate the train docked at Platform 1.

'But there's only four carriages at Platform 1,' said mum miserably.

'Dat's because dey other four hasn't gotten here yet. When dey get here, dey fix 'em to the back of de four dat's already over there.'

Mum was suddenly triumphant, 'So then they're the front and we have to sit in one of those four.'

'No, you can sit up de back o' dat one 'cause it ALL goin' to Hastings,' the cleaner laughed.

Ever the railway anorak, I chipped in excitedly, 'It's because this station is a terminus. Eastbourne's a dead-end, mum. What arrives here has to go out the same way it came in. They're splitting the trains in half. That was what all that bumping and banging was we heard after we got on.'

'De boy got it, ma darlin'! Dat's how dey do it. De boy got it!' shouted the cleaner joyfully and gave me a slap on the back that felt like it should have dislocated my spine. 'You just follow 'im, ma darlin',' she added and bustled off along the carriage, squeezing herself through the seats and singing happily as she collected the empty coke cans and crisp packets.

Tired, humiliated and still rather confused, mum led us into the burning heat of the August afternoon. She then pestered every BR employee she spotted, as well as a good many fellow travellers, to ensure that, this time, we were not only on the right train but in the right bit of it. She made me count the number of coaches a hundred times and even insisted we sat facing the direction in which the train was due to travel – as if that was going to make a difference to the perplexing choreography of BR's Southern Region. I think if she could have actually got us in with the driver, she would have done. Finally, we started the last short leg of the journey and our spirits began to revive. At last, the train reached what was to become my favourite part of a familiar journey, that section of the line between Glyne Gap and Bo-Peep where the tracks are virtually on the beach and the train, to this day, strikes up that marvellous clacketty-clack rhythm that seems to chant: 'You're nearly there. You're nearly there. You're nearly there'.

'The sea! The sea!' we yelled as the blue water sparkled and the white beach huts shone through the grime and grease of the train window. We were very, very late and, understandably enough, Aunty Joyce, had not remained at Warrior Square station after the train on which we should have arrived had come and gone; but she had left a hand-written message with one of the station staff and a request to watch out for a tired and confused looking family-of-three who could arrive at any time and from any direction. (You could do that sort of thing, back then.) Joyce's predictive description was obviously an accurate one for a young and immensely fat porter identified us immediately with a loud yell of, 'Hullo, Hullo! You the Wellseses, then?' He stood looking us up and down expectantly as if he had been tipped off that a troika of performing freaks was likely to alight at his station. Clearly disappointed that none of us was foaming at the mouth, he thrust a piece of paper into mum's hand and said, 'Phone this number, love, and she'll come get yer. Call box round the back. Got the coppers?'

While mum made the call my sister and I sat on the suitcases and observed the porter slyly. His ginger hair was like wire-wool and so tightly curled that he could lodge his ballpoint pen into the front of it while his BR regulation cap sat on the back of his head. He looked as if he was sprouting an embryonic dalek's eye. His uniform jacket was undone, he had an expired roll-up gummed to his lip and he was wearing plimsolls. He gave my sister a chewing gum and a saucy wink. I thought he was pretty cool.

Joyce came to get us and drove us straight back to her flat in her redoubtable Mini Estate. She whipped up bangers and Smash with spaghetti hoops and then offered to take my sister and I for our first look at the beach while mum 'unpacked' – which meant falling asleep from the sheer exhaustion and stress of a journey that, at a little over 70 miles, had taken over four hours and six trains – one of which hadn't even left the station. We were whacked, too, but all our fatigue evaporated as the smell of the sea tingled in our nostrils and we dragged poor Joyce down the hills at an ever-accelerating trot to the seafront.

Of course, that 'holiday' was, in fact, a very serious business for mum. She had a clutch of estate agents' details for potential house-buys and her mornings were spent flitting across the town – mostly St Leonard's – looking at properties which, realistically, had to be bungalows to avoid dad's having to negotiate any stairs.

๐ ๐ ๐

I don't recall the first day that we actually went swimming in the sea as residents of the town but I do recall blissful summer afternoons when mum would meet us at the door of

Mercatoria and we would head straight down to that section of the beach between Marine Court and London Road. She always arrived kitted out with our swimsuits, towels, Marmite sandwiches and lukewarm orange squash. We would clatter and clash down the shingle with mum calling out behind us, 'Where is it today, then?'

My sister and I would squint out to the sparkling horizon, each wanting to be the first to spot the *Royal Sovereign* light-platform, that curious 'T'-shaped edifice jutting from the waves some nine miles out to sea. It was some time before I actually realised that mum's 'Where is it today, then?' was a rhetorical question for our amusement and didn't mean that it moved about on the surface of the water from day to day. Actually, the light-platform moved to Hastings in the same year we did or, at least, its basic construction was finished in 1971 so it could replace the last of the *Royal Sovereign* lightships that, in one floating form or another, had done duty in that spot since 1875.

As children we were, of course, warned regularly about the tides and how one could be swept out to sea and drowned in an instant but, ironically, it was not the menace of the tide that was responsible for the first watery scare I was given on the beach. It was actually something of which I'd never heard.

My sister and I were in the sea as often and as quickly as was possible whether it was sunny, cloudy, windy or even drizzly (as long as it was a warmish drizzle). It had all started in earnest after the Easter holidays of our first year when we decided it was officially 'summer' and demanded the beach after school each day. Initially, we were happy to scrabble around in the surf but, as our confidence grew, we ventured farther beyond the point at which the waves started to break and into the smooth sea-green swell – although we were always careful not to go out of our depth.

Mum surprised us one day by using some of her catalogue commission to buy us an airbed which we competed for fiercely as soon as someone else had reduced themselves to a wheezing cripple by inflating it by mouth. It was thanks to that airbed that I received the cautionary lesson which ensured that my growing confidence did not develop into over-confidence – always a menace where water is concerned. That day, I had acquired use of the airbed by the simple expedient of pushing the sitting tenant – my sister – quickly and rather violently into the water. I reclined in triumph while she waded back to the beach to register her official complaint. I proceeded to show my contempt for her pitiful protests by striking a particularly casual posture, closing my eyes and enjoying the fierce sun on my body while the airbed rocked gently back and forth. Finally, I lifted my head and shielded my eyes against the sparkling blue fire of the sea and peered over to where mum was sitting with my dispossessed sister.

They weren't there.

I sat up in alarm, promptly lost my boat-balance and tumbled into some very cold water. Spluttering and with a rising sense of alarm, I found I was out of my depth. Clutching the airbed, I splashed clumsily shoreward until I felt the sharp shingle under my feet. I stood up and stared towards the spot which my erstwhile loved-ones had occupied.

They still weren't there.

I couldn't believe it. They'd packed up and gone just because I had extended the argument – forcefully, I admit – that it was my turn to use the airbed! My anger was overtaken by a rising fear. I was on my own. Had they taken my clothes away with them or just left them on the beach for seagulls to poo on? Did I have to walk home like this . . . and with no shoes? Tears of outrage and alarm pricked my eyes as I waded out of the water. I felt utterly incredulous, abandoned and frightened – not because I was alone but because they had left me alone. I picked my way gingerly along the beach, heading for the steps that would take me up to the promenade. I'd walked about 35 yards to my left when I stopped dead in my tracks. Mum and Miranda were sitting on the stones and eating sandwiches!

'Thought you'd come back when you saw the food coming out,' sneered my sister.

I looked at them hard. 'Why did you move?' I demanded fiercely.

'We haven't moved.'

'Yes, you have!'

'We haven't!'

'You did, too! I was floating right in front of you. I shut my eyes and when I opened them you'd packed up and moved back here.'

'We didn't, did we, mum!' retorted my sister hotly.

'Jem love, we didn't move,' mum laughed. 'You did. You floated off towards the pier. Everything floats down towards Hastings on this beach.'

I was outraged, largely because I was beginning to feel stupid – and my sister's smirking wasn't helping.

'Then you let me float off out to sea,' I sulked.

'No, just a few yards along the beach. I was watching you.'

'So was I,' said my sister. 'Should've seen yourself getting all frightened cos you couldn't see us. We could see you, though, you big girl's blouse!'

I kept my attention on mum as the best hope of some sympathy. 'You let me float along the beach and out to sea. I could've ended up in France . . . I could've been drowned.'

'We were watching you.'

It was mum's use of the first person plural that defeated me, there. The idea of my sister helping to keep a watchful eye on my safety was just too much. I slumped to the stones and sat in surly silence. It was a full thirty seconds before my injured pride could be persuaded to drop its objections and permit me to nibble exhaustedly on a Marmite sandwich.

At school, I was to learn all about longshore drift, that cross-current that moves the water from west to east down the coast and takes endless tons of shingle along for the ride. It's only checked by the placing of those ubiquitous and rather ugly groynes. It could, in its way, be just as menacing as an ebbing tide because one couldn't actually see the movement in real-time. On the airbed, I'd had no idea that I was slowly drifting down towards the pier although, with a flowing tide, there was no danger of my drifting out beyond the pier. I'd been duped because that whole section of the seafront between London Road and White Rock is uniform – the shingle, the colonnade of Bottle Alley, the promenade railings and the top of the seafront buildings behind. I was convinced that I had stayed static and that it was mum and Miranda who had changed positions. It was a lesson learned and I added it to my now reinvigorated anxiety about tides sweeping me out into the merciless deep waters and stayed vigilant while on the airbed thereafter.

There was endless entertainment to be had on the beach and it was down there one afternoon during our first summer that we watched, highly intrigued, the actions of a man and his two accompanying children. The tide was out and he and the kids had hopped and jumped some way out on to that area of exposed rock called Goat Ledge. He was squatting down and dangling a piece of string into a large crack in the stone. We watched fascinated as he suddenly twitched the string into view with a small crab hanging on to the end of it. The children squealed in delight and proffered their plastic buckets. The man quickly swung the string over one of them just as the crab dropped off the end. We hung about shyly nearby until the man noticed us and said, 'Hello. Want to see what we've got?'

Now, we weren't supposed to talk to strangers and, like all children, we took that sort of injunction very literally. It wouldn't have occurred to me to assess the situation objectively; to observe that this 'stranger' was with two children already, that he was in full view of everyone on the beach including mum who was reading her *Woman's Weekly* about 20 yards away. All I knew was that I had my little sister in my charge and was responsible for her. I could take no chances.

'Well, do you want to have a look?' smiled the man.

'Coo . . . Yes, please!' we chorused eagerly and leapt on to the rocks next to him, the fascination for his odd rock pool dipping just too compelling to resist. His children's buckets writhed and rattled with small dark green crustaceans.

'How do you do that?' I asked the children.

They proudly and eagerly showed us how to prise a mussel from the rocks, break it open with a stone (we didn't much care for that bit) and tie the resultant mess to a length of string or twine. Then their father taught us how to lower the line gently into the water of a rock pool, preferably under the overhang of the rock itself, and wait to feel the surprisingly strong tugs that came on the line. Then he demonstrated the knack of drawing up the line swiftly but smoothly until a perfectly formed miniature crab appeared gripping the appetising mussel mess with one of its pincers. Either little crabs infested the rock pools in their thousands or there were just a few particularly dim ones who couldn't learn the lesson. We didn't know but, in any event, crab fishing became an integral part of our afternoons on the beach – as long as the tide was out sufficiently for us to reach the rocks.

The tides were fascinating in themselves and we were very intrigued one day when mum told us that Aunty Alice had offered to take us on a special trip down to Bulverhythe to see the wreck of the *Amsterdam*. I was breathless with excitement because this maritime calamity was, according to what Alice had told mum, only rarely visible because it needed a particularly low tide to expose it to view.

'What? There's a shipwreck down at Bulverhythe?'

'Apparently so,' said mum.

'Why wasn't it on the news, then?' I asked.

'Because it's not really news,' said mum as she deftly folded the pillowcases she was extracting from the washing basket.

'A massive great whopping ship sinks on our doorstep and you don't think it's news?' I demanded.

'Jem, love,' said mum patiently. 'It didn't go down last night. It ran aground down there hundreds of years ago and sank into the mud or sand or whatever it is.'

I could hardly contain myself. Where was Alice? We needed to get down there fast! I had a picture in my mind of a *Marie Celeste* regurgitated by a freak combination of retreating sea and fickle mudbed. I could see it clearly – wet and sand-streaked sails still hanging in tattered strips from the masts and flapping uselessly in the onshore breeze. Oh yes! I could just picture its weather-beaten hull stuck-fast in the vice-like grip of a treacherous shore while the gun ports revealed the bronzed mouths of its cannon which had, no doubt, been primed by the captain to repel the evil wreckers who had betrayed the noble vessel to its destruction.

Alice parked her car in Bridge Way and I waited impatiently as she and mum put on their headscarves and tied them carefully under their chins, sharing the rear-view mirror to ensure their hair was protected from the breeze. I leapt up the steps to cross the footbridge over the railway and, from the top, scanned the beach and the tideline for a broken leviathan listing in the mud. It wasn't there.

I screwed my eyes up against the glare on the water. Was I missing something? Aha! A small group of individuals was gathering at the water's edge. That was it. We were early! The *Amsterdam* had yet to be given up to view by the elements.

Mum, Aunty Alice and my silent sister came over the shingle and we all went down on to the wet and shining sand to join the muffled group being buffeted by a strengthening breeze. I realised that a small man in a Russian hat and yellow wellies was addressing us, his reedy voice having to do battle with the wind and surf.

'. . . Was a Dutch East Indiaman en route to Java in . . .lost its rudder in Pevensey Bay . . . ran aground on a night in January 1749 . . . silver bullion . . .'

And then, to my horror, I looked down to the sand and on towards the endless procession of curling waves to see what appeared to be the tops of a load of fence posts arranged in a roughly elliptical shape.

And that was it? That was the wreck of the *Amsterdam*? I couldn't believe it.

'Aunty Alice, Aunty Alice,' I demanded. 'Where is it, then? Where's the boat?'

An elderly man with watering pale blue eyes took his churchwarden pipe from his mouth and used the stem to point at our feet. 'It's about thirty feet under all this muck, young man,' he said with a pronounced distaste. 'It's all mud here. Used to be a forest in prehistoric times, see.'

'What about the treasure?' I asked, beginning to be interested despite my ad hoc decision, made just seconds earlier, to go into a mighty sulk of disappointment.

'Long gone. Bars of pure silver, it's said,' nodded Mr Pipe. 'That all disappeared at a great rate of knots,' he added and then chuckled, presumably pleased at his nautically flavoured joke. He then clamped his pipe back in to his mouth and ignored me.

There the *Amsterdam* reposes to this day. It's always struck me as rather a shame that more wasn't – and isn't – being made of her. It's another of those odd Hastings features which is so nearly brilliant but which, through bad timing, bad judgement or plain bad luck, just hasn't been exploited. In fairness, it would be a job-and-half to do anything with her. Low tides actually low enough to make her accessible are rare and it would be a mighty job of engineering to excavate in anything approaching a serious way. Mind you, it's believed that the remains of three decks are still down there with much of the low-value cargo, the supplies and the personal possessions of those aboard still intact. Many people are surprised to learn that the luckless *Amsterdam* is regarded as hugely important as a site of marine archaeology because she is more than 60 per cent intact; in fact, she's the most intact East Indiaman known – she just happens to be submerged beneath several hundred tons of good old St Leonard's mud. And it's a fantastic story, too, comprising a state-of-the-art vessel, a maiden voyage, a colossal storm, suspected plague among those on board, a catastrophic running-aground, alleged mutiny of the crew, local smugglers raiding the cargo, the silver bullion, an actual gun battle on the beach at Bulverhythe and the enduring mystery of just how much of that silver stayed on board or was spirited away in to Hastings itself.

On that blustery day in 1971, though, I had to be content with my imagination and snapping a small piece of slimy wet wood from one of the ribs protruding from the beach as my personal souvenir. Yes, I know, I know . . . I've felt guilty about it ever since. If I could have put it back, I would have done so; but my souvenir crumbled away to dust within a fortnight of my possessing it.

But it is those after-school trips to the beach that reside in my memory. They were a real treat – even more so when, if we were lucky, they concluded with ice lollies on the way home. My favourites were the Fruity Blue – a frozen block of colourings, preservatives, additives and indeterminate flavourings which gave the lurid confectionery its name – and the Count Dracula which was black water ice wrapped round white ice cream with, at the very centre, a blob of vivid red jelly that looked disconcertingly like congealed blood. I don't think mum was particularly impressed by either of them especially when they frequently ended up decorating my school shirts and were, to quote her own eloquent words, 'a right bugger to get out'.

It might seem odd to today's youth that someone like me should wax so lyrical about something so mundane as eating an ice lolly on a summer's afternoon but these things were events in our lives – treats to which we looked forward with unfailing enthusiasm. On the basis of a loaf being a banquet to a starving man, a simple ice lolly or chocolate bar meant a great deal because it was a luxury; we couldn't take such things for granted and nothing dulls the appreciation faster or more comprehensively than taking something for granted.

Sweetshops, or, at least, bespoke sweetshops as I remember them, have all but disappeared. Utility is king and few traders can afford to indulge in the luxury of specialising in any one particular product. I suppose it was the unstoppable rise in the fortunes of the supermarkets that was at the bottom of it. Even back then, in the early 1970s, when supermarkets were still to be found in town centres and their cashiers rang up every item on individual key-press tills, the high street traders were feeling the pinch and the message was clear – diversify or die. A lot of them did die, too. I remember happy hours spent in several long-since vanished sweetshops in St Leonard's. There was one in London Road virtually opposite the Congregational church, another at the bottom of the same street next to what was, until recently, the Admiral Benbow pub and a third on the seafront close to the eastern end of the Marine Court colonnade.

A visit to the sweet shop was a grand thing. I would stand there looking at row upon row of screw-top jars lining the shelves all around the shop, those familiar names calling me – acid drops, peanut brittle, barley twists, rhubarb and custard, sherbet lemons – old friends, old faithfuls. I would make my selection and down the jar would come, the sweets clattering into the shop's scales as the needle on the dial crept round to the magic 4oz mark. Sometimes, if you were lucky and the shop keeper was feeling benign, he would tip the remaining sugar and sweet-splinters out of an empty jar and into a paper bag which he'd let you have for free. It was always an enjoyable experience. More often than not, it took an age to get served – especially if one of the shop's regular coffin-dodgers was fumbling for the few pennies needed to purchase his loose Mint Imperials – but we didn't mind because being in the sweet shop was an entertainment in itself.

By chance, recently, listening to the radio, I heard reference made to a website called 'A Quarter Of'. It's a site dedicated to confectionery in all its manifestations and which, among other things, tries to track down obscure, discontinued or hard-to-find sweets and chocolate bars. It also has a 'Does Anyone Remember?' page on which visitors can post nostalgic notes concerning the sweet treats of their youth. For me, that website was rather like discovering an old school photograph that one has not seen for many years. Names and images that hadn't entered my conscious mind for decades suddenly leapt off the screen as if it had been only yesterday. And, of course, I started pestering everyone who looked anywhere near my age with pensive 'Whatever happened to?' questions on the sweets of my youth. Where shall we start? Spangles (boiled sweets, square, fruit-flavoured), Glees – a bit like today's Skittles – and Pacers – a minty, chewy sweet. There were the old chocolate bars such as the dull but reliable Bar Six – a sort of glamourless relation of the Kit-Kat – and the much more sophisticated Fry's Five Centre, a multi-coloured, multi-flavoured version of the original Fry's Chocolate Cream (which first saw the light of day when Queen Victoria was still eating chocolate!). Then there was the Pyramint, with its definite Masonic overtones, and the curiously decorated Five Boys – a bar of chocolate with the face of a small boy engraven on each of its five segments and each featuring a different expression. The first one (or last, depending on your point of attack) was the wee chap weeping. I used to enjoy biting that one in half first, the ugly little git's fat face screwed up in such a way that I was quite certain that, whatever had made him cry, he had thoroughly deserved it!

Unlike most of the St Leonard's sweet shops, not all the confectionery of my youth was lost beyond redemption.

The Aztec bar, brought out to coincide with the Mexico City Olympics of 1968, made a brief reappearance in the 1990s but bombed a second time – now as extinct as the ancient civilisation it so frivolously commemorated. The Texan was another chocolate Lazarus. Texan had a great TV advert first time round. A long, tall Texan was seen in a variety of death-dealing situations; surrounded by whooping Apaches, captured by Mexican bandidos, etc. In all cases his last wish was to eat a Texan bar which, being so chewy, took him such an age to masticate that his captors had exhausted themselves in celebrating his imminent demise and fallen asleep. Texan thereupon strolls into the sunset and freedom. How cool was that! Like the Mexican, so the Texican – withdrawn. However, it made a similar reappearance in recent times. It wasn't the same; the packaging was different and it just didn't, well, chew in the same way. I dare say there was some rubber or plastic derivative worked into the hydrogenated vegetable fat that gave the original its jaw-aching longevity that has since been banned. You could put all sorts of interesting things into children's confectionery back then that you wouldn't get away with today. Shame.

The 'A Quarter Of' website was a slightly humbling experience. I felt rather ashamed that I had allowed my advancing years to purge the memory of these old friends. I certainly had fonder fondant recollections than those I had of the faces in the few old school photographs that I still possess. And if there's a moral to the story, it's not that you 'can't go back' but that if you do go back, make sure you know where you're going and go on your own terms.

Sweets, chocolate, ice cream and the sea – always synonymous for me and yet my true perception of the water on our doorstep took some time to arrive. In fact, after living by it for the best part of three years, I was formally introduced to the sea by a thirteen-year-old Swedish girl when I was aged just fourteen myself. Oddly enough, that introduction was effected a week after the girl, called Maria, had returned to her home in Gothenburg.

Maria had come to Hastings via the language school STS and stayed with us at no. 17 for three weeks in the late summer of 1974. I paid very little attention to her when she was with us but, just a few days after leaving Hastings, she sent us a letter – in her execrable and sadly unimproved English – thanking us for our hospitality. It included a photograph of her that mum had taken on Maria's camera on the beach in front of Marine Court. I found that picture curiously compelling but it was some little while before I realised why. It wasn't Maria that had caught my attention; it was what featured in the background. It was the sea. Suddenly, it was revealed to me as something more than an oversized paddling pool in which to fight my sister for possession of the family's airbed or fish for crabs. Superficially, the photo was typical of Maria being untypically Swedish. Instead of being the slim and evenly tanned young teenager with the trademark blue eyes, blonde hair and beautifully composed English that we expected of all the town's many Scandinavian visitors, Maria had a shock of almost Pre-Raphaelite red hair, dove-grey eyes, a loping gait and a maladroitness that would see her pour more breakfast cornflakes into her lap than she ever managed to get into her bowl. 'Many a slip 'twixt cup and lip', indeed! But for all her irritating incapability and, specifically, her knack of getting lost in parts of the town where she had no conceivable reason to be, she had a gamine charm and an individuality that meant you couldn't fail to like her. It may have been more luck than judgement on the part of my mother, but I realise now that that casual snapshot was actually excellent photography, marrying its subject to its setting in a way that allowed each to highlight something true and elemental about the other. I can see it now; a day of steel-grey hues, strong wind, white horses flecking the water far out to sea and low rain clouds with serrated edges massing ominously. Maria's hair streams out to one side while she cocks her head in the other direction with inscrutability in eyes as grey but as animated as the simmering elements of air and water behind her.

Suddenly, after three years of living by the sea, of seeing it every day, I became aware of it. I could see it as a force of nature, as something organic, something alive, something vast and unknowable and yet, at the same time, something as homely and as constant as a back garden. And it was Maria, looking studiedly bored for the photographic pose, who unlocked the door to something like an extra dimension in my mind. If teenagers grow physically in fits and starts, so perhaps they develop mentally the same way and that photo, I now believe, triggered a spurt of growth.

Now the English Channel is not the most romantic or exciting corner of the world's oceanic wilderness. It's 300 miles in length, 150 miles at its widest point and nowhere is it deep enough to submerge a building the height of St Paul's Cathedral. It's an oil-filmed marine motorway bereft of undersea volcanoes, coral reefs and weird prehistoric trenches that plunge to unguessable depths. In terms of wildlife, it holds no attractions whatever for those bizarre leviathans of the deep, the whales, or that sleek killing machine, the Great White Shark. Shy porpoises might occasionally be seen sporting at distance off the pier and there's always a chance that one of the fanatical night anglers might haul a seven-foot pilchard on to the beach and get his picture in the *Hastings and St Leonard's Observer* – but that's about it; or is it?

No, it isn't. The way to my discovery of the sea may have come from a photograph but that discovery proved anything but a two-dimensional moment frozen in time. For I learned that the sea, living by it and with it, was almost an added dimension to my life in itself: and not one frozen in time – in any sense. I understood that the oceans are almost as old as the planet itself and that they are the womb from which all life on Planet Earth sprung. Even the humble English Channel is a constantly changing, ceaselessly moving entity that has filtered its way into so many aspects of my life and my thoughts. On any day of any week of any year, the sea is true, its subtle partnership with the sky striking vivid images – to those who stop to look – as sharp as photographs, as fleeting as time itself. I understood the old story about Joan of Arc weeping at she watched a sunset fade because it would never be seen on earth again.

Image: a late, winter afternoon with the Channel a pewter plate piled high with clouds of buttered swede.

Image: A day of December; low tide at Bulverhythe with a sky so vast that it stunned the eye almost as fiercely as the rising sun – an early morning with air cold as razors, blue as a honed blade.

Image: The cliffs at Fairlight. Black turf falling away to the boom of surf, travelling to the shaded amber of a Paschal Moon rising out of the sea like the very face of innocence.

Image: White skies of August, the sun hidden by mist-into-cloud-into-mist until the horizon was drawn to my feet and the world beyond it had vanished, my eyes smarting as I tried to focus on the nothing that was everything.

Images, yes: but not of stasis. The very fleetingness of their creation seared them into my mind to travel with me, receding and returning in endless rhythm like the quiet breaths of the tides themselves.

10
Whipped Cream
On The Sausages

Hastings and St Leonard's bloomed in the summer months as seaside resorts – even those which have seen grander days – are wont to do. But for me, summertime in Hastings will always be synonymous with foreign students. We knew nothing about them before moving to the town but became a host family in only our second year. It was the beginning of a thirty-year association which saw us accommodating both the students and their group leaders throughout the summers. In the early 1980s I became a conversational tutor and, over a two-year period, worked for IST, EF and STS which further strengthened the association. The foreign student business became an integral part of our annual cycle and we loved every minute of it.

Now, I should say at this point that I'm quite aware that these seasonal visitors are no longer referred to as 'foreign students'; the word 'foreign' is, apparently, the stumbling block, here, as it is supposed to carry with it some sort of vague, xenophobic connotation – although no one has ever been able to explain to me quite why this should be. Today, these international visitors must be referred to as 'English-language students' – and please note the hyphen between the words 'English' and 'language'. If you leave it out and write 'English language students' you are indicating language students who are English rather than students of the English language who might be English but are more likely to be from outside England and therefore 'foreign' – which is the word we're not supposed to use anymore. It's complete bollocks but that, we are told, is now the rule. Well, it's not the rule with me. We called them 'foreign students' then and I call them 'foreign students' now. They're 'students' and they're 'foreign'. *Quad erat demonstrandum.* If the Political Correctness Police want to give me a caution, I'll live with it. There's nothing xenophobic about me now nor was there anything xenophobic about the Wells family back then. If we were guilty of anything in those days it was simple ignorance of our Continental neighbours. And here's one of those charming ironies of British life for the Indians, Pakistanis and Jamaicans that peppered the salt-streets of Hillingdon were not, as far as we were concerned, 'foreigners' while little Mr Gribalski in our corner shop – as white-skinned as we were – definitely was a 'foreigner'. Perhaps it was the echoes of empire that somehow made the immigrants from the Sub-Continent belong in a way that a Ukrainian Jew just didn't, even though we were ethnically, culturally and sociologically much closer to him than to the dark-skinned, turbaned and bindi-decorated newcomers. I think my parents were typical of their generation: they worried quietly about immigrants en masse and the damage they might do to their traditional lives and values yet when faced with an individual immigrant they saw no colour at all and judged as they always did, using the yardsticks of honesty, industry, moral rectitude, good manners and personal hygiene. Thus, by foreigners, we meant Europeans – and, remember, Britain didn't even join the Common Market (as the EU was called back then) until 1973 – so these 'foreigners' were a rarity and I think Mr Gribalski in our old corner shop had been the only one we'd ever properly met.

As residents of St Leonard's, we observed the hoards of students which arrived in the town with great objective interest and generous spirits. When they learned that they could make much needed cash by becoming a host family my parents positively embraced them and if mum or dad had had any reservations as to a clash of cultures they were almost immediately dispelled by our first guests – two Swedish girls who spoke English well, were appreciative of everything done for them and had impeccable manners in the British tradition of 'please', 'thank you' and 'excuse me'. They also understood the very British concept of queueing at bus stops and in shops – something that not all European countries have developed to the extent of the British and one of the things that did tend to cause slight friction in the town – particularly with the older generation, members of whom could find themselves unceremoniously bundled out of the way when a bus arrived. Mum was enchanted by these 'Stepford-Daughters' and I caught her, on more than one occasion, casting glances of longing in the general direction of her own offspring.

The influx of students began as a trickle at Easter and gradually filled the town with a cacophony of loud and excited European voices. We would see our 'guests' crocodiling through the Old Town, the town centre and along the seafront, the blue bags identifying the EF contingents while the yellow bags advertised the STS students – by far the two biggest players at the time.

Mum had been tipped off by the mother of one of my classmates that the language schools were always on the look-out for decent host families and she lost no time in submitting domestic CVs to the likes of EF, STS, Embassy and various others. So, from 1971 onwards, from April to August, no. 17 took on the appearance of an airport departure lounge with foreign students, aged from twelve to nineteen, and from all over the Continent coming in and going out. The breakfast table was more like a United Nations cafeteria with, at various times, guests from Portugal, Russia, Spain, France, Belgium, Switzerland, West Germany, Italy, Austria, Poland, the Czech Republic and Romania. There were also a good many Swedes,

Danes and Norwegians – even the occasional visitor from the mysterious and little known Finland – a country with a language like nothing we'd ever heard before. (Actually, I later learnt that its closest linguistic relation is Hungarian. Work that one out!). Over the years, as the concept of the Global Village developed, they came from farther afield; exotic South Americans from Colombia and Brazil and even three trainee nurses from India who, after their first meal with us, brought to the table each day jars of chutneys and pickles so fearsomely hot that they must have been all but radioactive! Poor things: they never complained but they must have found our food bland to the point of tastelessness.

Initially though, we hosted mainly Scandinavians and almost always female Scandinavians because mum worked on a cunning theory that figure-conscious teenage girls would be cheaper to feed. She feared that too many beefy Björns would eat into the profits – quite literally. For a boy entering his adolescence, I found it both alarming and strangely exciting to join the breakfast table each morning in the company of those exquisite Nordic beauties all examining the Marmite and the marmalade and discussing in their sing-song native tongues what these strange concoctions might be. The standard of English varied enormously. The Scandinavians proved the most advanced in their grasp of both grammar and vocabulary with the Germans not so far behind. The Italians trailed a distant third but, as they spent most of their time happily singing at the tops of their voices and waving their hands about, it didn't seem to matter. Indeed, the hostelry that no. 17 became taught me a great deal about our Continental neighbours who, up to that time, if I'd thought about them at all, I had generally considered to be slightly odd and rather excitable tribes which occupied the landmass that was kept away from England by the reassuring barrier of the English Channel. It was then also that I realised that English was, indeed, the nearest thing there was to an international language. The Scandinavians, in particular, had long since worked that out and the children who stayed with us did so because their parents had acknowledged that fluent English was an absolute 'must' if their children were going to make all they could of themselves in the world. As one of them said simply, 'Who's going to bother to learn Swedish?' Point made.

The routine of their time with us was usually the same. They'd be at their classes in the morning and involved in some visit – Battle Abbey or Canterbury Cathedral – during the afternoon. Evenings were normally for discos or, weather permitting, barbecues on the beach. The Scandinavians, in particular, went to the beach at every given opportunity, fascinated by the 'tidvatten' as they called it – literally 'time-water'. We finally learned that it was the tides that fascinated them so. The Baltic, their own sea, is pretty much tideless and the Swedes never lost interest in the ebb and flow of our waters. We even showed them how to fish for the little crabs in the rock pools just as we had been shown ourselves.

Poor mum did find feeding them something of a headache. They seemed to view everything they were offered with a sort of polite but reticent curiosity and she had to keep a running list of things that had proved definite non-starters. Top of the list of familiar British food items that the foreign students either couldn't fathom or hated – usually both – included:

Pork pies	Mushy peas
Cornish pasties	Pickled onions
Salt 'n' vinegar crisps	Tinned pilchards
Pork scratchings	Lemon curd
Tea with milk in it	Sage and onion stuffing
Powdered instant coffee	Tinned spaghetti
Corned beef	Sausages
Sliced white bread	Marmite
Pork luncheon meat	

It seemed that only the Germans could be persuaded to try sausages – probably because they came from a country with its own proud sausage tradition (they have approximately 1,500 different types of wurst, I was to discover) but I fear they looked upon the standard Walls snorker with a sort of slightly indulgent pity.

But if our European visitors expressed polite reservations over the hale and hearty, stuffed collagen tube that was the British banger (the pig's 'eye-hole, ear-hole and arse-hole' as dad so eloquently referred to them), that recalcitrance paled into insignificance when confronted with that balm of Beelzebub – Marmite. And if they needed any confirmation that the British harboured strange tastes and that the apocryphal reputation that our native cuisine had attracted was well-deserved, they found it encapsulated in that one word. This curious foodstuff first appeared in the nation's grocery shops in the first decade of the twentieth century and has polarised the opinions of the natives ever since. You either love it or hate it and Marmite actually created a highly successful advertising campaign based on that very idea. To a man, our foreign guests took one doubtful sniff, blenched visibly and thenceforth avoided it like the plague, viewing it as they would have viewed some slow, evil-smelling unguent distilled from Lord-knows-what filth by the local witch. Of course, if you're British, Marmite is just one of those things that has always been there, like the royal family, queues at the post office and Status Quo. No one knows exactly what it is, still less why it is. It's ostensibly a vegetable extract but it's so well muscled mum even used it as a stock cube substitute to make gravy when she ran out of Oxo. All we knew was that it had something to do with yeast and was so strongly flavoured that too much burnt your mouth. For me, Marmite on toast for tea on a winter's afternoon is one of those 'comfort memories' that has remained with me and, as a child, I viewed it as being as solid and reliable as my parents and just as homely. Delicate Scandinavian noses might have recoiled at the pungent odour emanating from that little glass jar with its yellow top, but I felt none of the embarrassment that so frequently afflicted me when our homely little idiosyncrasies met with that guileless Continental disdain. Marmite was different. Our students might pass it over but that was their loss. It was as if the answer to some great cosmic imponderable had been laid before them had they only the wit to interpret it as such; but they had missed the opportunity for enlightenment. Those of us who had been inculcated into the cult of Marmite could only smile sadly at their squandered chances of yeasty illumination.

At the other end of the taste spectrum, though, British jams and, particularly, marmalade were a huge hit with our guests and we would see them, at the end of their stays with us, cramming jar after jar of strawberry jam and thick-cut Oxford marmalade into their suitcases, eager to spread the word – and the bread – for the folks back home.

There is no doubt that our European visitors arrived representative of their distinct food cultures while the best we could manage was a food attitude – and that attitude was mostly indifference. Quite why is the enduring puzzle. One can blame the war – and I shall – but plenty of places were inconvenienced by that little spat to a far more distressing degree than the UK. Was it the traditionally high cost of eating out? The lack of café culture? Geographic isolation? Laziness? I don't know – but the problem wasn't a new one. Look in the history books and there are many references to foreign ambassadors to the courts of our earlier monarchs keeping grumpy diaries and writing despairing letters home in which they complain as much about the abysmal food as the appalling weather.

In the early 1970s the food items used for Wells family meals were as limited as the TV channels. Ironically, I would argue that the choice today still compares with TV channels;

there's a bewildering array of fare of which you've never heard and you still can't find anything you fancy. Modern Britain is spoilt for choice and, in my humble opinion, rather spoilt by choice. When you see couples in Sainsbury's hissing at each other over the choice between sun-dried tomatoes and sun-blushed tomatoes you get to feel there's a serious priorities problem.

Our weekly menu was as set in stone as the nation's bank holidays (except, of course, the May Day bank holiday which did not at that time exist – it was only formally adopted in England in 1978). It was unalterable and unchallengeable; it never occurred to any of us to suggest otherwise. In fact, the only kitchen drama I recall came following a letter from Aunty Mary in Canada which contained a recipe for something she called meatloaf. Unusually, our deeply cuisine-conservative mother decided to try it out and was delighted to produce a savoury, dark-brown breeze block which could be carved like a joint, cubed and put into sauce or sliced cold for sandwiches – all at the expense of half a pound of cheap mince, a couple of eggs and bread crumbs pounded out of the remains of last week's Mother's Pride. Mary's Meatloaf, as it was dubbed, usurped the Thursday-night spot which had been honourably held for many years by corned beef hash – a bottom-of-the-barrel standby pressed into service each week because our shopping day was Friday and by Thursday the cupboards were looking rather bare.

One must remember also that mum had spent her latter teenage years learning the housewife's arts from her own mother while the bombs were falling on London and the nation lived in the bleak fear of invasion and the equally bleak reality of rationing. Wasting food was not simply lazy and indulgent, it was actively aiding the enemy because so much of what the country ate had to be brought to our shores by ships which sailed in the daily risk of a torpedo. Kitchen cunning and thrifty larder-management was drummed into a generation of young girls as the best weapon they could use to thwart Hitler. For young women like my mum, the lesson never left them. When I started to take an interest in food and cooking as a teenager, mum's tuition and guidance had a deep bias towards economy and efficiency. (Even today, the cooking which gives me the greatest pleasure is that which produces a half-decent meal from ingredients which might otherwise have been discarded.)

The thrift theme was also readily apparent when mum did the weekly shop on Friday afternoons. After school, she would walk us into town along the seafront and we'd head for the Tesco store in Wellington Square – now Poundstretcher. It was the lure of those damned Green Shield stamps again . . . sheets of the wretched things generated by the family shopping list. My mouth used to dry out at the mere thought of them. With no working barcode system then, everything was rung through the till individually and packed into carriers. We would then lumber back through the town centre, past the Memorial, to the bus stop – all three of us hoping fervently (if silently) that we didn't encounter the Dunlops about the same business. The town centre road plan was very different then and all the buses heading west into St Leonard's for Silverhill and Hollington picked up at a row of bus stops outside Debenhams – or the Plummers department store as it was then. Not quite all the buses, though, for our local service, the no. 74, took the long way to West St Leonard's via Cambridge Road, Falaise Road and St Margaret's Road. More often than not, mum would only remember that she'd forgotten to buy dad's fags while we were on the way home. She'd then have to get off the bus at Christ Church and dive into the tobacconist. However, such was the length of time taken by the queueing crones to board the bus, buy a ticket and seat themselves without falling over someone else's shopping trolley, walking sticks or dog, mum would be back before the driver was ready to pull away. The Friday Tesco adventure was important because, unlike our previous home in Hillingdon, there was no 'corner shop' to which one of the children could be dispatched should mum realise that she had run out of flour, sugar or stock cubes. Pretty much everything required for the week needed to be bought in that one shopping expedition – and the manifest never altered.

The supermarkets of my childhood and youth had names which sound oddly in the ear today: Wavy Line, International, Mace – and, of course, even the larger ones were small by the standards of today's city-state outlets in which you can buy everything from green-lipped mussels to car insurance, from a single custard apple to an A4 paper laminator. But one thing the supermarkets back then shared in common with the smaller shops was seasonal produce. Today, of course, anything and everything is available on 365 days of the year, literally; but back then it was well nigh impossible to get hold of runner beans in November or Brussels sprouts in May. Because of it, certain things became not only a treat but a mark of the passage of the year. That's not to say that there was no imported food – of course there was; all bananas are imported for obvious reasons – but we waited for the food that was in season because it was cheap, it was good quality and its advent was like the reappearance of a faithful old friend. For instance, we all looked forward to the first new potatoes of the year. The Jersey Royals came first followed by the English new potatoes – spring was maturing into summer and there was no going back to frost and freezing fog from that point. There was the English spring lamb. Strawberries meant June, Wimbledon, my parents' wedding anniversary and the finest month in the English calendar (if you're lucky). The summer settled and the runner beans appeared to chaperone the Sunday joint while the dining room windows opened to the soft air and silence of the Sabbath. Tomatoes, cucumbers, radishes, peas and broad beans; gooseberries, raspberries and apricots – all spoke of high summer and long holidays. Blackberries in the hedgerows were the start of autumn and free to all finders. The old boys on the allotments warned us not to pick them after 29 September because 'it's Michaelmas when the Devil spits on 'em to claim 'em for his own.' As the year turned, apples and pears weighed down the trees and, later, swedes, leeks and parsnips appeared on the plates. Last and honourably least, the much-maligned sprout is still as much the essence of Christmas for me as the smell of extinguished candles and the exotic scent of satsumas. Ah, the simple pleasures. Who was it who said: 'When you have everything, you have nothing'?

Now, it might seem by today's standards that our meals were repetitive, their component parts unimaginative and our general food outlook desperately unadventurous; but we didn't see it like that. If mum and dad were the war generation, then we were the children of the war generation and it was drummed into us from earliest days that we were lucky to have it, we had to eat it and we should be bloody grateful for it – whatever it happened to be. If there were things we didn't like, we ate round them or tried to sneak them onto someone else's plate. Mum wasn't a bad cook; she was a typically post-war English housewife for whom vegetables required boiling to the point of pulp and salad was religiously constructed as a 'lettuce-tomato-cucumber-and-half-a-hard-boiled-egg' still-life on a plate. It wasn't that she couldn't be bothered to experiment, it wouldn't have occurred to her to try. These were the days before food was a hobby and chefs were TV stars. With the exception of the fearsome Fanny Craddock, the first TV chef I remember seeing was Graham Kerr, the so-called Galloping Gourmet. By today's standards his cooking was rather conservative but he had the charisma to go with the coriander and he drew in a huge TV audience. Even so, the nation saw him, I think, as a one-off eccentric rather than a prophet. Dad just saw him as a poof.

Kitchens were as basic as the food produced in them. There were few freezers and I'd never seen a microwave oven. The nearest thing to ready-meals were either boil-in-the-bag concoctions or dried packets of exotica like the Vesta Chow Mein which came in as many sections as one of my Airfix kits. Even the Pot Noodle, that cult culinary item now synonymous with nutritional bankruptcy, was seen by mum as a brash and flippant indulgence akin to buying ready-grated cheese.

For the Wells family, the day of plenty was Sunday because Sunday lunch was always a roast at 1 p.m. sharp. It was a formal occasion augmented by dad's one wild extravagance of the week, a bottle of Tizer. I remember that we always had to refer to the midday meal as 'lunch' while what was eaten in the early evening was 'dinner'. It was one of my parents' few outward nods to snobbery because, as mum would say, it was working class people (who almost certainly lived in her despised 'council houses') who ate dinner in the middle of the day.

○ ○ ○

Now, I will digress briefly here, dear reader, for a word of clarification if not explanation. You will find dotted throughout this book references to my mother's rather tart comments about 'council houses' and the people who resided within them. I don't want to malign her for this apparent snobbery for she was but typical of her generation; a generation in which it was the woman of the house, the wife and mother, who was the guardian of the family's standards and the bulwark of its respectability. I have no idea why this should be and I shan't burden anyone with my theories. However, in this important aspect of our lives, it was mum who was the supreme arbiter: she set the tone and she set the rules. Things were either right or they were wrong – and if they were wrong, as like as not they were 'common'. Some classic examples of behaviour that was 'common' are:

Putting the milk bottle on to the tea table without first decanting the milk into a jug

Spreading butter on to a slice of bread before it has been cut
    from the loaf
Drinking tea from a saucer because it's too hot to drink from
    a cup
Splatting tomato ketchup all over one's food instead of
    pouring it neatly on to the side of one's plate
Putting ketchup on a Christmas dinner
Calling ketchup 'Red Slapper'
Referring to 'pudding' or 'dessert' as 'afters'
Using the *Daily Mirror* as a table cloth
Using the *Daily Mirror* as toilet paper
Having the *Daily Mirror* delivered to your home
Reading the *Daily Mirror*

These social judgments were handed down without any of
us thinking to dispute them – and some of them were pretty
arbitrary. For instance, it was all right for a woman to smoke
but it was 'common' for her to do so in the street. Red was
a 'common' colour and chewing-gum was a 'common'
confectionery. The most withering verdict that mum could
hand down was, 'Ooh, she's a common woman, that one.'
I think that our move to the rather snooty St Leonard's-on-
Sea heightened mum's anti-'common' radar and we were all
constantly on the alert; but it seemed that it was at the table
that we most ran the risk of falling into 'common' behaviour
and our meal-ritual was thus well constructed, well practised
and familiar –particularly on a Sunday.

    And so were the meals themselves. Whatever we had to call
them, those Sunday lunches progressed through the weeks
with the same unshakeable uniformity with which they
were consumed; beef, pork, lamb, chicken, beef, pork, lamb,
chicken ad infinitum. Furthermore, which ever one it was
then decided Monday's dinner because Monday was leftovers
day; beef became cottage pie while lamb became shepherd's
pie and so forth. Tuesday was bacon, tinned spaghetti and

toast; Wednesday was sausage and mash; Thursday became meatloaf, chips and tinned tomatoes while Friday was, for reasons already given, good old fish and chips. And it was good old fish and chips, too; real fish and chips with potatoes which were peeled and cut up while the fish was fresh and coated in home-made bread crumbs. The whole lot was fried in lard . . . Wonderful!

Saturday, when everyone was at home, also saw the main meal of the day advanced from 6 p.m. to 1 p.m. but with far less formality that on Sunday. It was always chump ends – dirt cheap chops which even the world's worst cook can't destroy (not that dad was ever required to cook for us on any regular basis). They were served with boiled potatoes – mashed, if mum was feeling angry at dad and wanted to give something a good pounding – and cabbage. There was a bonus, too, at the weekend. We got pudding! Sunday's roast was always rounded off with ice cream, normally Neopolitan but occasionally Raspberry Ripple if mum was overcome by frivolity while in Tesco. Saturday's dessert was more basic – usually custard with a dollop of chocolate spread in it and garnished with 'top-of-the-milk'. Whatever happened to top-of-the-milk, that couple of inches of cream at the top of every bottle? It disappeared with the bottles, I suppose, and the national rise in cholesterol obssessing. It was a real treat and always the subject of fierce competition between us kids, the dispute frequently ending with mum rather spitefully shaking the bottle violently so that nobody got it. Mind you, that particular act of 'scorched earth' conflict resolution was abandoned one day after she shook the bottle in irritation at our bickering unaware that the little blue tit bandits who watched for the milkman every day had already started to open the aluminium foil cap. The whole room got top-of-the-milk that day!

What our foreign guests made of it all is impossible to say but, of their memories of Britain, I doubt the pleasures of the table ranked high in their nostalgic anecdotes. But there was one exception to the Marmite-haters, sausage-abstainers and general abhorrers of our national cuisine who stayed with us; but she was pretty exceptional in other respects, too. She was an Italian girl called Amelia who thoroughly enjoyed her first English sausages but only after she had layered them liberally with the Bird's Dream Topping which was actually on the table to go with the dessert bowl of peaches. Amelia was, as I said, something of an exception. She enjoyed sun-bathing topless in the back garden; she also enjoyed sun-bathing topless in the front garden, the latter location causing something of a stir in the neighbourhood. Topless sunbathing was just not something that the average British citizen had encountered. Consequently, when the parties of chattering teenage Italian or Swedish girls descended on the beach and unlimbered, it didn't tend to take long for them to be noticed. Under tight-lipped observation from wives, middle-aged men would stare rigidly out into the sparkling sea until their eyes were streaming and the veins in their necks were bulging. Meanwhile, the hopelessly inarticulate male youth of the town would gather in small groups on the beach to show off and to express their appreciation of the bathulkopian beauty on display by throwing small pebbles at the nearest exposed breasts.

I think it unlikely that poor Amelia drew such attention as the kindest way to describe her would be as an acnied scarecrow in a red, pantomime fright-wig. She produced bottles of beer to drink at breakfast and went in daily terror of the dog we acquired soon after we lost dad, a rather handsome Golden Retriever cross we'd named Bunty. With the sort of sixth sense that animals possess, Bunty seemed to know that Amelia was terrified of her and would lurk in various places about the house ready to ambush joyfully her 'victim'. In the early mornings, Amelia's bedroom door would open a crack and a wary Italian eye would scan the hallway. Satisfied the dog was occupied elsewhere, Amelia would spring out of her bedroom and make a bolt for the bathroom – which is precisely where Bunty would be quietly waiting for her. The girl would wail in terror and dismay while the dog would bark and bound at her, delighted at having encountered her 'friend'. Bunty loved Amelia: Amelia hated Bunty. She wasn't too keen on Timothy the cat, either. On another morning, we heard a scream of alarm and dashed to its source. Mum shooed us away from the toilet from whence had come the call for help. She told us later that Amelia hadn't quite closed the toilet door properly and Timothy had pushed it open to sit down in front of where Amelia was sitting down, fixing her with his gimlet stare. Apparently, Italian women deem it very bad luck to be viewed by a cat while their knickers are round their ankles.

Amelia's English was generally OK, not so some of our other guests. There was Inge from Düsseldorf who, at eighteen, was allowed some considerable autonomy and was old enough to have her own door key if the householder was happy to issue one. Mum was; so we hardly ever saw her. The only English I ever heard her speak was on her first morning when, at the breakfast table, she all but barked at mum, 'Vun day ekk, vun day cornflek!'

It was an injunction which we took to mean that she required boiled eggs and cereal served on alternate mornings. Whether we were right or not was never really tested for, on the occasions Inge did join us for her meals, she generally managed a very passable imitation of a plague of locusts and demolished just about everything edible on the table – except the Marmite. Even so, we didn't quite dare to try our sausages on Inge. Although we took in foreign students while dad was still with us, we entered into it on a seriously commercial basis during the summer following his death, the now legendary summer of 1976. Mum bedded down on a settee in the front room (which was at the back, remember) and that freed up the twin-bedded room she had shared with dad. My sister and I stayed where we were so the third bedroom meant we could take three students at a time as long as two were happy to share. Two students who were more than happy to share were the slightly older Italians Gianni and Marinella. Looking back it's quite obvious that they were an item and had conned the language school into billeting them under the same roof because they claimed to be 'related'. They were supposed to be in separate rooms but a little wheeler-dealing bought off our third guest – who happened to be the highly Teutonic Inge and who had no intention of sharing a room with another female – especially an Italian. Inge got a room to herself and so did the 'kissing cousins'. I think they emerged from that room about once every 48 hours. I don't think they attended a single language class and I remember mum serving them their sporadic meals with rather pursed lips. She didn't complain, though. After all, she was keeping her end of the deal and if Gianni and Marinella had better things to do than learn English and admire Leeds Castle in the rain – well, as long as their meals were on the table and the required domestic facilities were available, she had done her duty.

It was much needed revenue but it wasn't the doss some people had told us it would be. Mum worked damned hard at it and made sure she followed all the language school rules to the letter so that those 'children in a foreign land', as she saw them, not only got a decent house in which to stay but a 'home' as well, inviting them to share and join in with Wells family life. Not surprisingly, the majority chose to decline the offer as it seemed to comprise a sulky, argumentative teenage girl, an older teenage boy obsessed with playing his Led Zeppelin albums at top volume and a large, boisterous dog which became borderline hysterical with delight whenever anyone came through the door.

✿
Epilogue

t would be easy to state bluntly that the Hastings of today is not the town that the Wells family found on its arrival during the very first days of 1971; easy and rather pointless. Of course the town has changed: nothing concerning human beings stays static over a period of forty years. It's the nature of change that goes to the heart of the age-old question: was it better back then? And of course, the answer to that is that I'm hardly qualified to answer. I saw the Hastings and St Leonard's of the 1970s as a child while I see the town today with the sadness and the wisdom that exactly fifty years on the planet brings to one. Forty years have battered, weathered and stained Jeremy Wells as well as Hastings and St Leonard's.

Were the summers hotter and sunnier back then?

Did we have regular white Christmases?

Could you really have two pints of mild-and-bitter in the pub, smoke twenty Kensitas while watching *The Towering Inferno* at the cinema, grab fish and chips afterwards plus a cab home and still have change out of two quid?

Was there really a furriers shop in Silchester Road?

The actual answers to these questions are:

No.

No.

No

And, extraordinarily, yes.

But fur has passed out of fashion – and so has Silchester Road and its attendant streets that make up central St Leonard's – now one of the most deprived parts of a town which freely admitted just a couple of years ago that it was number 39 in a list of the most deprived areas of the country.

Did I see that coming? Did I see it happening?

Memory is a tricky blighter. That's why we humans developed nostalgia which, as I hinted at the very start of this book, takes something from the heart as well as from the head. That way we can use the past to find both points of reference and a place of refuge when what we see about us is not to our taste. So, for me, the summers of my childhood were made of endless sunny days, all my Christmases were white, money went further and Silchester Road was always a dump. That's the place I have made my camp and I'll fight anyone who wants to argue.

But what is the reality? Has age withered this place? Has custom made stale its infinite variety? I could say that for me, as an impatient, ambitious young man, the best thing about Hastings and St Leonard's was the leaving of it; but, you see, I'm still here.

It's worse than that – I came back to it.

As I said, many pages ago, I'm neither a sociologist nor a philosopher so I'm simply going to leave you with this.

It was one of those cold evenings of late summer – cold in the way that only seaside towns can get, lulling people with a golden afternoon and then cheating them with a grey, chilled evening. I had just moved home and had decided to end a hectic day of no little family and domestic upheaval by celebrating new locations and reaffirming old loyalties with the nation's second favourite panacea (after 'a nice cup of tea') – a takeaway.

For some reason it brought to mind that, nearly forty years previously, my original family had done something very similar; on that occasion cementing ourselves into our new home – that squat, cranially-bludgeoned bungalow – with a fish-and-chip supper.

Fish-and-chips: that phrase, along with nice cup of tea, has always been a sort of 'all clear' sounded to tell me that whatever unpleasantness, trauma, disturbance or distress had been imposed upon the family members, it was now over. The cup of tea and, on more serious occasions, the fish-and-chip supper signalled that peace accords had been signed, the enemy bombers were clear of our skies, the dark clouds had rolled away and the horizons were once again clean and clear, free from menace and uncertainty.

The actual takeaway I plumped for on that chilly September evening was an Indian one for, as consistent surveys have shown us, the British loyalty to cod and two penn'orth has long since been importuned by the more exotic chicken tikka masala and its retinue of onion bhaji, naan bread, pilau rice and poppadoms. So an Indian it was and, while waiting for the order, I stepped out of the restaurant for a cigarette. I found myself next to a youngish chap whose expanding waistline and receding hairline proclaimed him a family man. He had come out of the pasta restaurant next door to poison his lungs while he waited for food to appear before him.

We stood next to each other looking over the seafront to a grey, sullen and featureless English Channel, the whole prospect striking me as really rather uninspiring. My companion in tobacco, though, clearly had a different and altogether more engaging prospect before his eyes. He took the cigarette out of his mouth and, drawing in a lungful of air, remarked to the evening, 'Lovely to be by the sea. All that sky and the air . . . almost stings the nose when you sniff it.'

'Not a local man, then?' I inquired casually.

'Nah, London.'

'Oh yes? Whereabouts?'

'Out on the western edge. Hillingdon.'

I turned to look at him as he contemplated the darkling horizon. 'It's funny you should say that,' I told him. 'Because that's where my lot came from when we moved down here at the start of the '70s.'

We had a short and rather desultory conversation about places we both might have known which were few, for obvious reasons, before he said, 'The wife and I are toying with the idea of moving down here, permanent like. I'd have to keep working in town but I think it might be worth the aggro. For the kids, like.'

He stood, his cigarette seemingly forgotten, as he breathed in the air and stared out to sea.

There was a flash from the Marina speed camera as two chavs sped past in a beaten up Corsa while a cold gust of wind rattled an empty can of White Lightning along the pavement. There came the splatter of a seagull doing what comes naturally to a bird on the wing and, from somewhere along the unpopulated seafront, the hysterical wailing of an approaching police siren smote my ears. Feeling cold, hungry and curiously enervated, I left my companion to his reverie and turned to go back into the restaurant for my order. As I did, I caught the two words he sighed to himself as he, in turn, dropped his butt and turned away from that dismal marine prospect.

'Bleeding lovely,' he said.

Hastings Logic? You've got it!

'Come and join us, brother,' I thought. 'Come and join us!'

● ● ●